Index to CHILDREN'S PLAYS IN COLLECTIONS

second edition

by

Barbara A. Kreider

The Scarecrow Press, Inc.
Metuchen, N.J.   1977

Library of Congress Cataloging in Publication Data

Kreider, Barbara.
 Index to children's plays in collections.

  Bibliography: p.
  1. Children's plays--Indexes. I. Title.
PN1627.K7 1977   016.812'041   76-49666
ISBN 0-8108-0992-3

Copyright © 1977 by Barbara A. Kreider

Manufactured in the United States of America

ACKNOWLEDGMENTS

The compiler of this index thanks the following librarians who offered her valuable suggestions and worked with her in locating play collections: Ann Alder, Shelley Amos, Carol Carlson, Margaret Ceresa, Del Chaussé, Rosemary Glenn, Jim Harris, Kim Iwamoto, Virginia Newcomb, Norma Pless, Gail Sims, Elise Smith, Vera Mae Thoms, and Jean Wenburg.

She also gives special thanks to Van, Susan, and Keith, whose patience and encouragement made possible the completion of this work.

CONTENTS

Introduction / Guide to Use	vii
Summary of Subject Headings	x
The Index (Authors, Titles, and Subjects)	1
Cast Analysis	181
Directory of Publishers	221
Bibliography of Collections	223

INTRODUCTION / GUIDE TO USE

This second edition is greatly enlarged and expanded. It covers ten years, 1965 through 1974, and includes not only one-act plays and skits but also monologs and dialogs if they were in the collections indexed. To the first edition (published in 1972), 950 plays from 42 collections have been added, making a total of 1450 plays.

Bibliographies used by the compiler to ascertain which play collections were published from 1965 through 1974 are Books for Elementary School Libraries (American Library Association, 1969); Books in Print (R. R. Bowker Co., the 1965-1975 vols.); Children's Catalog, 1971, and Supplements, 1972 and 1973 (H. W. Wilson Co.); and Elementary School Library Collection, 6th ed. (Bro-Dart Foundation). Only those collections published in the United States with copyright dates of the years 1965-1974 are indexed.

All collections that could be located have been indexed, and no attempt has been made to select plays on merit. The authors, titles, and subjects of all plays are included in one alphabet.

Sample author entry:

    Alderman, Elinor R. The wonderful witchware store.
    In Kamerman, S. Fifty Plays for Holidays. 5 char+

This entry tells the index user that Elinor R. Alderman wrote a play entitled "The Wonderful Witchware Store"; that it appears in the collection Fifty Plays for Holidays, edited by S. Kamerman; and that it has 5 characters and extras. "Extras" include nonspeaking characters, characters listed in groups, and both singing and speaking choruses.

Sample title entry:

    The miniature darzis. Gregg, L.

Introduction   viii

Sample subject entry:

    TAILORS
        Gregg, L. The miniature darzis

        The user should note that the "subjects" chosen under which to arrange the various plays in the Index proper are not limited strictly to subjects but include the following: themes, e.g. JUSTICE; type of play, e.g. MELODRAMA or MYSTERY; occasion for which play was written, e.g. BOOK WEEK or THANKSGIVING; period in which play was set, e.g. CIVIL WAR; setting (geographical) of a play, e.g. IRELAND; historical or legendary person involved, e.g. ROBIN HOOD; special cast, e.g. GIRL SCOUTS; and genre, e.g. SKITS--PANTOMIME or VERSE PLAYS.

        For the benefit of those users who wish to browse for an idea, a summary listing of subject headings is provided on page x.

        If a play is sought and found under other than the main entry--e.g. under title--the user must consult the main entry to find the collection in which the play appears and the size of the cast. Occasionally (see, e.g., The silver key) the main entry is under the title but usually is under an author.

        If a collection includes only plays on a particular subject, the book title, rather than the titles of the individual play, is entered under the subject. For example:

    UNITED NATIONS
        Fisher, A. United Nations Plays and Programs

        Following the Index proper is the Cast Analysis section, in which the plays are arranged by the numbers of characters involved. This section is divided into four types of cast: all-female, all-male, and mixed casts, and puppet plays. Under each of these four types the arrangement is from few to many characters by specific number. Further, entries under a sub-arrangement such as 5 characters are immediately followed by entries under the sub-arrangement 5 characters and extras.

        A Directory of Publishers section then follows, giving complete names and addresses for publishers whose collections are analyzed in this Index.

At the end of the book is a Bibliography giving full publication data plus grade-level indicators for all collections indexed.

SUMMARY OF SUBJECT HEADINGS

Accidents
Actors and Actresses
Adam and Eve
Adventure
Advertising
Africa
Airplanes
Alcott, Louisa May
Alden, John
Alfred the Great, King of
  England
Allah
Alphabet
Ambition
American Education Week
Andersen, Hans Christian
Anger
Animals
Antiques
Appalachia
Apples
Appleseed, Johnny
Arabia
Arbor Day
Archery
Argentina
Arguments
Arithmetic
Armistice Day
Art
Arthur, King
Artists
Astronomy
Atomic War
Audience Participation Skits
Austria
Automobiles

Autumn

Baker's Dozen
Ballads
Balloons
Banks and Banking
Barbers
Baseball
Beards
Beauty
Beauty Pageants
Bells
Bible
Birds
Birthdays
Black Americans
Boasting
Boats
Book Week
Books
Books--Care of
Bookworms
Booth, John Wilkes
Bottles
Boxing
Boys
Brains
Bravery
Brotherhood Week
Brothers
Brothers and Sisters
Bunyan, Paul
Burglary
Burr, Aaron

x

xi Summary of Subjects

Caesar, Julius--Spoof
Calendar
California
Camping
Candy
Careers
Caribbean
Cartoons
Carver, George Washington
Cats
Cavalry
Character Building
Characters in Literature
Checkers
Chemistry Sets
Child Labor
Children
China
Choral Plays
Christmas
Christmas in Other Countries
Christmas Spirit
Christmas Trees
Circus
Civil War
Cleverness
Clive, Robert
Clocks
Cloth
Clowns
Clubs [Associations]
Colds
Colors
Columbus, Christopher
Columbus Day
Comedy
Computers
Connecticut--History
Conscience
Constitution
Contentment
Contests
Cookies
Cooking
Cooperation
Counting
Courtesy

Cousins
Cowboys
Crime
Crowd Psychology
Crying
Cyclops
Czechoslovakia

Dancing
Darwin, Charles
Days of the Week
Death
December
Declaration of Independence
Democracy
Denmark
Department Stores
Despair
Detectives
Devil
Devil--Spoof
Dialogues
Diamonds
Dictionary
Diet
Discrimination
Doctors
Documentary Plays
Dogs
Dolls
Donkeys
Dragons
Dramatic Scenes
Dreams and Dreamers
Dwarfs

Easter
Ecology
Education
Eggs
Egypt
Elections
Elections--Satire
Elves
England

Summary of Subjects

English Language
Epidemics
Equality
Esther, Queen
Etiquette
Evil
Explorations
Eyes

Fables
Fables--Spoof
Fairies
Fairs
Fairy Tales
Fairy Tales--Spoof
Faith
Family Life
Fantasy
Farces
Faust--Spoof
Fear
Fighting
Fire
Fire Prevention
First Aid
Fish
Flags
Flags--United States
Floods
Florida
Flowers
Folk Heroes
Folk Songs
Folk Tales
Folk Tales--Spoof
Fools
Football
Forest Fire Prevention
Fortune
Fourth of July
France
Franklin, Benjamin
Freedom
French Revolution
Friendship
Frogs and Toads

Garden of Eden
Gardening
Generation Gap
George, Saint
Georgia
Germany
Gettysburg, Pa.
Ghost Towns
Ghosts
Giants
Gifts
Girl Scouts
Girls
Glasses
Glue
Goats
Gods and Godesses
Gold
Goldilocks
Good and Evil
Gossip
Governesses
Government
Government--World
Graduation
Grammar
Greece
Greed
Grief
Ground-Hog Day
Growing Up
Guilt
Gypsies

Hair
Hale, Sarah Josepha
Halloween
Hallucinations
Hamilton, Alexander
Hamlet
Happiness
Harlem
Hats
Health
Heroes and Heroines
Hiking

Summary of Subjects

Hillbillies
Hippies
Hippopotamuses
History-Comedy
History--United States see United States--History
Hobbies
Holidays
Holland
Home
Honesty
Honor
Hope
Horses
Human Nature
Human Rights
Hunger
Hunt, Robert
Husband and Wife
Hygiene

Imagination
Independence [personal]
India
Indiana
Indians
Individuality
Indonesia
Insurance
Intelligence
Inventions
Involvement
Ireland
Irony
Israel--Ancient
Italy

Jackson, Andrew
Japan
Java
Jealousy
Jefferson, Thomas
Jesters
Jesus Christ-Nativity
Joan of Arc

Jokes
Journalism
Justice
Kabuki [Japanese drama]
Kentucky--History
Kidnapping
Kindness
Kindness to Animals
Kings and Queens
Knights and Knighthood
Knights and Knighthood--Satire
Knowing Yourself see Self-Knowledge
Korea

Laughter
Leaders
Legends
Leprechauns
Liberty
Liberty Bell
Library
Life
Lincoln, Abraham
Lincoln's Birthday
Litter
London
Loneliness
Louisiana Territory
Love
Loyalty
Lucifer--Spoof
Luck

Magic
Magicians
Mail
Mardi Gras
Marriage
Massachusetts
Maturing see Character Building; Growing up
May Day
Mayflower
Mediaeval Miracle Plays

Summmary of Subjects xiv

Meek, Joe
Melodrama
Memorial Day
Mermaids
Mexican Americans
Mexico
Mice
Migrant Workers
Mime see Pantomime;
 Skits--Pantomime
Minorities
Miracle Play
Miracles
Missouri
Misunderstandings
Money
Monologues
Monologues [1 actor =2 parts]
Monroe, James
Monsters
Months see Calendar; Time;
 specific months
Moon
Moore, Dr. Clement Clarke
Morality Play
Mosquitoes
Motels
Mother Goose
Mothers
Mother's Day
Movies
Murder
Murillo
Mushrooms
Music
Musical Comedy
Musical Plays
Musical Terms
Mystery
Mythology
Mythology--Spoof

Napoleon Bonaparte
Nature
Negroes see Black American

Neighbors
Netherlands see Holland
New Year
New York (City)
Newbery Award Books
Newspapers
Newspapers--School
Night Before Christmas
Nightingale, Florence
Nonsense
Norway
Numbers see Counting
Numbers--History
Nursery Rhymes
Nursery Rhymes--Farce
Nurses

Obedience
Ocean
Ocean Voyages
Oklahoma
Old Age
Old Men
Old Women
Opera--Farce
Oppression
Optimism
Oregon--History
Orphans

Painting
Paintings
Panama Canal
Pan-American Day
Pancakes
Pantomime
Parent and Child
Patrick, Saint
Peace
Peanuts
Penguins
Penn, William
Pennsylvania
Percy, George
Persia

Summary of Subjects

Peru
Pets
Physics
Piano
Pie
Pilgrims
Pioneers
Pirates
Planets
Play within a Play
Plays in Verse see Verse
   Plays
Poetry
Poison
Poland
Pollution
Pony Express
Poor see Poverty
Post Office
Potatoes
Poverty
Power
Practical Jokes
Prayer
Pretending
Pride
Princes and Princesses
Princesses see Princes
   and Princesses
Prisoners
Prizes
Promptness
Prospectors
Publishers
Punch and Judy
Punctuation
Puppet Plays
Puppets
Purim

Queens see Kings and
   Queens
Quilts

Rabbits

Radio Plays
Rain
Rainbow
Recreation
Red Cross
Reed, Walter
Repentance
Responsibility
Restaurants
Revenge
Revere, Paul
Revolutionary War [American]
Riddles
Rings
Robin Hood
Robots
Rock Music Plays
Rome
Ross, Betsy
Rulers
Russia

Safety
Sailors
Saint Patrick's Day
Salt
Sanitation
Santa Claus
Satire
Scandinavia
Scarecrows
School
Science
Science Fiction
Scientists
Scotland
Sculpture see Art
Sea
Seasons
Secretaries
Secrets
Self-Confidence
Self-Interest
Self-Knowledge
Self-Pity
Senses

Summary of Subjects

Servants
Sewing
Shadows
Shakespeare, William
Shakespeare, William--Spoof
Shakespeare's Plays
Sharing
Sheep
Ships
Shoemakers
Shoes
Sicily
Silent Night (Song)
Silk
Sillies see Fools
Silver
Simplicity
Singing see Songs
Sisters
Skits
Skits--Audience Participation see Audience Participation Skits
Skits--Pantomime
Slavery
Sleep
Smith, John
Smog
Smuggling
Snakes
Snobbery
Society
Solar System
Soldiers
Solomon, King
Songs
Sorrow
Soup
The South
Space
Space Fantasy
Space Flight
Spain
Spiders
Spies
Spies--Industrial
Spinning

Sports
Spring
Standish, Miles
Stars
Statue of Liberty
Stealing see Thieves
Strength
Students
Suicide
Summer
Supernatural
Superstition
Surprises
Suspense
Switzerland

Tailors
Talking
Tax Evasion
Teachers
Teenagers
Teeth
Television
Tell, William
Temper
Tennis
Terrell, Mary Church
Texas
Thanksgiving
Theater
Thieves
Thrift
Time
Toads see Frogs and Toads
Tourists
Toys
Traditions
Tragedy
Trains
Transportation
Trash
Treason
Treasure
Trees
Trials
Trickery

Summary of Subjects

Trojan War
Trolls
Truth and Falsehood
Turkey [nation]
Turtles
Twelfth Night--Rock Version
Twins

Wolves
Women's Liberation
Words
World War II
Worms
Wrestling
Wright, Orville and Wilbur
Writers

Ulysses
Unhappiness
United Nations
United States
United States--History
Unity
Unselfishness

Young Men
Young Women
Youth

Valentine's Day
Vanity
Verse Plays
Veteran's Day
Villains
Virginia
Virginia--History
Vocabulary see Words
Voting

Wagers
Wales
Wallpaper
War
Washington, D.C.
Washington, George
Washington, Martha
Washington's Birthday
Weather--Spoof
The West
Whales
Wind
Winter
Wisdom
Wishes
Witch Hunts--New England
Witches
Wives

THE INDEX

ABC for safety. Hark, M.
Aase searches for her son. Ibsen, H.
Abe buys a barrel. Peterson, M.
Abe Lincoln in Illinois. Sherwood, R.
Abe's winkin' eye. Fisher, A.
Abigail stands fast. Stuart, M.
Accident of birth. Fisher, A.
ACCIDENTS
    Miller, H.   Safety clinic
ACTORS AND ACTRESSES
    Barbee, J.   Enter Juliet
    Conrad, E.   Show boat
    Garver, J.   Howling success
    Miller, H.   Broadway turkey
    Nolan, P.   Take it from the beginning
    Schaaf, A.   Jump for Joy
    Weik, M.   The rehearsal
    Wilde, C.   Susan goes Hollywood
Adalmina's pearl. Ashrand, K.
ADAM AND EVE
    Milton, J.   Eve decides to eat the fruit of the tree of knowledge
Admiral and the feathered pilots. Ross, L.
ADVENTURE
    Baum, L.   Wizard of Oz
    Boiko, C.   All hands on deck
    Carroll, L.   Through the looking glass
    Colson, J.   Robin Hood in Sherwood Forest
    Dumas, A.   Count of Monte Cristo
    Glass, G.   Ghost town treasure
    _____.   Miss Pickerell goes to Mars
    _____.   Pippi Longstocking
    _____.   Saturdays
    Jacob, E.   Robin Hood tricks the sheriff
    Love, S.   One-eyed giant
    The silver key
    Simonds, N.   Peter Rabbit

ADVERTISING

    Stevenson, R. Kidnapping of David Balfour
    Twain, M. Tom Sawyer and Injun Joe
    _____. Tom Sawyer, pirate
    Verne, J. Around the world in eighty days
    _____. Five weeks in a balloon
    Wyss, J. Swiss Family Robinson
ADVERTISING
    Dias, E. Hippie and the bard
    _____. Madison Avenue merry-go-round
    Murry, J. National everything
Aesop, man of fables. Phillips, E.
AFRICA
    Verne, J. Five weeks in a balloon
    Winther, B. African trio
African garden. Childress, A.
African trio. Winther, B.
AFRO-AMERICANS see BLACK AMERICANS
Ah See and the six-colored heaven. Boiko, C.
AIRPLANES
    Ickler, L. Kitty Hawk--1903
Airport adventure. Murray J.
Aladdin and his wonderful lamp. Thane, A.
ALCOTT, LOUISA MAY
    Goldsmith, S. Louisa Alcott's wish
ALDEN, JOHN
    Ramsey, H. In the name of Miles Standish
Alderman, Elinor R. Hamelot. In Burack, A. Skits, Comedies and Farces for Teen-agers. 16 char
_____. The wonderful witchware store. In Kamerman, S. Fifty Plays for Holidays. 5 char+
Alexander, Sue. Frog princess. In Alexander, S. Small Plays for You and a Friend. 2 char
_____. Goom-bya, room-bya, zerko! In Alexander, S. Small Plays for You and a Friend. 2 char
_____. Hello, little dog. In Alexander, S. Small Plays for You and a Friend. 2 char
_____. What's in my soup? In Alexander, S. Small Plays for You and a Friend. 2 char
_____. Zabba, zabba, zoom! In Alexander, S. Small Plays for You and a Friend. 2 char
ALFRED THE GREAT, KING OF ENGLAND
    Holmes, R. In the days of King Alfred
    Thane, A. King Alfred and the cakes
Ali Baba and the forty thieves. Felsheim, J.
Alice in Puzzleland. Fisher, A.
Alice in Wonderland. Worcester, N. (Play title: Mad tea party)

Alice's adventures in Wonderland. Carroll, L.
All about animals. Carlson, B.
All about mothers. Boiko, C.
All-American thank you. Miller, H.
All hands on deck. Boiko, C.
All houses are haunted. Woster, A.
All in favor. Schwartz, M.
All in the UN. Fisher, A.
All points west. Boiko, C.
All the world around. Fisher, A.
All washed up. Howard, V.
ALLAH
    Asbrand, K. Silver coffeepot
ALPHABET
    Boiko, C. The "T" party
Amahl and the night visitors. Menotti, G.
AMBITION
    Nolan, P. In-group
    Shakespeare, W. Lady Macbeth receives a letter from her husband
    _____. Richard alone
America is a song. Nolan, P.
AMERICAN EDUCATION WEEK
    Cole, E. Welcome, parents
    Pyle, M. Three royal r's
And Christmas is its name. Nolan, P.
Andersen, Hans Christian. Emperor's nightingale. In Thane, A. Plays from Famous Stories and Fairy Tales. 14 char
_____. Princess and the pea. In Mahlman, L. Puppet Plays for Young Players. 5 char
_____. Swineherd. In Smith, M. 7 Plays and How to Produce Them. 14 char; in Thane, A. Plays from Famous Stories and Fairy Tales. 14 char
_____. Tinderbox. In Mahlmann, L. Puppet Plays for Young Players. 11 char
ANDERSEN, HANS CHRISTIAN
    Boiko, C. One hundred words
Anderson, Robert A. Gold mine at Jeremiah Flats. In Burack, A. Skits, Comedies and Farces for Teen-agers. 10 char
_____. Trouble in outer space. In Durrell, D. Teen-Age Plays for Classroom Reading. 9 char
Androcles and his pal. Fontaine, R.
Angel in the looking glass. Fisher, A.
Angel of mercy. Lipnik, E.

ANGER

ANGER
    Ibsen, H. Aase searches for her son
    Pope, A. Belinda bemoans the loss of a lock of her hair
    Shakespeare, W. Richard alone
ANIMALS
    Asbrand, K. Friendly as can be
    Bennett, R. The hare and the tortoise
    _____. Lion and the mouse
    _____. Winter Wizards
    Boylan, A. Musicians of Bremen
    Fisher, A. On strike
    Hark, M. Christmas in the woods
    Howard, H. Little circus donkey
    Howard, V. In the jungle
    Jarvis, S. Giant's cat
    Pantopuck. Owl's birthday
    Philpott, V. The egg
    Roberts, W. Musicians of Bremen Town
    Werner, S. Home, sweet home
    see also specific animals
Anonymous [plays specified as by "anonymous" in collections have a main entry in this index under title]
Another Cinderella. Fontaine, R.
Another man's family. Cable, H.
Another way. Carlson, B.
Another way to weigh an elephant. Blumenfeld, L.
ANTIQUES
    Nicholson, J. Teapot trouble
Anton Chekhov sort of evening
Antony and Cleopatra. Shakespeare, W. (title given in collection: Cleopatra's death scene)
Anywhere and everywhere. Boiko, C.
Apache silver. Love, S.
Apolinar, Danny; Driver Donald; and Hester, Hal. Your own thing. In Swortzell, L. All the World's a Stage. 10 char
APPALACHIA
    White, A. Deaf woman's courtship
APPLES
    Nolan, P. Boshibari and the two thieves
APPLESEED, JOHNNY
    Hark, M. Visit of Johnny Appleseed
    Howard, V. Johnny Appleseed in danger
    Nolan, P. Johnny Appleseed
    Whittaker, H. Gift from Johnny Appleseed

ARABIA
    Asbrand, K. Silver coffeepot
    Thane, A. Aladdin and his wonderful lamp
ARBOR DAY
    Boiko, C. Trouble in tree-land
    Fisher, A. On strike
    Hark, M. Day for trees
    McCarty, S. Tree friends
    Oscar, J. Weeping willow's happy day
ARCHERY
    Nolan, P. Robin Hood and the match at Nottingham
ARGENTINA
    Peterson, M. Pedro and the burro
ARGUMENTS
    Carlson, B. Shut the door
Ariadne exposed. Nightingale, E.
ARITHMETIC
    Chaloner, G. Court of King Arithmetic
    Kane, E. How we got our numbers
    Nesbit, E. Long and short division
Arkwood two-four-two-four. Howard, V.
ARMISTICE DAY
    Streacker, L. Bob's armistice parade
Arnold E. W. Make him smile. In Burack, A. One Hundred Plays for Children. 9 char
Around the world. Howard, V.
Around the world in eighty days. Verne, J.
ART
    Murray, J. Mad about art
    _____. Triumph for Trimbley
    Myrick, N. Day is bright
ARTHUR, KING
    Love, S. King Arthur
    Malory, T. Crowning of King Arthur
    Morley, O. King Arthur and his knights
The artist. Howard, V.
ARTISTS
    Huff, B. Case of the missing masterpiece
    Shore, M. Watch out for Aunt Hattie
Asbrand, Karin. Adalmina's pearl. In Durrell, D. Thirty plays for Classroom Reading. 5 char
_____. China comes to you. In Burack, A. One Hundred Plays for Children. 19 char
_____. Crystal flask. In Burack, A. One Hundred Plays for Children. 8 char
_____. Friendly as can be. In Kamerman, S. Little Plays for Little Players. 9 char

ASTRONOMY

_____. Little hero of Holland. In Burack, A. One Hundred Plays for Children. 21 char
_____. Pandora's box. In Kamerman, S. Children's Plays from Favorite Stories. 10 char
_____. Silver coffeepot. In Kamerman, S. Children's Plays from Favorite Stories. 15 char
_____. What's a penny? In Burack, A. One Hundred Plays for Children. 9 char

ASTRONOMY
    Rittenhouse, C. Children of the sun
    Sanderlin, O. Follow the North Star

ATOMIC WAR
    Fisher, A. Caves of the earth

Atwater, Richard and Florence. Mr. Popper's penguins. In Glass, G. From Plays into Reading. 10 char

AUDIENCE PARTICIPATION SKITS
    Bowers, E. Nobility
    McGee, C. King with the terrible temper
    _____. Lion hunt
    _____. Spasm in three speeds
    _____. Trip to Mexico
    Pylant, A. Starring you

AUSTRIA
    Hollingsworth, L. Silent night

Automa. Henderson, N.

AUTOMOBILES
    Fontaine, R. Love seeks a way

AUTUMN
    Bennett, R. Pixie in a trap
    _____. Rainbow's end
    Boiko, C. Crocus who couldn't bloom
    Neman, D. Green Leaf's lesson

AVARICE see GREED

Avon calling! Olfson, L.

- B -

Baby Bird. Sperling, L.
Background for Nancy. Manning, S.
Backward people. Howard, V.
Baher, Constance Whitman. Cinder-rabbit. In Kamerman, S. Fifty Plays for Holidays. 12 char
_____. Robin Hood outwits the sheriff. In Kamerman, S. Dramatized Folk Tales of the World. 19 char
Bailey, go home. Cable, H.
Bailiff's daughter of Islington. White, A.

Bakeless, Katherine Little. Most memorable voyage. In Burack, A. Four Star Plays for Boys. 10 char+
BAKER'S DOZEN
　　Rowland, E. Precedent in pastries
Baker's neighbor. Thane, A.
Baking contest. Simon, S.
Ballad for the shy. Dias, E.
BALLADS
　　White, A. Saucy Sailor and Other Dramatized Ballads
BALLOONS
　　McMeekin, I. Runaway balloon
　　Ross, L. Washington and the first flight in America
　　Verne, J. Five weeks in a balloon
BANKS AND BANKING
　　Fontaine, R. Where banking is a pleasure
Barbee, Lindsey. Columbus sails the sea. In Burack, A. One Hundred Plays for Children. 5 char+
―――――. Enter Juliet. In Durrell, D. Teen-Age Plays for Classroom Reading. 9 char
―――――. Flag of the United States. In Burack, A. One Hundred Plays for Children. 14 char+
―――――. Friday foursome packs a box. In Burack, A. Christmas Plays for Young Actors. 7 char
―――――. Guide for George Washington. In Burack, A. One Hundred Plays for Children. 6 char
―――――. Holly hangs high. In Burack, A. One Hundred Plays for Children. 7 char
―――――. Letter to Lincoln. In Burack, A. One Hundred Plays for Children. 7 char
―――――. Princess who couldn't dance. In Kamerman, S. Little Plays for Little Players. 6 char
BARBERS
　　Miller, H. Busy barbers
Barbour, Floyd. Bird cage. In Childress, A. Black Scenes. 2 char
Barnett, Grace T. Treasure in the Smith house. In Kamerman, S. Fifty Plays for Junior Actors. 5 char
Baron Barnaby's box. Colson, J.
Barr, June. Cinderella. In Kamerman, S. Little Plays for Little Players. 8 char
―――――. Lion and the mouse. In Durrell, D. Thirty Plays for Classroom Reading. 8 char; in Kamerman, S. Little Plays for Little Players. 7 char
―――――. Old Mother Hubbard. In Kamerman, S. Children's Plays from Favorite Stories. 8 char+
―――――. Present for mother. In Burack, A. One Hundred Plays for Children. 7 char; in Kamerman, S. Little Plays for Little People. 7 char

_____. Rapunzel. In Kamerman, S. Children's Plays from Favorite Stories. 5 char
_____. Three little kittens. In Kamerman, S. Children's Plays from Favorite Stories. 4 char
Barrington, Patrick. I had a hippopotamus. In McGee, C. Drama for Fun. 10 char
Barrows, Marjorie. Valentine tree. In Kamerman, S. Fifty Plays for Holidays. 8 char+
Baseball. Taylor, L.
BASEBALL
    Cable, H. Fairest pitcher of them all
    Taylor, L. Baseball
Baum, L. Frank. Wizard of Oz. In Burack, A. Popular Plays for Classroom Reading. 14 char; in Kamerman, S. Fifty Plays for Junior Actors. 16 char; in Mahlmann, L. Puppet Plays for Young Players. 13 char+; in Sanders, S. Creating Plays with Children. 13 char+
Beach, Marcia Moray. On the fence. In Kamerman, S. Fifty Plays for Junior Actors. 7 char
Beaded moccasins. Bennett, R.
Bealmear, J. H. Covetous councilman. In Kamerman, S. Dramatized Folk Tales of the World. 4 char
BEARDS
    Spamer, C. Dwarfs' beards
BEAUTY
    Nolan, P. View of the sea
Beauty and the beast. Hughes, T.
BEAUTY PAGEANTS
    Olfson, L. Meet Miss Stone-age!
BEHAVIOR see HUMAN BEHAVIOR
Belinda bemoans the loss of a lock of her hair. Pope, S.
Bell of Dolores. Campbell, C.
Bellah, Melanie. Blue toadstool. In Kamerman, S. Little Plays for Little Players. 6 char
BELLS
    Weathers, W. Vision of the silver bell
Ben Franklin, peace-maker. Howard H.
Benjamin Franklin. Walsh, H.
Bennett, Anna Elizabeth. Little witch. In Glass, G. From Plays into Reading. 13 char
Bennett, Helen Cotts. Rumpelstiltskin. In Burack, A. One Hundred Plays for Children. 9 char
_____. Sleeping Beauty. In Burack, A. One Hundred Plays for Children. 17 char
Bennett, Rowena. Beaded moccasins. In Bennett, R. Creative Plays and Programs for Holidays. 3 char+
_____. Child who was made of snow. In Bennett, R.

Creative Plays and Programs for Holidays. 3 char+
———. Christmas pie. In Bennett, R. Creative Plays and Programs for Holidays. 11 char
———. City mouse and the country mouse. In Bennett, R. Creative Plays and Programs for Holidays. 5 char; in Kamerman, S. Children's Plays from Favorite Stories. 5 char
———. Fire-face and the Indians. In Bennett, R. Creative Plays and Programs for Holidays. 2 char+
———. First Easter eggs. In Bennett, R. Creative Plays and Programs for Holidays. 8 char+; in Ross, L. Holiday Puppets. 7 char
———. French doll's surprise. In Bennett, R. Creative Plays and Programs for Holidays. 3 char
———. Good morning, Mr. Rabbit. In Bennett, R. Creative Plays and Programs for Holidays. 9 char
———. Hare and the tortoise. In Bennett, R. Creative Plays and Programs for Holidays. 3 char
———. In the witch's house. In Bennett, R. Creative Plays and Programs for Holidays. 3 char; in Kamerman, S. Little Plays for Little Players. 3 char
———. King's holiday. In Bennett, R. Creative Plays and Programs for Holidays. 6 char
———. Lion and the mouse. In Bennett, R. Creative Plays and Programs for Holidays. 2 char; in Burack, A. One Hundred Plays for Children. 2 char
———. Littlest artist. In Bennett, R. Creative Plays and Programs for Holidays. 4 char+; in Kamerman, S. Little Plays for Little Players. 4 char+
———. Magic weaver. In Bennett, R. Creative Plays and Programs for Holidays. 6 char+
———. Miss Muffet and the spider. In Bennett, R. Creative Plays and Programs for Holidays. 4 char
———. On New Year's Eve. In Bennett, R. Creative Plays and Programs for Holidays. 1 char+
———. Out of the clock. In Bennett, R. Creative Plays and Programs for Holidays. 5 char
———. Piccola. In Bennett, R. Creative Plays and Programs for Holidays. 5 char
———. Pixie in a trap. In Bennett, R. Creative Plays and Programs for Holidays. 7 char
———. The plot. In Bennett, R. Creative Plays and Programs for Holidays. 7 char+
———. Prince of hearts. In Bennett, R. Creative Plays and Programs for Holidays. 8 char
———. Pudding-bag string. In Bennett, R. Creative Plays and Programs for Holidays. 9 char+

_____. Rainbow's end. In Bennett, R. Creative Plays and Programs for Holidays. 4 char
_____. Rumpelstiltskin. In Bennett, R. Creative Plays and Programs for Holidays. 6 char+; in Kamerman, S. Children's Plays from Favorite Stories. 6 char+
_____. Runaway pirate. In Burack, A. Four Star Plays for Boys. 4 char+; in Durrell, D. Thirty Plays for Classroom Reading. 5 char
_____. Santa's send-off. In Bennett, R. Creative Plays and Programs for Holidays. 5 char
_____. Scarecrow and the witch. In Bennett, R. Creative Plays and Programs for Holidays. 4 char+
_____. School for scamperers. In Bennett, R. Creative Plays and Programs for Holidays. 5 char+
_____. Shoemaker and the elves. In Bennett, R. Creative Plays and Programs for Holidays. 5 char
_____. Snowman who played Santa. In Bennett, R. Creative Plays and Programs for Holidays. 4 char
_____. Snow-white and Rose-red. In Bennett, R. Creative Plays and Programs for Holidays. 7 char
_____. Thanksgiving pageant. In Bennett, R. Creative Plays and Programs for Holidays. 7 char
_____. Three terrors. In Bennett, R. Creative Plays and Programs for Holidays. 5 char; in Ross, L. Holiday Puppets. 5 char
_____. Valentine for Mary. In Bennett, R. Creative Plays and Programs for Holidays. 6 char
_____. Visitors for Nancy Hawks. In Bennett, R. Creative Plays and Programs for Holidays. 4 char
_____. Waking the daffodil. In Bennett, R. Creative Plays and Programs for Holidays. 5 char
_____. What will the toys say? In Bennett, R. Creative Plays and Programs for Holidays. 7 char+
_____. Winter wizards. In Bennett, R. Creative Plays and Programs for Holidays. 7 char
_____. Ye olden festival of Christmas. In Bennett, R. Creative Plays and Programs for Holidays. 17 char+
Benson, Islay. Long live Christmas. In Kamerman, S. Fifty Plays for Holidays. 32 char+
Beowulf. Love, S.
Best Bargain in the world. Fisher, A.
Best gift of all. Smith, M.
Best of sports. Cable, H.
Beware the genies! Boiko, C.
Beyond mutiny. Peterson, M.
BIBLE
    Fisher, A. Three and the dragon

BIBLE

    Howard, V. Daniel in the lion's den
    ―――――. David and Goliath
    ―――――. David's battle with Goliath
    Milton, J. Eve decides to eat of the fruit of the tree of knowledge
    Preston, C. In a manger laid
    White, A. Prodigal son
    Zeligs, D. Queen Esther saves her people
Bible pantomimes. Howard, V.
Bierce, Ambrose. Shipwreck. In Gilfond, H. Plays for Reading. 10 char
Bierling, J. C. Eleanor. No braver soldier. In Burack, A. One Hundred Plays for Children. 11 char
Big Paul Bunyan. Thane, A.
Big Red Riding Hood. Cable, H.
Big shoo. Boiko, C.
Big stone. Leuser, E.
Biggs, Louise. Key to understanding. In Kamerman, S. Fifty Plays for Junior Actors. 28 char
Billy-club puppets. Lorca, F.
Bird cage. Barbour, F.
BIRDS
    Anderson, H. Emperor's nightingale
    Bennett, R. Pixie in a trap
    Boiko, C. Number one Apple Tree Lane
    Carlson, B. Happy nesting
    ―――――. Why the owl is sacred in Hawaii
    ―――――. Why the nightingale sings gloriously
    Jarvis, S. M. Lion and the birds
    Sperling, L. Baby bird
Birthday gift. MacLellan, E.
Birthday pie. Miller, H.
Birthday surprises. Howard, V.
BIRTHDAYS
    Boiko, C. Melinda's incredible birthday
    Martens, A. Thirteen
    Miller, H. Mother Goose bakeshop
    ―――――. One to grow on
    ―――――. Wait and see
    Nolan, P. Licha's birthday serenade
    Pantopuck. Owl's birthday
Bishop's candlesticks. Hugo, V.
Biskie the snowman. Lehman, J.
BLACK AMERICANS
    Childress, A. Black Scenes
    Glass, G. Early life of George Washington Carver
    Hughes, L. Soul gone home

BLACK 12

Black idol. Love, S.
Blaine, Betty Gray. Rosy-cheeked ghost. In Kamerman, S. Fifty Plays for Junior Actors. 12 char+
Blanton, Catherine. Dulce man. In Burack, A. One Hundred Plays for Children. 5 char+
Blown with the breeze. McNair, J.
Blue toadstool. Bellah, M.
Blumenfeld, Lenore. Another way to weigh an elephant. In Burack, A. Popular Plays for Classroom Reading. 8 char
BOASTING
    Bennett, R. Runaway pirate
Boat club dance. Robinson, C.
BOATS
    Conrad, E. Show boat
Bobby and the Lincoln speech. Hark, M.
Bobby and the Lincoln speech. Pendleton, E.
Bob's armistice parade. Streacker, L.
Boiko, Claire. Ah See and the six colored heaven. In Boiko, C. Plays and Programs for Boys and Girls. 18 char
_____. All about mothers. In Boiko, C. Children's Plays for Creative Actors. 16 char+
_____. All hands on deck. In Boiko, C. Children's Plays for Creative Actors. 11 char; in Burack, A. Popular Plays for Classroom Reading. 12 char
_____. All points west. In Boiko, C. Children's Plays for Creative Actors. 16 char+
_____. Anywhere and everywhere. In Boiko, C. Children's Plays for Creative Actors. 29 char+
_____. Beware the genies! In Boiko, C. Plays and Programs for Boys and Girls. 12 char+
_____. Big shoo. In Boiko, C. Children's Plays for Creative Actors. 14 char+
_____. Book that saved the earth. In Boiko, C. Plays and Programs for Boys and Girls. 7 char; in Kamerman, S. Fifty Plays for Holidays. 7 char
_____. Care and feeding of Mother. In Boiko, C. Plays and Programs for Boys and Girls. 8 char
_____. Christmas revel. In Boiko, C. Children's Plays for Creative Actors. 16 char+
_____. Cinder-riley. In Boiko, C. Children's Plays for Creative Actors. 7 char+; in Kamerman, S. Fifty Plays for Junior Actors. 7 char+
_____. Clean sweep. In Boiko, Children's Plays for Creative Actors. 24 char
_____. Crocus who couldn't bloom. In Boiko, C. Chil-

dren's Plays for Creative Actors. 19 char
___. Cupivac. In Boiko, C. Children's Plays for Creative Actors. 17 char+
___. Destination: Christmas! In Boiko, C. Plays and Programs for Boys and Girls. 33 char+
___. Exterior decorator. In Boiko, C. Children's Plays for Creative Actors. 20 char
___. Franklin reversal. In Boiko, C. Children's Plays for Creative Actors. 9 char
___. Honorable cat's decision. In Boiko, C. Plays and Programs for Boys and Girls. 18 char
___. Hotel Oak. In Plays and Programs for Boys and Girls. 21 char
___. How mothers came to be. In Boiko, C. Plays and Programs for Boys and Girls. 17 char+
___. How to choose a boy. In Boiko, C. Plays and Programs for Boys and Girls. 14 char
___. Insatiable dragon. In Boiko, C. Children's Plays for Creative Actors. 7 char+
___. Jack Jouette's ride. In Boiko, C. Plays and Programs for Boys and Girls. 13 char+
___. Lady Moon and the thief. In Boiko, C. Plays and Programs for Boys and Girls. 14 char+; in Kamerman, S. Dramatized Folk Tales of the World. 14 char+
___. Lion to lamb. In Boiko, C. Children's Plays for Creative Actors. 22 char
___. Little red hen. In Boiko, C. Plays and Programs for Boys and Girls. 12 char+
___. Long table. In Boiko, C. Plays and Programs for Boys and Girls. 23 char+
___. Marvelous time machine. In Boiko, C. Children's Plays for Creative Actors. 10 char
___. May basket fantasia. In Boiko, C. Plays and Programs for Boys and Girls. 24 char
___. Meet the pilgrims! In Boiko, C. Children's Plays for Creative Actors. 10 char
___. Melinda's incredible birthday. In Boiko, C. Plays and Programs for Boys and Girls. 15 char+
___. Mother Goose's Christmas surprise. In Boiko, C. Children's Plays for Creative Actors. 13 char
___. Next stop--spring! In Boiko, C. Plays and Programs for Boys and Girls. 27 char+
___. Number one Apple Tree Lane. In Boiko, C. Plays and Programs for Boys and Girls. 9 char+
___. On camera, Noah Webster! In Boiko, C. Plays and Programs for Boys and Girls. 19 char+

_____. One hundred words. In Plays and Programs for Boys and Girls. 10 char
_____. Operation litterbug. In Boiko, C. Children's Plays for Creative Actors. 10 char
_____. Pandora's perilous predicament. In Boiko, C. Plays and Programs for Boys and Girls. 17 char
_____. Penny wise. In Boiko, C. Children's Plays for Creative Actors. 17 char
_____. Pepe and the cornfield bandit. In Boiko, C. Plays and Programs for Boys and Girls. 12 char+; in Kamerman, S. Dramatized Folk Tales of the World. 12 char+
_____. Peter, Peter, Peter! In Boiko, C. Children's Plays for Creative Actors. 12 char
_____. Punctuation proclamation. In Boiko, C. Children's Plays for Creative Actors. 12 char+
_____. Roman romance. In Boiko, C. Plays and Programs for Boys and Girls. 9 char
_____. Runaway bookmobile. In Boiko, C. Children's Plays for Creative Actors. 8 char+
_____. Scaredy cat. In Boiko, C. Children's Plays for Creative Actors. 10 char+
_____. Search for the sky-blue princess. In Plays and Programs for Boys and Girls. 14 char+
_____. Small crimson parasol. In Boiko, C. Children's Plays for Creative Actors. 10 char+
_____. Snowflake. In Boiko, C. Plays and Programs for Boys and Girls. 17 char+
_____. Snowman who overstayed. In Boiko, C. Children's Plays for Creative Actors. 11 char+
_____. Song goes forth. In Boiko, C. Plays and Programs for Boys and Girls. 20 char
_____. Spaceship Santa Maria. In Boiko, C. Children's Plays for Creative Actors. 16 char
_____. Star bright. In Boiko, C. Children's Plays for Creative Actors. 11 char+
_____. Sun up! In Boiko, C. Children's Plays for Creative Actors. 21 char
_____. The "T" party. In Boiko, C. Children's Plays for Creative Actors. 11 char
_____. Take me to your marshal. In Boiko, C. Plays and Programs for Boys and Girls. 10 char; in Burack, A. Popular Plays for Classroom Reading. 11 char
_____. Tale of two drummers. In Boiko, C. Children's Plays for Creative Actors. 12 char
_____. Tall-tale tournament. In Boiko, C. Plays and Programs for Boys and Girls. 15 char+

15 BONAPARTE

———. Terrible Terry's surprise. In Boiko, C. Children's Plays for Creative Actors. 15 char
———. Trouble in tree-land. In Boiko, C. Children's Plays for Creative Actors. 15 char
———. Wayward Witch. In Boiko, C. Children's Plays for Creative Actors. 3 char+
———. What ever happened to Mother Nature? In Plays and Programs for Boys and Girls. 14 char
———. Who will bell the cat? In Boiko, C. Plays and Programs for Boys and Girls. 9 char
———. Wild rabbit chase. In Boiko, C. Plays and Programs for Boys and Girls. 20 char+
———. Wonderful circus of words. In Boiko, C. Children's Plays for Creative Actors. 28 char
———. Yes, yes, a thousand times yes! In Burack, A. Skits, Comedies, and Farces for Teen-agers. 10 char
———. Young Abe's destiny. In Boiko, C. Children's Plays for Creative Actors. 7 char
BONAPARTE, NAPOLEON
    Walsh, H. Louisiana
Book revue. Hark, M.
Book that saved the earth. Boiko, C.
BOOK WEEK
    Bennett, R. City mouse and the country mouse
    ———. Hare and the tortoise
    ———. Lion and the mouse
    ———. Rumpelstiltskin
    ———. Snow-white and Rose-red
    Boiko, C. Book that saved the earth
    ———. Runaway bookmobile
    D'Arcy, A. Wonders of storybook land
    Fisher, A. Once upon a time
    ———. Treasure hunt
    Hark, M. Book revue
    ———. Books a la mode
    ———. Off the shelf
    Miller, H. Damsels in distress
    ———. Library circus
    Moore, E. Mr. Longfellow observes book week
    Nicholson, J. Haunted bookshop
    Spamer, C. Pop-up books
    Woster, A. Hubbub on the bookshelf
BOOKS
    Boiko, C. Book that saved the earth
    ———. Runaway bookmobile
    ———. Chaloner, G. Bookworm
    Clapp, P. Magic bookshelf

BOOKS 16

    D'Arcy, A. Wonders of storybook land
    Fisher, A. Once upon a time
    _____. Treasure hunt
    Hark, M. Book revue
    _____. Books a la mode
    _____. Off the shelf
    Miller, H. Damsels in distress
    _____. Library circus
    Molloy, L. Fortune of Merrylegs and Tawnywhiskers
    Nicholson, J. Haunted bookshop
    Spamer, C. Pop-up books
    Woster, A. Hubbub on the bookshelf
Books a la mode. Hark, M.
BOOKS--CARE OF
    Hark, M. Off the shelf
The bookworm. Chaloner, G.
BOOKWORMS
    Chaloner, G. Bookworm
    Woster, A. Hubbub on the bookshelf
BOOTH, JOHN WILKES
    Love, S. Man who shot the president
Born in a stable. Preston, C.
Boshibari and the two thieves. Nolan, P.
Boston tea party. Howard, V.
BOTTLES
    Pyle, M. Clever Peter
Bowers, Ethel. Nobility. In McGee, C. Drama for Fun.
    5 char
Bow-wow blues. Dias, E.
Box of chocolates. Howard, V.
BOXING
    Boyd. J. Featherweight champ
    McGee, C. Interview with Punchy McPugg
Boy who could not tell a lie. Very, A.
Boyd, Jan Nisbet. Featherweight champ; or, tickled to
    death. In McGee, C. Drama for Fun. 4 char
Boylan, Eleanor. Jack the giant killer. In Boylan, E. How
    to Be a Puppeteer. 3 char
_____. Musicians of Bremen. In Boylan, E. How to Be
    a Puppeteer. 7 char
_____. Prince and the dragon. In Boylan, E. How to
    Be a Puppeteer. 4 char
_____. Rip Van Winkle. In Boylan, E. How to Be a
    Puppeteer. 10 char+
_____. Runaway pancake. In Boylan, E. How to Be a
    Puppeteer. 5 char
_____. Three billy goats gruff. In Boylan, E. How to

BOYS
    Be a Puppeteer. 4 char
    Bennett, R. Snowman who played Santa
    Boiko, C. Marvelous time machine
    Collodi, C. Pinocchio
    ————. Pinocchio goes to school
    Colson, J. Top of the bill
    Coyle, R. Matter of conscience
    Definition of a boy
    Dickens, C. Oliver Twist
    Glass, G. Henry and the night crawlers
    ————. Lemonade trick
    Hark, M. Stuff of heroes
    Jarvis, S. M. Turkeys are tricky
    Sanders, S. Tragedy in the graveyard
    Twain, M. Tom Sawyer and Injun Joe
    ————. Tom Sawyer, pirate
    see also BROTHERS; BROTHERS AND SISTERS; CHILDREN

Bradbury, Ray. The meadow. In Maloney, E. Plays to Remember. 6 char
Bradley, Polly Lewis. Professor Countdown takes off. In Burack, A. Skits, Comedies and Farces for Teenagers. 4 char+

BRAINS
    Williams, G. Kettle of brains
Branch, William. To follow the phoenix. In Childress, A. Black Scenes. 2 char

BRAVERY
    Bierling, J. No braver soldier
    Boiko, C. All hands on deck
    ————. Tale of two drummers
    Boylan, E. Jack the giant killer
    Colbo, E. Heroine of Wren
    Dumas, A. The Duel
    Hall, H. The valiant
    Hark, M. Stuff of heroes
    Howard, V. David and Goliath
    ————. Oliver Twist asks for more
    Leuser, E. Courage piece
    Melchior, H. Little Ki and the serpent
    Miller, H. Rabbit who refused to run
    Musil, R. Invisible dragon of Winn Sinn Tu
    Nolan, F. Gates of Dinkelsbuehl
    ————. Leak in the dike
    ————. Son of William Tell
    Orczy, B. Scarlet Pimpernel

Watts, F. Miss Louisa and the outlaws
Breaking the ice. In McGee, C. Drama for Fun. 2 char+
Bride of Gorse-Bracken Hall. Olfson, L.
Bridge to Killybog Fair. Watts, F.
Bright, Robert. Richard Brown and the dragon. (Play title: How to put out a dreadful dragon, written by G. Glass). In Glass, G. From Plays into Reading. 10 char
Broadway turkey. Miller, H.
Broken broomstick. Miller, H.
Brontë, Charlotte. Jane Eyre. In Olfson, L. Classics Adopted for Acting and Reading. 5 char
Brontë, Emily. Wuthering Heights. In Olfson, L. Classics Adopted for Acting and Reading. 5 char
Broom market day. Molloy, L.
Broth of Christkindli. Leuser, E.
BROTHERHOOD WEEK
    Clapp, P. Other side of the wall
BROTHERS
    Huntsberry, W. Minor developments
    Leuser, E. Five brothers
BROTHERS AND SISTERS
    Bennett, R. Beaded moccasins
    Fontaine, R. Loafer
    Garver, J. My fair Linda
    Simonds, N. Hansel and Gretel
    Thane, A. Hansel and Gretel
Brown, Thelma Lucille. Talent tree. In Burack, A. One Hundred Plays for Children. 8 char
Browne, Theodore. Natural man. In Childress, A. Black Scenes. 2 char+
Brownie who found Christmas. Thane, A.
Browning, Robert. My last duchess. In Kline, P. Theatre Student: Scenes to Perform. 1 char
_____. Pied piper of Hamlin. In Thane, A. Plays from Famous Stories and Fairy Tales. 8 char+
Brydon, Margaret Wylie, and Esther Ziegler. Dreadful dragon. In Kamerman, S. Fifty Plays for Junior Actors. 15 char+
_____, _____. May witch. In Kamerman, S. Fifty Plays for Holidays. 8 char
_____, _____. Reluctant ghost. In Durrell, D. Favorite Plays for Classroom Reading. 11 char
Buck, Doris F., and Foulk, C. W. Floating stone. In Burack, A. One Hundred Plays for Children. 10 char
Buechler, James. Stone soup. In Kamerman, S. Dramatized Folk Tales of the World. 8 char+
Builder of the wall. Roberts, H.

BUILDING

Building the Panama Canal. Howard, V.
Bulla, Clyde. Ghost town treasure. In Glass, G. From
 Plays into Reading. 9 char
Bullins, Ed. Son come home. In Childress, A. Black
 Scenes. 2 char
Bunnyland brigade. Spamer, C.
BUNYAN, PAUL
 Thane, A. Big Paul Bunyan
BURGLARY
 Nicholson, J. Ghost walks tonight
 _____. Mysterious stranger
Burlingame, Cora. Three wishes. In Burack, A. One
 Hundred Plays for Children. 9 char
_____. Yellow fever. In Burack, A. Four-Star Plays
 for Boys. 12 char
Burnett, Frances Hodgson. Little princess. In Olfson, L.
 Dramatized Classics for Radio-Style Reading, Vol. II.
 10 char; in Thane, A. Plays from Famous Stories
 and Fairy Tales. 12 char
BURR, AARON
 Walsh, H. Louisiana
Burtle, Gerry Lynn. Mystery of the gumdrop dragon. In
 Kamerman, S. Fifty Plays for Junior Actors. 19 char
The bus. Howard, V.
Bus stop. Howard, V.
Busy barbers. Miller, H.
But, doctor. Howard, V.

- C -

Cable, Harold. Another man's family. In Cable, H. Plays
 for Modern Teen-Age Actors. 18 char+
_____. Bailey, go home. In Cable, H. Plays for Mod-
 ern Teen-Age Actors. 18 char
_____. Best of sports. In Cable, H. Plays for Modern
 Teen-Age Actors. 8 char
_____. Big Red Riding Hood. In Cable, H. Plays for
 Modern Teen-Age Actors. 6 char
_____. Deputy for Broken Bow. In Cable, H. Plays
 for Modern Teen-Age Actors. 9 char
_____. Fairest pitcher of them all. In Cable, H. Plays
 for Modern Teen-Age Actors. 24 char
_____. Last stop. In Cable, H. Plays for Modern
 Teen-Age Actors. 9 char
_____. Little Jackie and the beanstalk. In Cable, H.
 Plays for Modern Teen-Age Actors. 20 char

CAESAR 20

    _____. Peace, pilgrim. In Cable, H. Plays for Modern Teen-Age Actors. 15 char+
    _____. Reform of Sterling Silverheart. In Cable, H. Plays for Modern Teen-Age Actors. 10 char
    _____. Reluctant Columbus. In Cable, H. Plays for Modern Teen-Age Actors. 12 char+
    _____. Way-out Cinderella. In Cable, H. Plays for Modern Teen-Age Actors. 9 char
    _____. Way, way down south. In Cable, H. Plays for Modern Teen-Age Actors. 10 char+
    _____. Young forever. In Cable, H. Plays for Modern Teen-Age Actors. 8 char

CAESAR, JULIUS--SPOOF
    Fontaine, R. Great Caesar
    Olfson, Lewy. Great Caesar's ghost!

Cake bake. Howard, V.

CALENDAR
    Boiko, C. Clean sweep
    Faux, D. Littlest month
    Fox, D. Littlest month
    Hartley, C. Children of the calendar
    Oser, J. King's calendar
    see also specific months

CALIFORNIA
    Howard, V. California gold discovery
    Saroyan, W. Man with the heart in the highlands

California gold discovery. Howard, V.
Call to a bride. Howard, V.
Call Washington 1776. Miller, H.
Calling all cooks. Howard, V.
Calling all spies. Howard, V.
Campbell, Camilla. Bell of Dolores. In Kamerman, S. Fifty Plays for Holidays. 16 char+
    _____. Morning maker. In Kamerman, S. Little Plays for Little Players. 4 char+
Campbell, Josephine E. Pink roses for Christmas. In Burack, A. Christmas Plays for Young Actors. 4 char

CAMPING
    Carlson, B. Or make pot holders
    Fontaine, R. Camping pictures

Camping pictures. Fontaine, R.
Canadian fairy tale. In Philpott, A. Eight Plays for Hand Puppets. 5 char

CANDY
    Burtle, G. Mystery of the gumdrop dragon
    Spamer, C. Candy canes

Candy canes. Spamer, C.

Can't get there from here, mebbe. Fontaine, R.
Can'tsee Poorsight. McGee, C.
Capell, Loretta Camp. Tongue-cut sparrow. In Kamerman, S. Children's Plays from Favorite Stories. 17 char+
Captain Castaway's captives. Miller, H.
Care and feeding of mother. Boiko, C.
CAREERS
    Brown, T. Talent tree
Carefree high school orchestra. Fontaine, R.
CARIBBEAN
    Cable, H. Bailey, go home
Carlson, Bernice. All about animals. In Carlson, B. Funny-Bone Dramatics. 2 char
————. Another way (the Mayflower Compact) In Carlson, B. Play a Part. 4 char+
————. Fit for a king. In Carlson, B. Funny-Bone Dramatics. 10 char
————. Follow-the-leader. In Carlson, B. Funny-Bone Dramatics. 2 char+
————. Ghosts. In Carlson, B. Play a Part. 7 char+
————. Golden spike. In Carlson, B. Play a Part. 5 char+
————. Golden tooth. In Carlson, B. Play a Part. 3 char+
————. Goodbye, Snikke-snak. In Carlson, B. Play a Part. 4 char+
————. Happy nesting. In Carlson, B. Play a Part. 9 char+
————. Home cooking. In Carlson, B. Funny-Bone Dramatics. 2 char
————. Impossible! unacceptable! preposterous! In Carlson, B. Play a Part. 6 char+
————. In the dumps. In Carlson, B. Funny-Bone Dramatics. 2 char
————. It had to be. In Carlson, B. Funny-Bone Dramatics. 3 char
————. Justice for all. In Carlson, B. Play a Part. 3 char+
————. Let her ride! In Carlson, B. Play a Part. 7 char+
————. Let's fool someone. In Carlson, B. Play a Part. 3 char
————. Make your own bed. In Carlson, B. Funny-Bone Dramatics. 2 char
————. Marked trail. In Carlson, B. Funny-Bone Dramatics. 3 char
————. Murky monster foiled again. In Carlson, B.

CARLSON 22

_____. Play a Part. 9 char+
_____. My treasure. In Carlson, B. Funny-Bone Dramatics. 3 char+
_____. Nothing! In Carlson, B. Funny-Bone Dramatics. 3 char
_____. O little town. In Carlson, B. Play a Part. 8 char+
_____. On myself. In Carlson, B. Funny-Bone Dramatics. 2 char
_____. Operation satellite. In Carlson, B. Play a Part. 5 char+
_____. Or make pot holders. In Carlson, B. Play a Part. 2 char
_____. Pirates. In Carlson, B. Play a Part. 6 char
_____. Rebecca of Sunnybrook Farm. In Carlson, B. Play a Part. 3 char
_____. Remember the Christmas tree. In Carlson, B. Play a Part. 7 char+
_____. Robin Hood meets Little John. In Carlson, B. Play a Part. 4 char+
_____. Rock the baby, Granny. In Carlson, B. Play a Part. 5 char+
_____. Salt in the soup. In Carlson, B. Play a Part. 6 char
_____. Seven Simons. In Carlson, B. Funny-Bone Dramatics. 8 char
_____. Ship like this. In Carlson, B. Funny-Bone Dramatics. 3 char
_____. Shut the door! In Carlson, B. Funny-Bone Dramatics. 4 char
_____. Smithtown, U.S.A. In Carlson, B. Funny-Bone Dramatics. 2 char
_____. Summer maker. In Carlson, B. Play a Part. 6 char+
_____. The $10,000 dog. In Carlson, B. Funny-Bone Dramatics. 3 char
_____. There's always a leader. In Carlson, B. Play a Part. 11 char+
_____. To build a federal city. In Carlson, B. Play a Part. 8 char+
_____. To play the piano. In Carlson, B. Funny-Bone Dramatics. 2 char
_____. Touch one. In Carlson, B. Funny-Bone Dramatics. 3 char
_____. Trailing arbutus. In Carlson, B. Play a Part. 4 char
_____. Turn south at Voorhees' farm. In Carlson, B.

Play a Part. 5 char+
_____. What is it? In Carlson, B. Play a Part. 4 char+
_____. Where there are no snags. In Carlson, B. Play a Part. 3 char+
_____. Who will be king? In Carlson, B. Play a Part. 4 char+
_____. Why catch a Leprechaun? In Carlson, B. Funny-Bone Dramatics. 4 char+
_____. Why don't you? In Carlson, B. Funny-Bone Dramatics. 2 char
_____. Why the leaves of the aspen tree quake in a breeze. In Carlson, B. Play a Part. 5 char
_____. Why the nightingale sings gloriously. In Carlson, B. Play a Part. 4 char+
_____. Why the owl is sacred in Hawaii. In Carlson, B. Play a Part. 5 char+
Carroll, Gladys Hasty. Merry, merry, merry. In Burack, A. One Hundred Plays for Children. 24 char
Carroll, Lewis. Alice's adventures in Wonderland. In Mahlmann, L. Puppet Plays for Young Players. 17 char
_____. Through the looking-glass. In Olfson, L. Classics Adopted for Acting or Reading. 8 char
Carter, Steve. One last look. In Childress, A. Black Scenes. 9 char+
CARTOONS
    Wilde, C. Comic strip antics
CARVER, GEORGE WASHINGTON
    Glass, G. Early life of George Washington Carver
Case for two detectives. Murray, J.
Case of mistaken identity. Murray, J.
Case of the frustrated corpse. Wallace, R.
Case of the giggling goblin. Miller, H.
Case of the missing masterpiece. Huff, B.
Cask of Amontillado. Poe, E.
Cast up by the sea. Dias, E.
Cat and the queen. Molloy, L.
Catastrophe Clarence. Shore, M.
CATS
    Barr, J. Three little kittens
    Bennett, R. Pudding-bag string.
    Boiko, C. Who will bell the cat?
    Elfenbeim, J. Puss-in-boots
    Glass, G. Dick Whittington and his cat
    Hark, M. Too many kittens
    Harper, J. First cat on Mars

Hughes, T. Sean
Miller, H. Country store cat
———. Three little kittens
Murray, J. Scaredy cat
Newman, D. Yankee-doodle kitten
Perrault, C. Puss in boots
Thane, A. Dick Whittington and his cat
Very, A. Golden bell for mother
———. Puss-in-boots
Cavalcade of human rights. Fisher, A.
CAVALRY
    Dias, E. Hold back the redskins
Caves of the earth. Fisher, A.
Celebrated jumping frog of Calaveras County. Twain, M.
Cervantes, Miguel de. Don Quixote. In Olfson, L. Dramatized Classics for Radio-Style Reading. 14 char
Chaloner, Gwen. Bookworm. In Kamerman, S. Fifty Plays for Junior Actors. 16 char
———. Court of King Arithmetic. In Kamerman, S. Fifty Plays for Junior Actors. 22 char
Chandler, Anna Curtis. Chinese Rip Van Winkle. In Burack, A. One Hundred Plays for Children. 12 char+
CHARACTER BUILDING
    Dias, E. Christmas spirit
    ———. Gift of laughter
    ———. Little man who wasn't there
    Leuser, E. Tommy's adventure
    Miller, H. Shady shadows
    Pendleton, E. Jingle bells
    Waite, H. Christmas house
    see also GROWING UP; RESPONSIBILITY
CHARACTERS IN LITERATURE
    D'Arcy, A. Wonders of storybook land
    Mahlmann, L. Magic shoes
    Moore, E. Mr. Longfellow observes book week
    Nicholson, J. Haunted bookshop
    Nolan, P. Anton Chekhov sort of evening
    ———. Whole city's down below
Cheatham, Val. Snow White and friends. In Burack, A. Skits, Comedies and Farces for Teen-Agers. 7 char
CHECKERS
    Nolan, P. Trash and treasure
Chekhov, Anton. The Upheaval. In Gilfond, H. Plays for Reading. 6 char
CHEMISTRY SETS
    Glass, G. Lemonade trick
Chermak, Sylvia. Peter and the wolf. In Kamerman, S. Dramatized Folk Tales of the World. 9 char+

CHILD LABOR
    Howard, V. Oliver Twist asks for more
Child who was made of snow. Bennett, R.
Childhood. Wilder, T.
CHILDREN
    Beach, M. On the fence
    Fisher, A. One-ring circus
    Glass, G. Pippi Longstocking
    _____. Saturdays
    Hark, M. Christmas snowman
    _____. Cupies and hearts
    _____. Our own four walls
    Heath, A. Gypsy look
    Henderson, N. Look behind the mask
    Hoppenstedt, E. Poet's nightmare
    Lehman, J. Biskie the snowman
    Miller, H. Circus daze
    _____. Shirley Holmes and the FBI
    Nicholson, J. Teapot trouble
    Nolan, P. Gates of Dinkelsbuehl
    Pyle, M. Mrs. Gibbs advertises
    _____. Not on the menu
    Thane, A. Brownie who found Christmas
    Wilder, T. Childhood
    see also BOYS; BROTHERS; BROTHERS AND SISTERS; GIRLS; PARENT AND CHILD; SISTERS; TEEN-AGERS
Children of Chocolate Street. Kane E.
Children of the calendar. Hartley, C.
Children of the sun. Rittenhouse, C.
Children on the moon. Hoff, S.
Children who found new friends. Howard, V.
Childress, Alice. African garden. In Childress, A. Black
    Scenes. 2 char
CHINA
    Andersen, H. Emperor's nightingale
    Asbrand, A. China comes to you
    Blumenfeld, L. Another way to weigh an elephant
    Boiko, C. Ah See and the six-colored heaven
    _____. Insatiable dragon
    _____. Lady Moon and the thief
    Brydon, M. Dreadful dragon
    Chandler, A. Chinese Rip Van Winkle
    Cochrane, L. Moon dragon
    Fitz-Adcock, I. Royal cloth of China
    Hagy, L. Fire in a paper
    Huff, B. Feast of the thousand lanterns

CHINA 26

    McFarlan, E. Pear tree
  ―――――. Tiger catcher
Melchior, H. Little Ki and the serpent
Miller, H. Wishing stream
Musil, R. Invisible dragon of Winn Sinn Tu
Newman, D. Plum Blossom and the dragon
Nicholson, M. Wise wife
Nolan, F. Double nine of Chih Yuan
Richards, L. Chop-chin and the golden dragon
China comes to you. Asbrand, K.
Chinese Rip Van Winkle. Chandler, A.
Chisholm, James R. Enchanted, I'm sure. In Burack, A. Skits, Comedies and Farces for Teen-Agers. 6 char; in Durrell, D. Teen-Age Plays for Classroom Reading. 7 char
―――――. Prince is where you find him. In Kamerman, S. Fifty Plays for Junior Actors. 13 char
―――――. Shades of ransom. In Durrell, D. Favorite Plays for Classroom Reading. 10 char
Choosing of Easter Rabbit. Werner, S.
Chop-chin and the golden dragon. Richards, L.
CHORAL PLAYS
    Breaking the ice
    Barrington, P. I had a hippopotamus
    Boiko, C. Lion to lamb
    ―――――. Sun up!
    Definition of a boy
    Eskimo
    Fly and a flea
    Grabe, Mrs. K. I know an old woman
    Local frog stages comeback
    McGee, C. Evolution
    On being a senior adult
    Tree toad loved a she-toad
    Two frogs
    Youngster named Danny
CHRISTMAS
    Barbee, L. Holly hangs high
    Bennett, R. The child who was made of snow
    ―――――. Christmas pie
    ―――――. Piccola
    ―――――. Pudding-bag string
    ―――――. Santa's send-off
    ―――――. Shoemaker and the elves
    ―――――. Snowman who played Santa
    ―――――. What will the toys say?
    ―――――. Ye olden Festival of Christmas

Benson, I.   Long live Christmas
Boiko, C.   Christmas revel
———.   Destination: Christmas!
———.   Mother Goose's Christmas surprise
———.   Star bright
Burack, A.   Christmas Plays for Young Actors
Carlson, B.   O little town
Carroll, G.   Merry, merry, merry
Colbo, E.   First New England Christmas tree
Dias, E.   Christmas spirit
———.   Video Christmas
Dickens, C.   Christmas carol
DuBois, G.   Two strangers from Nazareth
Fisher, A.   Angel in the looking-glass
———.   Christmas cake
———.   Christmas tree for kitty
———.   Merry Christmas elf
———.   Spirit of Christmas
———.   Time out for Christmas
Hark, M.   Christmas Eve news
———.   Christmas in the woods
———.   Christmas party
———.   Junction Santa Claus
———.   Santa Claus parade
———.   That Christmas feeling
Howard, V.   Happy holidays for little women
Howells, W.   Christmas every day
Hughes, T.   Coming of the kings
Kane, E.   Children of Chocolate Street
Leuser, E.   Legend of the Christmas rose
———.   Mixing stick
McCarty, E.   Little cake
McGee, C.   Night before Christmas
MacLellan, E. Clock's secret
Menotti, G.   Amahl and the night visitors
Miller, H.   Christmas peppermints
———.   Lost Christmas cards
———.   Mistletoe mystery
———.   Red Carpet Christmas
———.   Red flannel suit
———.   S.O.S. from Santa
———.   Santa calls a conference
———.   Toy scout jamboree
———.   Wake up, Santa Claus!
Mills, G.   Christmas comes to Hamelin
Moessenger, B. Man in the red suit
Neman, D.   One night in Bethlehem

Nolan, J. Happy Christmas to all
Patterson, E. No room at the inn
Preston, C. Born in a stable
───── . In a manger laid
───── . Old Christmas
Roberts, H. Lonely fir tree
Ross, L. Three kings
Sagoff, S. Hand-me-down Hildy
Thane, A. Brownie who found Christmas
───── . Elves and the shoemaker
Waite, H. Christmas house
Watts, F. Santa and the efficiency expert
see also CHRISTMAS IN OTHER COUNTRIES; CHRISTMAS SPIRIT; CHRISTMAS TREES; SANTA CLAUS
Christmas cake. Fisher, A.
Christmas carol. Dickens, C.
Christmas comes to Hamelin. Mills, G.
Christmas eve news. Hark, M.
Christmas every day. Howells, W.
Christmas house. Hoppenstedt, E.
CHRISTMAS IN OTHER COUNTRIES
Boiko, C. Destination: Christmas!
Nolan, P. And Christmas is its name
Very, A. Everywhere Christmas
Christmas in the woods. Hark, M.
Christmas party. Hark, M.
Christmas peppermints. Miller, H.
Christmas pie. Bennett, R.
Christmas revel. Boiko, C.
Christmas snowman. Hark, M.
CHRISTMAS SPIRIT
Barbee, L. Friday foursome packs a box
Dias, E. Christmas spirit
───── . Video Christmas
Fisher, A. Merry Christmas elf
───── . Spirit of Christmas
Leuser, E. Broth of Christkindli
Miller, H. Red flannel suit
Nolan, P. And Christmas is its name
Paradis, M. Santa goes to town
Pendleton, E. Jingle bells
Pyle, M. Perambulating pie
St. Clair, R. Spirit of Christmas
Christmas spirit. Dias, E.
Christmas train. Howard, H.
Christmas tree for kitty. Fisher, A.

CHRISTMAS TREES
    Carlson, B. Remember the Christmas tree
    Colbo, E. Littlest fir
    Fisher, A. Christmas tree for kitty
Cinder-rabbit. Baher, C.
Cinder-riley. Boiko, C.
Cinderella. Barr, J.
Cinderella. Cable, H. (Play title: Way-out Cinderella)
Cinderella. D'Arcy, A.
Cinderella. Newman, D.
Cinderella. Thane, A.
Cinderella revisited. Olfson, L.
CIRCUS
    Colson, J. Top of the bill
    Miller, H. Circus daze
    Nicholson, M. Crying clown
Circus daze. Miller, H.
City mouse and the country mouse. Bennett, R.
CIVIL RIGHTS see HUMAN RIGHTS
CIVIL WAR
    Dias, E. Visitor to Gettysburg
    Miller, H. Pink parasol
    Very, A. President Lincoln's children
Clapp, Patricia. Girl whose fortune sought her. In Kamerman, S. Children's Plays from Favorite Stories. 6 char
_____. Magic bookshelf. In Kamerman, S. Fifty Plays for Junior Actors. 10 char
_____. Other side of the wall. In Kamerman, S. Fifty Plays for Holidays. 7 char+
Clark, Barrett H. Fires at Valley Forge. In Burack, A. Four-Star Plays for Boys. 9 char
Clean sweep. Boiko, C.
Cleanest town in the West. Dias, E.
Cleary, Beverly. Ellen Tebbits (Play title: Ellen's secret, written by G. Glass); In Glass, G. From Plays into Reading. 8 char
_____. Henry Huggins. (Play title: Henry and the night crawlers, written by G. Glass) In Glass, G. From plays into reading. 9 char
Clemens, Samuel see Twain, Mark
Cleopatra's death scene. Shakespeare, W.
Clever Peter. Pyle, M.
CLEVERNESS
    Buechler, J. Stone soup
    Feather, J. Quick-witted Jack
    Nicholson, M. Princess Nimble-wit

CLIVE 30

  ――――――. Wise wife
  Nolan, P. Highland fling
  ――――――. Magic of Salamanca
  Slattery, M. Patchwork princess
CLIVE, ROBERT
  Love, S. Clive of India
CLOCKS
  Miller, H. Trouble in Tick Tock Town
  Clock's secret. MacLellan, E.
CLOTH
  Carlson, B. My treasure
CLOWNS
  Colson, J. Top of the bill
  Nicholson, M. Crying clown
CLUBS [Associations]
  Schwartz, M. All in favor
Cockrane, Louise. Karagiosis and the dragon. In Cochrane, L. Shadow Puppets in Color. 6 char+
  ――――――. Moon dragon. In Cochrane, L. Shadow Puppet in Color. 3 char+
  ――――――. Story of Rama and Sita. In Cochrane, L. Shadow Puppets in Color. 6 char+
Colbert, Mildred. Salt in the sea. In Burack, A. One Hundred Plays for Children. 17 char
Colbo, Ella Stratton. First New England Christmas tree. In Burack, A. One Hundred Plays for Children. 8 char+
  ――――――. Heroine of Wren. In Burack, A. One Hundred Plays for Children. 6 char; in Durrell, D. Thirty Plays for Classroom Reading. 7 char
  ――――――. Littlest fir. In Burack, A. Christmas Plays for Young Actors. 7 char
COLDS
  Kane, E. Piffle! It's only a sniffle!
Cole, Eva. Welcome, parents. In Kamerman, S. Fifty Plays for Holidays. 12 char
Collodi, Carlo. Pinocchio. In Mahlmann, L. Puppet Plays for Young Players. 13 char
  ――――――. Pinocchio goes to school. In Thane, A. Plays from Famous Stories and Fairy Tales. 9 char+
The colonel. Howard, V.
COLORS
  Hark, M. Rainbow colors
Colson, J. G. Baron Barnsby's box. In Kamerman, S. Dramatized Folk Tales of the World. 9 char
  ――――――. Message from Robin Hood. In Kamerman, S. Fifty Plays for Junior Actors. 11 char+

————. Robin Hood in Sherwood Forest. In Burack, A.
Four-Star Plays for Boys. 13 char+
————. Top of the bill. In Burack, A. Four-Star Plays
for Boys. 5 char
COLUMBUS, CHRISTOPHER
    Bakeless, K. Most memorable voyage
    Barbee, L. Columbus sails the sea
    Bennett, R. The plot
    Boiko, C. Spaceship Santa Maria
    Cable, H. Reluctant Columbus
    Dias, E. Ghost from Genoa
    Fisher, A. Day of destiny
    ————. Weaver's son
    Howard, V. Columbus' discovery of America
    MacLellan, E. Return of the Nina
    Olfson, L. Sail on! Sail on!
    Peterson, M. Beyond mutiny
    Roberts, H. For the glory of Spain
    Ross, L. Admiral and the feathered pilots
COLUMBUS DAY
    Fisher, A. Day of destiny
    ————. Weaver's son
    Ross, L. Admiral and the feathered pilots
Columbus' discovery of America. Howard, V.
Columbus sails the sea. Barbee, L.
Come to the fair! Murray, J.
COMEDY
    Alderman, E. Hamelot
    Alexander, S. Small Plays for You and a Friend
    Blumenfeld, L. Another way to weigh an elephant
    Boiko, C. Book that saved the earth
    ————. Cupivac
    ————. Franklin reversal
    ————. Scaredy cat
    ————. Take me to your marshal
    ————. Terrible Terry's surprise
    Brydon, M. Reluctant ghost
    Cable, H. Bailey, go home
    Chisholm, J. Prince is where you find him
    ————. Shades of ransom
    Dias, E. Gift of laughter
    ————. Hippie and the bard
    ————. Madison Avenue merry-go-round
    ————. Printer's devil
    Dorand, J. Surprise party
    Draper, C. Emperor's daughters
    Driver, D. Your own thing

DuBois, G.   Last Laugh
Elfenbeim, J.   Ten-penny tragedy
Fletcher, J.   Jailer's daughter falls in love with a prince
Garver, J.   Howling success
Glass, G.   Lemonade trick
─────────.   Mr. Popper's penguins
─────────.   Pippi Longstocking
Grahame, K.   Reluctant dragon
Hale, L.   Lady who put salt in her coffee
Hark, M.   Father keeps house
─────────.   Our own four walls
─────────.   Too many kittens
─────────.   When do we eat?
Heath, A.   Much ado about ants
Howard, H.   Doctor Know-All
Huntsberry, W.   Minor developments
Irving, W.   Legend of Sleepy Hollow
Jarvis, S.   Supper with the queen
Lawrence, J.   Inside a kid's head
McGee, C.   Dr. Quack's medicine show
Martens, A.   George slept here, too
Miller, H.   Ghost in the house
─────────.   Puppy love
─────────.   Valentine for Kate
Molière.   Would-be gentleman
Molloy, L.   Cat and the queen
─────────.   Jenny-by-the-day
Murray, J.   Come to the fair!
─────────.   Healthy, wealthy, and wild
─────────.   Mad about art
─────────.   National everything
─────────.   Publisher's choice
─────────.   Triumph for Trimbly
Nicholson, J.   Ghost walks tonight
─────────.   Valentine stardust
Nolan, P.   Courters
─────────.   Happy ending
─────────.   Hi down there
─────────.   Magic of Salamanca
O'Casey, S.   End of the beginning
Olfson, L.   My son, the prince
Perrault, C.   Puss in boots
Philpott, V.   The egg
Pope, A.   Belinda bemoans the loss of a lock of her hair
Pyle, M.   Not on the menu

Robinson, C.   Boat club dance
Rostand, E.   Nose speech
Schwartz, M.   Twin cousins
Shakespeare, W.   Comedy of errors
————.   Midsummer night's dream
————.   Taming of the shrew
Sheridan, R.   The rivals
Shore, M.   Catastrophe Clarence
Simon, S.   Doctor farmer
Stockton, F.   Transferred ghost
Swintz, M.   King's creampuffs
————.   Panic in the palace
————.   Posies for the potentate
Taylor, L.   Baseball
————.   Not for one sandwich
————.   Telephone
Thane, A.   Dummling and the golden goose
Twain, M.   Tom Sawyer, pirate
Weik, M.   The bridge
————.   King's garden
————.   Moonlight
————.   The rehearsal
————.   River risin'!
White, A.   Deaf woman's courtship
————.   Eight bells
————.   Nice girls don't chase the boys
————.   Willie's gane to Melville castle
Whitworth, V.   Mechanical maid
Wilde, O.   Importance of being earnest
————.   On being too frequently proposed to
Worcester, N.   Mad tea party
Comedy of errors.   Shakespeare, W.
Comedy skit.   Taylor, L.
Comedy team.   Howard, V.
Comic strip antics.   Wilde, C.
Coming of the kings.   Hughes, T.
Complaint desk.   Howard, V.
COMPUTERS
    Boiko, C.   Cupivac
    Henderson, N.   Automa
    Olfson, L.   Try data-date!
CONNECTICUT--HISTORY
    Hall, M.   Hearts of oak
Conrad, Edna and Mary Van Dyke.   Show boat.   <u>In</u> Conrad,
    E.   History on the Stage.   21 char+
CONSCIENCE
    Coyle, R.   A matter of conscience

CONSTITUTION
    Toles, M. We, the people
CONTENTMENT
    Nolan, P. Happiest hat
CONTESTS
    Boiko, C. Big shoo
    _____. Christmas revel
    Nolan, P. Highland fling
COOKIES
    Carlson, B. Nothing!
    _____. Touch one
    Miller, H. Magic cookie jar
COOKING
    Fisher, A. Christmas cake
    Jarvis, S. Supper with the queen
    Slattery, M. King in the kitchen
    Werner, S. King's bean soup
Cooper, Esther. Greta and the prince. In Durrell, D. Thirty Plays for Classroom Reading. 6 char
_____. Little white cloud. In Kamerman, S. Little Plays for Little Players. 5 char
_____. Magic spell. In Burack, A. One Hundred Plays for Children. 6 char
_____. Witch's pumpkin. In Burack, A. One Hundred Plays for Children. 3 char
Cooper, James Fenimore. The spy. In Walsh, Henry H. Six Plays in American History. 17 char
COOPERATION
    Davis, L. David and the second Lafayette
    Fisher, A. Special edition
    Howard, H. Christmas train
    Leuser, E. Mixing stick
Corbett, Scott. Lemonade trick. In Glass, G. From Plays into Reading. 9 char
Corey, Caroline H. Dancing princesses. In Kamerman, S. Children's Plays from Famous Stories. 19 char
Corson, Hazel W. Dame Fortune and Don Money. In Kamerman, S. Dramatized Folk Tales of the World. 14 char+
_____. Fish in the forest. In Burack, A. Popular Plays for Classroom Reading. 19 char; in Kamerman, S. Dramatized Folk Tales of the World. 13 char+
_____. Triumph for two. In Kamerman, S. Dramatized Folk Tales of the World. 18 char
Count of Monte Cristo. Dumas, A.
COUNTING
    Carlson, B. Seven Simons
    see also NUMBERS--HISTORY

Country store cat. Miller, H.
Couple of right smart fellers. Olfson, L.
COURAGE see BRAVERY
Courage piece. Leuser, E.
Court of King Arithmetic. Chaloner, G.
Courters. Nolan, P.
COURTESY
    Hark, M. Doctor Manners
    Howard, H. Ben Franklin, peace-maker
    see also ETIQUETTE
Courtesy at the wheel. Howard, V.
COUSINS
    Heath, A. Gypsy look
Covetous councilman. Bealmear, J.
COWBOYS
    Cable, H. Deputy for Broken Bow
    Fontaine, R. How the West was won
    Miller, H. Half-pint cowboy
    _____. Jimmy Cinders
Coyle, Rollin W. Matter of conscience. In Durrell, D.
    Favorite Plays for Classroom Reading. 6 char
The crabfish. White, A.
CRIME
    Chisholm, J. Enchanted, I'm sure
    Love, S. Black idol
    Murray, J. Dead of night
    _____. Triumph for Trimbly
    see also BURGLARY; DETECTIVES; MURDER;
    THIEVES
Crimson feather. Watts, F.
Crocus who couldn't bloom. Boiko, C.
Cross princess. MacLellan, E.
Crow and the corn. Rhodes, J.
CROWD PSYCHOLOGY
    Tolstoy, L. Little girls wiser than men
Crowded house. Jacob, E.
Crowning of King Arthur. Malory, T.
CRYING
    Asbrand, K. Crystal flask
    Nicholson, M. Crying clown
Crying clown. Nicholson, M.
Crystal flask. Asbrand, K.
Cumming, William D.
    see Love, Stewart, and William D. Cumming
Cupid in demand. Miller, H.
Cupid's post office. Hark, M.
Cupies and hearts. Hark, M.

CUPIVAC

Cupivac. Boiko, C.
Curse of hag hollow. Miller, H.
CYCLOPS
    Love, S. One-eyed giant
Cyrano de Bergerac. Bostand, E. (Play title: Nose speech)
CZECHOSLOVAKIA
    Corson, H. Triumph for two

- D -

Dame Fortune and Don Money. Corson, H.
Damsels in distress. Miller, H.
The dancers. Howard, V.
DANCING
    Carlson, B. Rock the baby, Granny
    Nolan, P. Highland fling
    Robinson, C. Boat club dance
    Weik, M. King's garden
    Wilde, C. Junior prom
Dancing princesses. Corey, C.
Dangerous game. Miller, C.
Daniel in the lion's den. Howard, V.
D'Arcy, Alice. Cinderella. In Burack, A. One Hundred Plays for Children. 16 char
_____. Wonders of storybook land. In Burack, A. One Hundred Plays for Children. 19 char
Daring sailormen. Howard, V.
DARWIN, CHARLES
    Carlson, B. What is it?
The daubers. Ward, T.
D'Aulnoy, Mme. Princess Rosette. In Glass, G. From Plays into Reading. 24 char
David and Goliath. Howard, V.
David and the second Lafayette. Davis, L.
David Swan. Hawthorne, N.
David's battle with Goliath. Howard, V.
Davis, Lavinia R. David and the second Lafayette. In Burack, A. One Hundred Plays for Children. 13 char+
_____. St. Patrick and the last snake in Ireland. In Kamerman, S. Little Plays for Little Players. 13 char
_____. A turtle, a flute, and the general's birthday. In Kamerman, S. Fifty Plays for Junior Actors. 16 char+
Davis, Ossie. Purlie Victorious. In Childress, A. Black Scenes. 5 char
Day Canary met Sparrow. Sperling, L.

DAY

Day for trees. Hark, M.
Day is bright. Myrick, N.
Day of absence. Ward, D.
Day of destiny. Fisher, A.
Day the moonmen landed. Ryback, R.
DAYS OF THE WEEK
    Miller, H. Real princess
Dead of night. Murray, J.
Deaf woman's courtship. White, A.
Dear Judy. Howard, V.
Dear Lottie. Dias, E.
Dear Mr. Loveletter. Howard, V.
DEATH
    Henry, O. Last leaf
    Marlowe, C. Death of Zenocrate
    Nolan, P. Our sister, Sitya
    ————. Whole city's down below
    Poe, E. Masque of the red death
    Shakespeare, W. Cleopatra's death scene
    ————. To be or not to be
Death of Zenocrate. Marlowe, C.
DECEMBER
    Fisher, A. Time out for Christmas
DECLARATION OF INDEPENDENCE
    Slingluff, M. Naughty Susan
    see also REVOLUTIONARY WAR [American]
Definition of a boy. In McGee, C. Drama for Fun. 2 char+
Deming, Dorothy. First aid first. In Kamerman, S. Little Plays for Little Players. 4 char
————. Grey ghosts. In Burack, A. One Hundred Plays for Children. 6 char
————. Old man river. In Burack, A. One Hundred Plays for Children. 7 char
DEMOCRACY
    Hall, M. Hearts of oak
    Schwartz, M. All in favor
DENMARK
    Carlson, B. Goodbye, Snikke-snak
    Shakespeare, W. Hamlet
Dennis, Alice. Wind wand. In Kamerman, S. Little Plays for Little Players. 5 char
DEPARTMENT STORES
    Murray, J. One in a million
Deputy for Broken Bow. Cable, H.
DESPAIR
    Ibsen, H. Aase searches for her son

DESTINATION 38

  Shakespeare, E. To be or not to be
Destination: Christmas! Boiko, C.
DETECTIVES
  Doyle, A. Sherlock Holmes and the red-headed league
  _____. Sherlock Holmes and the stockbroker's clerk
  Fontaine, R. Who killed Doc Robin
  Murray, J. Miss Forsythe is missing
  Nicholson, J. Mysterious stranger
  Olfson, L. Ten-year-old detective
DEVIL
  Hughes, T. Sean, the fool, the devil, and the cats
DEVIL--SPOOF
  Nolan, P. Happy ending
Dial M for mother. Miller, H.
DIALOGUES
  Howard, V. Bus stop
  _____. Comedy team
  _____. Fred and Lois
  _____. Funny business
  _____. Girl talk
  _____. Help wanted
  _____. Ranch romance
  _____. Saturday chatter
  _____. Schoolwork
DIAMONDS
  MacLellan. Secret of the windmill
Dias, Earl J. Ballad for the shy. In Durrell, D. Teen-Age Plays for Classroom Reading. 13 char
_____. Bow-wow blues. In Dias, E. One-Act Plays for Teen-Agers. 7 char
_____. Cast up by the sea. In Dias, E. One-Act Plays for Teen-Agers. 8 char
_____. Christmas spirit. In Dias, E. One-Act Plays for Teen-Agers. 8 char
_____. Cleanest town in the West. In Dias, E. One-Act Plays for Teen-Agers. 9 char
_____. Dear Lottie. In Dias, E. One-Act Plays for Teen-Agers. 6 char
_____. Express to Valley Forge. In Durrell, D. Favorite Plays for Classroom Reading. 7 char
_____. Ghost from Genoa. In Kamerman, S. Fifty Plays for Holidays. 5 char
_____. Gift of laughter. In Dias, E. One-Act Plays for Teen-Agers. 8 char
_____. Hippie and the bard. In Dias, E. One-Act Plays for Teen-Agers. 7 char

DICK

———. Hold back the redskins. In Dias, E. One-Act Plays for Teen-Agers. 13 char
———. Landslide for Shakespeare. In Dias, E. One-Act Plays for Teen-Agers. 16 char
———. Little man who wasn't there. In Dias, E. One-Act Plays for Teen-Agers. 7 char
———. Madison Avenue merry-go-round. In Dias, E. One-Act Plays for Teen-Agers. 9 char
———. The mantle. In Dias, E. One-Act Plays for Teen-Agers. 13 char
———. Martha Washington's spy. In Kamerman, S. Fifty Plays for Holidays. 7 char
———. Printer's devil. In Dias, E. One-Act Plays for Teen Agers. 6 char
———. Treasure at Bently Inn. In Dias, E. One-Act Plays for Teen-Agers. 11 char
———. Video Christmas. In Dias, E. One-Act Plays for Teen-Agers. 7 char+
———. Visitor to Gettysburg. In Kamerman, S. Fifty Plays for Holidays. 7 char
Dick Whittington and his cat. Glass, G.
Dick Whittington and his cat. Thane, A.
Dickens, Charles. Christmas carol. In Burack, A. Christmas Plays for Young Actors. 24 char+; in Burack, A. Popular Plays for Classroom Reading. 19 char; in Olfson, L. Classics Adopted for Acting and Reading. 16 char
———. Magic fishbone. In Kamerman, S. Fifty Plays for Junior Actors. 8 char+
———. Martin Chuzzlewit. In Olfson, L. Dramatized Classics for Radio-Style Reading. 9 char
———. Oliver Twist. In Burack, A. Popular Plays for Classroom Reading. 18 char; in Howard, V. Complete Book of Children's Theater. 12 char+
DICTIONARY
    Boiko, C. On Camera, Noah Webster!
DIET
    Hark, M. Nursery rhyme diet
———. Pleasant dreams
see also HEALTH
Directions. Howard, V.
DISCRIMINATION
    Davis, O. Purlie Victorious
Dish for the king. Hark, M.
Dizzy dinners. Howard, V.
Doctor farmer. Simon, S.
Doctor for Lucinda. Mantle, M.

DR. 40

Dr. Heidegger's experiment. Hawthorne, N.
Doctor Know all. Howard, H.
Doctor Manners. Hark, M.
Dr. Quack's medicine show. McGee, C.
DOCTORS
    Fontaine, R. Emergency
    _____. Eyes have it
    _____. Oh, Medico!
    _____. Personality problem
    Geiger, M. In the fog
    Simon, S. Doctor farmer
Doctor's office. Taylor, L.
DOCUMENTARY PLAYS
    Henderson, N. Get on board, little children
DODGSON, Charles L. see Carroll, Lewis
DOGS
    Alexander, S. Hello, little dog
    Andersen, H. Tinderbox
    Boiko, C. How to choose a boy
    Carlson, B. The $10,000 dog
    Dias, E. Bow-wow blues
    Garver, J. Howling success
    Miller, H. Puppy love
    Pyle, M. Mrs. Gibbs advertises
Dog's house. Jarvis, S.
The dolls. Hark, M.
DOLLS
    Hark, M. The dolls
    Miller, H. Dolly saves the day
    see also TOYS
Dolly saves the day. Miller, H.
Don Quixote. Cervantes, M.
Don Quixote saves the day. Howard, V.
DONKEYS
    Howard, H. Little circus donkey
    Jarvis, S. Mr. Maybe
    Jarvis, S. M. I think I know
    McArthur, J. Fiesta the first
    Peterson, M. Old Four-legs
Don't be afraid. Taylor, L.
Dorand, John. Surprise party. In Burack, A. Skits,
  Comedies and Farces for Teen-agers. 8 char; in
  Durrell, D. Teen-Age Plays for Classroom Reading.
  9 char
_____. Teen and twenty. In Burack, A. Skits, Come-
  dies and Farces for Teenagers. 9 char; in Durrell,
  D. Teen-Age Plays for Classroom Reading. 10 char

Double nine of Chih Yuan. Nolan, P.
Downing, Robert. Shop girl's revenge. In Burack, A.
 Skits, Comedies and Farces for Teen-agers. 7 char
Doyle, A. Conan. Sherlock Holmes and the red-headed
 league. In Burack, A. Popular Plays for Classroom
 Reading. 7 char
―――――. Sherlock Holmes and the stockbroker's clerk. In
 Olfson, L. Dramatized Classics for Radio-Style Reading,
 Vol. II. 6 char
DRAGONS
    Boiko, C. Insatiable dragon
    Boylan, E. Prince and the dragon
    Brydon, M. Dreadful dragon
    Cochrane, L. Karagiosis and the dragon
    Glass, G. How to put out a dreadful dragon
    Grahame, K. Reluctant dragon
    Miller, H. Tomboy and the dragon
    Musil, R. Invisible dragon of Winn Sinn Tu
    Richards, L. Chop-chin and the golden dragon
DRAMATIC SCENES
    Carlson, B. Pirates
―――――. Rebecca of Sunnybrook Farm
Childress, A. Black Scenes
Kline, P. Theatre Student: Scenes to Perform
Draper, Cena Christopher. Emperor's daughters. In Kamerman, S. Children's Plays from Favorite Stories. 11 char
Dreadful dragon. Brydon, M.
DREAMS AND DREAMERS
    Bradbury, R. The meadow
    Carroll, L. Alice's adventures in Wonderland
    Steinbeck, J. Leader of the people
Drive in the country. Howard, V.
Driver, Donald; Hal Hester; and Danny Apolinar. Your own thing. In Swortzell, L. All the World's a Stage. 10 char
DuBois, Graham. Governor Bradford's scissors. In Kamerman, S. Fifty Plays for Holidays. 9 char
―――――. Last laugh. In Durrell, D. Teen-Age Plays for Classroom Reading. 8 char
―――――. Perfect gift. In Burack, A. Christmas Plays for Young Actors. 12 char
―――――. St. Patrick saves the day. In Kamerman, S. Fifty Plays for Holidays. 11 char
―――――. Two strangers from Nazareth. In Kamerman, S. Fifty Plays for Holidays. 10 char
The duel. Dumas, A.

DULCE 42

Dulce man. Blanton, C.
Dumas, Alexandre. Count of Monte Cristo. In Olfson, L.
 Classics Adopted for Acting and Reading. 13 char
 _____. The duel. In Gilfond, H. Plays for Reading.
 11 char
Dummling and the golden goose. Thane, A.
Dunsany, Lord. Jest of Hahalaba. In Maloney, H. Plays
 to Remember. 4 char
Duvall, Lucille M. Valentine's Day. In Kamerman, S.
 Fifty Plays for Junior Actors. 9 char+
DWARFS
 Spamer, C. Dwarfs' beards
Dwarfs' beards. Spamer, C.

- E -

Early life of George Washington Carver. Glass, G.
EASTER
 Baher, C. Cinder-rabbit
 Bennett, R. First Easter eggs
 _____. Good morning, Mr. Rabbit
 Boiko, C. Wild rabbit chase
 Hark, M. Father's Easter hat
 _____. Magic egg
 Knight, L. Flibber turns the tables
 Miller, H. Forgetful Easter rabbit
 _____. Peter Rabbit volunteers
 _____. Rabbits who changed their minds
 Spamer, C. Bunnyland brigade
 Tolstoy, L. Little girls wiser than men
 Werner, S. Choosing of Easter Rabbit
ECOLOGY
 Boiko, C. Beware the genies!
 _____. Hotel Oak
 _____. What ever happened to Mother Nature?
 Carlson, B. Marked trail
 Fisher, A. On strike
 see also LITTER; POLLUTION
EDUCATION
 Henderson, N. Automa
 Pyle, M. Three royal r's
Efficiency expert. Fontaine, R.
The egg. Philpott, V.
EGGS
 Bennett, R. First Easter eggs
 Philpott, V. The egg

EGYPT
    Fisher, A. What happened in Egypt
Eight bells. White, A.
Election day in Spooksville. Ryback, R.
ELECTIONS
    Fisher, A. Voice of liberty
    Murray, J. Mechanical man
    Reay, N. Mr. Bates goes to the polls
ELECTIONS--SATIRE
    Rybak, R. Election day in Spooksville
Elfenbein, Josef A. King who couldn't be fooled. In Kamerman, S. Children's Plays from Favorite Stories. 9 char
    _____. Puss-in-boots. In Kamerman, S. Children's Plays from Favorite Stories. 6 char
    _____. Ten-penny tragedy. In Burack, A. Popular Plays for Classroom Reading. 9 char
Ellen Tebbits. Cleary, B.
Ellen's secret. Glass, G.
ELVES
    Dennis, A. Wind wand
    Jarvis, S. M. Fisherman and the elf
    Kane, E. Elves and the shoemaker
    Mahlmann, L. Magic shoes
    Newman, D. Mrs. Santa's Christmas gift
    Spamer, C. Candy canes
    Thane, A. Elves and the shoemaker
    see also LEPRECHAUNS
Elves and the shoemaker. Kane, E.
Elves and the shoemaker. Thane, A.
Emergency. Fontaine, R.
EMOTIONS see HUMAN BEHAVIOR
Emperor's daughters. Draper, C.
Emperor's new robes. Foley, M.
Emperor's nightingale. Andersen, H.
Empty bowls. Fisher, A.
Enchanted, I'm sure. Chisholm, J.
End of the beginning. O'Casey, S.
ENGLAND
    Baher, C. Robin Hood outwits the sheriff
    Boiko, C. Christmas revel
    Dickens, C. Oliver Twist
    Ferguson, D. Most special dragon
    Holmes, R. In the days of King Alfred
    Leuser, E. D. Wise people of Gotham
    Love, S. Fifth of November
    Molloy, L. Stolen tarts

  Morley, O. King Arthur and his knights
  Nolan, P. Robin Hood and the match at Nottingham
  Sheridan, R. The rivals
  Thane, A. King Alfred and the cakes
  Twain, M. Prince and the pauper
  White, A. The crabfish
ENGLISH LANGUAGE
  Boiko, C. The "T" party
  Hall, M. Language shop
  _____. Trial of Billy Scott
  Miller, H. Captain Castaway's captives
Enoch Arden. Tennyson, A.
Enright, Elizabeth. The Saturdays. In Glass, G. From Plays into Reading. 13 char
Enter George Washington. Hark, M.
Enter Juliet. Barbee, L.
EPIDEMICS
  Fisher, A. What happened in Egypt
Equal rights. Olfson, L.
EQUALITY
  Barbour, F. Bird cage
  Branch, W. To follow the phoenix
  Fisher, A. Accident of birth
  Mitchell, L. Land beyond the river
  see also FREEDOM; HUMAN RIGHTS
The Eskimo. In McGee, C. Drama for Fun. 2 char+
ESTHER, QUEEN
  Zeligs, D. Queen Esther saves her people
ETIQUETTE
  Boiko, C. Terrible Terry's surprise
  Hark, M. Doctor Manners
  Jarvis, S. M. Lion and the mosquitoes
  Miller, H. Case of the giggling goblin
  _____. Visit to Goldilocks
  see also COURTESY
Eve decides to eat the fruit of the tree of knowledge. Milton, J.
Everyman's prayer. In Kline, P. Theatre Student: Scenes to perform. 1 char
Everywhere Christmas. Very, A.
EVIL
  Asbrand, K. Pandora's box
  Shakespeare, W. Lady Macbeth receives a letter from her husband
  _____. Richard alone
Evolution. In McGee, C. Drama for Fun. 2 char+
The experts. Howard, V.

EXPLANATIONS

Explanations. Howard, V.
EXPLORATIONS
    Bakeless, K. Most memorable voyage
    Ross, L. Admiral and the feathered pilots
Express to Valley Forge. Dias, E.
Exterior decorator. Boiko, C.
EYES
    Miller, H. Country store cat
The eyes have it. Fontaine, R.

- F -

FABLES
    Asbrand, K. Adalmina's pearl
    Barr, J. Lion and the mouse
    Bennett, R. Lion and the mouse
    Boiko, C. Star bright
    _____. Who will bell the cat?
    Fisher, A. Way to Norwich
    Howard, H. What he deserves
    Hughes, T. Tiger's bones
    Jarvis, S. Dog's house
    _____. Foolish Fred
    _____. Mr. Maybe
    _____. Six wise travelers
    _____. Sun and the wind
    _____. Who helped the lion?
    Phillips, E. Aesop, man of fables
    Rhodes, J. Crow and the corn
    Richards, L. Chop-chin and the golden dragon
    _____. With all my heart
    Sperling, L. Day Canary met Sparrow
    Walker, B. Lion's den
    _____. Rabbit and the wolf
    _____. Which price is mine?
FABLES--SPOOF
    Fontaine, R. Androcles and his pal
Fair today, followed by tomorrow. Fontaine, R.
Fairest pitcher of them all. Cable, H.
FAIRIES
    Shakespeare, W. Midsummer night's dream
FAIRS
    Murray, J. Come to the fair!
FAIRY TALES
    Andersen, H. Princess and the pea
    _____. The tinderbox

FAIRY TALES 46

Asbrand, K. Crystal flask
―――――. Little hero of Holland
Baher, C. Cinder-rabbit
Barr, J. Cinderella
―――――. Rapunzel
Barrows, M. Valentine tree
Bennett, H. Rumpelstiltskin
―――――. Sleeping beauty
Bennett, R. French doll's surprise
―――――. Magic weaver
―――――. Shoemaker and the elves
―――――. Snow-white and Rose-red
Boiko, C. Ah See and the six-colored heaven
―――――. Cinder-riley
―――――. Little red hen
―――――. One hundred words
―――――. Small crimson parasol
Boylan, E. Musicians of Bremen
Brydon, M. Dreadful dragon
Burlingame, C. Three wishes
Canadian fairy tale
Capell, L. Tongue-cut sparrow
D'Arcy, A. Cinderella
Dennis, A. Wind wand
Dickens, C. Magic fishbone
Gertler, L. Punch and the heartless giant
Glass, G. Golden touch
Gregg, L. Miniature darzis
Holmes, R. Little Red Riding Hood
Howells, W. Christmas every day
Jacob, E. Snow White
King, W. Little Snow White
―――――. Snow White
Mahlmann, L. Jack and the beanstalk
―――――. Magic mushrooms
―――――. Snow White and the seven dwarfs
Miller, H. Jiminy Cinders
―――――. Magic cookie jar
―――――. Princess and the pea
―――――. Real princess
Nesbit, E. Long and short division
Newman, D. Cinderella
―――――. Magic goose
Perrault, C. Sleeping beauty
Pyle, H. Apple of contentment
Rowland, E. Hans, who made the princess laugh
Sanders, S. Hansel and Gretel

Simonds, N. Hansel and Gretel
Slattery, M. Patchwork princess
―――――. Queen's mirror
Stockton, F. Old Pipes
Thane, A. Cinderella
―――――. Dummling and the golden goose
―――――. Jack and the magic beanstalk
―――――. Rumpelstiltskin
―――――. Saucy scarecrow
Tichenor, T. Jack and the beanstalk
Turnbull, L. Magic shoes
Werner, S. Choosing of Easter Rabbit
FAIRY TALES--SPOOF
Cable, H. Big Red Riding Hood
―――――. Fairest pitcher of them all
―――――. Way-out Cinderella
Cheatham, V. Snow White and friends
Fontaine, R. Another Cinderella
―――――. Let sleeping beauties lie
McGee, C. Gransel and Hettal
Olfson, L. Cinderella revisited
―――――. My son, the prince
―――――. Once and future frog
Sayers, N. The story of Gransel and Hettal
FAITH
St. Clair, R. Miss Muffett's wish
Sperling, L. Baby Bird
The family. Hoff, S.
Family affair. Ward, M.
FAMILY LIFE
Barnett, G. Treasure in the Smith house
Cable, H. Another man's family
Campbell, J. Pink roses for Christmas
Carlson, B. O little town
Colbo, E. First New England Christmas tree
Dias, E. Video Christmas
Dorand, J. Surprise party
Fisher, A. Abe's winkin' eye
Garver, J. Turkey, anyone?
Hark, M. Father keeps house
―――――. When do we eat?
Hoff, S. The family
Howard, V. Happy holidays for little women
Nolan, P. Anton Chekhov sort of evening
Van Druten, J. I remember Mama
Ward, M. Mr. Lazy Man's family
Famous words. Howard, V.

FANTASY

Baum, L. Wizard of Oz
Bierce, A. Shipwreck
Boiko, C. Big shoo
———. Book that saved the earth
———. Cupivac
———. Exterior decorator
———. Insatiable dragon
———. Lady Moon and the thief
———. Marvelous time machine
———. Scaredy cat
———. Spaceship Santa Maria
———. Terrible Terry's surprise
Cable, H. Reluctant Columbus
Carroll, L. Alice's adventures in Wonderland
Chandler, A. Chinese Rip Van Winkle
Dias, E. Little man who wasn't there
Hark, M. The dolls
———. Three wishes for Mother
Shakespeare, W. The tempest
Smith, G. Star Light and the sandman
 see also SCIENCE FICTION; SUPERNATURAL

FARCES

Alderman, E. Hamelot
Boiko, C. Yes, yes, a thousand times yes!
Dias, E. Bow-wow blues
Henry, O. Romance of a busy broker
Murray, J. Case for two detectives
———. Spies and dolls
Nolan, P. Boshibari and the two thieves
———. French cabinetmaker
———. This younger generation
———. Tree to the sky
O'Casey, Sean. End of the beginning
Olfson, L. Avon calling!
———. Cinderella revisited
———. Great Caesar's ghost!
———. Incredible housing shortage
———. My son, the prince
Swintz, M. Panic in the palace
La farza del Miss Muffet. Olfson, L.
Fatal quest. McGee, C.
Father hits the jackpot. Garver, J.
Father keeps house. Hark, M.
Father's Easter hat. Hark, M.

FAUST--SPOOF

Nolan, P. Happy ending

Faux, Damally. Littlest month. In Durrell, D. Thirty
 Plays for Classroom Reading. 14 char
Fay, Maxine. Saving the old homestead. In Kamerman, S.
 Fifty Plays for Junior Actors. 10 char
FEAR
 Miller, H. Rabbit who refused to run
Feast of the thousand lanterns. Huff, B.
Feather, Jean. One wish too many. In Kamerman, S.
 Dramatized Folk Tales of the World. 5 char
─────. Quick-witted Jack. In Kamerman, S. Dramatized Folk Tales of the World. 31 char+
Feathertop. Hawthorne, N.
Featherweight champ; or, tickled to death. Boyd, J.
Felsheim, Jerry. Ali Baba and the forty thieves. In Durrell, D. Thirty Plays for Classroom Reading. 8 char
Ferguson, David. Most special dragon. In Kamerman, S.
 Dramatized Folk Tales of the World. 7 char
Fiesta. McArthur, J.
Fiesta the first. McArthur, J.
Fifth of November. Love, S.
FIGHTING [Quarrels]
 Fisher, A. Special edition
FILMS
 McGee, C. The stand-in
Final edition. Sayre, G.
Finn McCool. Lynch, M.
FIRE
 Boiko, C. Insatiable dragon
Fire-face and the Indians. Bennett, R.
Fire in a paper. Hagy, L.
FIRE PREVENTION
 Deming, D. Grey ghosts
 Urban, C. Who started the fire?
 see also FOREST FIRE PREVENTION
Fires at Valley Forge. Clark, B.
FIRST AID
 Deming, D. First aid first
First aid first. Deming, D.
First cat on Mars. Harper, J.
First Easter eggs. Bennett, R.
First flight of the Wright brothers. Howard, V.
First flowers. Wilson, M.
First New England Christmas tree. Colbo, E.
FISH
 Olfson, L. Bride of Gorse-Bracken Hall
Fish in the forest. Corson, H.
Fisher, Aileen. Abe's winkin' eye. In Fisher, A. Holiday Programs for Boys and Girls. 8 char

FISHER   50

_____. Angel in the looking glass. In Burack, A. Christmas Plays for Young Actors. 8 char; in Fisher, A. Holiday Programs for Boys and Girls. 8 char
_____. Caves of the earth. In Fisher, A. Holiday Programs for Boys and Girls. 7 char+
_____. Christmas cake. In Fisher, A. Holiday Programs for Boys and Girls. 4 char
_____. Christmas tree for kitty. In Fisher, A. Holiday Programs for Boys and Girls. 6 char+
_____. Day of destiny. In Fisher, A. Holiday Programs for Boys and Girls. 10 char
_____. Ghosts on guard. In Fisher, A. Holiday Programs for Boys and Girls. 7 char
_____. Hearts, tarts and valentines. In Fisher, A. Holiday Programs for Boys and Girls. 9 char+
_____. King's toothache. In Durrell, D. Thirty Plays for Classroom Reading. 15 char
_____. Merry Christmas elf. In Fisher, A. Holiday Programs for Boys and Girls. 12 char+
_____. Mother of Thanksgiving. In Fisher, A. Holiday Programs for Boys and Girls. 16 char
_____. Mother's Day off and on. In Fisher, A. Holiday Programs for Boys and Girls. 5 char
_____. New hearts for old. In Fisher, A. Holiday Programs for Boys and Girls. 6 char
_____. On Halloween. In Fisher, A. Holiday Programs for Boys and Girls. 12 char+
_____. On strike. In Fisher, A. Holiday Programs for Boys and Girls. 8 char
_____. Once upon a time. In Fisher, A. Holiday Programs for Boys and Girls. 16 char
_____. One-ring circus. In Burack, A. One Hundred Plays for Children. 9 char; in Durrell, D. Thirty Plays for Classroom Reading. 10 char
_____. Play without a name. In Fisher, A. Holiday Programs for Boys and Girls. 21 char
_____. Special edition. In Burack, S. One Hundred Plays for Children. 8 char
_____. Spirit of Christmas. In Fisher, A. Holiday Programs for Boys and Girls. 8 char
_____. Three and the dragon. In Fisher, A. Holiday Programs for Boys and Girls. 12 char
_____. Time for Mom. In Kamerman, S. Fifty Plays for Holidays. 8 char+
_____. Time out for Christmas. In Fisher, A. Holiday Programs for Boys and Girls. 28 char
_____. Treasure hunt. In Fisher, A. Holiday Programs

for Boys and Girls. 24 char
———. Unexpected guests. In Fisher, A. Holiday Programs for Boys and Girls. 12 char; in Ross, L. Holiday Puppets. 12 char
———. Voice of liberty. In Fisher, A. Holiday Programs for Boys and Girls. 10 char
———. Washington marches on. In Fisher, A. Holiday Programs for Boys and Girls. 33 char+
———. Way to Norwich. In Burack, A. One Hundred Plays for Children. 11 char
———. Weaver's son. In Fisher, A. Holiday Programs for Boys and Girls. 5 char
———. Young Abe Lincoln. In Kamerman, S. Fifty Plays for Holidays. 17 char+
———, and Olive Rabe. Accident of Birth. In Fisher, A. United Nations Plays and Programs. 11 char
———, ———. Alice in Puzzleland. In Fisher, A. United Nations Plays and Programs. 16 char
———, ———. All in the UN. In Fisher, A. United Nations Plays and Programs. 21 char
———, ———. All the world around. In Fisher, A. United Nations Plays and Programs. 15 char+
———, ———. Best bargain in the world. In Fisher, A. United Nations Plays and Programs. 5 char
———, ———. Cavalcade of human rights. In Fisher, A. United Nations Plays and Programs. 39 char+
———, ———. Empty bowls. In Fisher, A. United Nations Plays and Programs. 26 char
———, ———. Fresco for UNESCO. In Fisher, A. United Nations Plays and Programs. 6 char+
———, ———. Get-together dinner. In Fisher, A. United Nations Plays and Programs. 5 char
———, ———. Getting in line. In Fisher, A. United Nations Plays and Programs. 14 char
———, ———. Invasion from the stratosphere. In Durrell, D. Thirty Plays for Classroom Reading. 8 char+; in Fisher, A. United Nations Plays and Programs. 7 char+
———, ———. Let there be bread. In Fisher, A. United Nations Plays and Programs. 26 char
———, ———. Nickel and a dime. In Fisher, A. United Nations Plays and Programs. 11 char
———, ———. Of gods and men. In Fisher, A. United Nations Plays and Programs. 8 char
———, ———. Skills to share. In Fisher, A. United Nations Plays and Programs. 8 char

FISHERMAN 52

_____, _____. Story of a well. In Fisher, A. United Nations Plays and Programs. 7 char+
_____, _____. Thanks a million. In Fisher, A. United Nations Plays and Programs. 13 char+
_____, _____. Turning the tables. In Fisher, A. United Nations Plays and Programs. 7 char
_____, _____. What happened in Egypt. In Fisher, A. United Nations Plays and Programs. 7 char
The Fisherman. Howard, V.
Fisherman and the elf. Jarvis, S. M.
Fit for a king. Carlson, B.
Fitz-Adcock, Irma. Royal cloth of China. In Durrell, D. Favorite Plays for Classroom Reading. 17 char
Five brothers. Leuser, E.
Five senses. Hark, M.
Five weeks in a balloon. Verne, J.
Flag of the United States. Barbee, L.
FLAGS
    Fisher, A. Alice in Puzzleland
FLAGS--UNITED STATES
    Barbee, L. Flag of the United States
    MacLellan, E. Needle fights for freedom
    Miller, H. Old Glory grows up
    Newman, D. Yankee-doodle kitten
Fletcher, John. Jailer's daughter falls in love with a prince. (Two noble kinsmen) In Kline, P. Theatre Student: Scenes to Perform. 1 char
Fletcher, Lucille. Sorry, wrong number. In Maloney, H. Plays to Remember. 11 char
Flibber turns the tables. Knight, L.
Flight fifteen. Howard, V.
Floating stone. Foulk, C.
FLOODS
    Deming, D. Old man river
FLORIDA
    Cable, H. Young forever.
FLOWERS
    Bennett, R. Waking the daffodil
    Boiko, C. Crocus who couldn't bloom
    _____. Search for the sky-blue princess
    Clapp, P. Girl whose fortune sought her
    Hoff, S. Wild flowers
    MacLellan, E. Small shoes and small tulips
    Wilson, M. First flowers
Fly and a flea. In McGee, C. Drama for Fun. 3 char
Flying Dutchman. Heine, H.

FOLK HEROES
 Boylan, E. Rip Van Winkle
 Howard, V. Johnny Appleseed in danger
 _____. Return of Rip Van Winkle
 Irving, W. Rip Van Winkle
 Lynch, M. Finn McCool
 Nolan, P. Johnny Appleseed
 Thane, A. Big Paul Bunyan
 Whittaker, H. Gift from Johnny Appleseed

FOLK SONGS
 White, A. Crabfish
 _____. Deaf woman's courtship
 _____. Nice girls don't chase the boys
 _____. Sailor's return
 _____. Wonderous apple tree

FOLK TALES
 Bennett, R. Hare and the tortoise
 _____. Lion and the mouse
 Boiko, C. Pepe and the cornfield bandit
 _____. Snowflake
 _____. Tall-tale tournament
 Boylan, E. Rip Van Winkle
 Campbell, C. Morning maker
 Carlson, B. Justice for all
 _____. Salt in the soup
 Glass, G. Dick Whittington and his cat
 _____. How to put out a dreadful dragon
 _____. Princess Rosette
 Howard, H. Doctor Know All
 Hughes, T. Beauty and the beast
 Irving, W. Rip Van Winkle
 Kamerman, S. Dramatized Folk Tales of the World
 Martin, P. Invitation to supper
 _____. Little Ugo and the foolish ones
 Nolan, P. Golden voice of Little Erik
 _____. Son of William Tell
 _____. Stanislaw and the wolf
 Pirandello, L. The jar
 Sanders, S. Three sillies
 Thane, A. Dick Whittington and his cat
 _____. King Alfred and the cakes
 _____. Magic nutmeg-grater
 _____. Three wishes

FOLK TALES--SPOOF
 Cable, H. Little Jackie and the beanstalk
Follow-the-leader. Carlson, B.
Follow the North Star. Sanderlin, O.

Folmsbee, Beulah. Goblin parade. In Burack, A. One Hundred Plays for Children. 8 char+
Fontaine, Robert. Androcles and his pal. In Fontaine, R. Humorous Skits for Young People. 4 char
―――――. Another Cinderella. In Fontaine, R. Humorous Skits for Young People. 6 char
―――――. Camping pictures. In Fontaine, R. Humorous Skits for Young People. 4 char
―――――. Can't get there from here, mebbe. In Fontaine, R. Humorous Skits for Young People. 3 char
―――――. Carefree high school orchestra. In Fontaine, R. Humorous Skits for Young People. 7 char+
―――――. Efficiency expert. In Fontaine, R. Humorous Skits for Young People. 7 char
―――――. Emergency. In Fontaine, R. Humorous Skits for Young People. 4 char
―――――. Eyes have it. In Fontaine, R. Humorous Skits for Young People. 4 char
―――――. Fair today, followed by tomorrow. In Fontaine, R. Humorous Skits for Young People. 5 char
―――――. Good morning, Your Honor. In Fontaine, R. Humorous Skits for Young People. 5 char
―――――. Graduation address. In Fontaine, R. Humorous Skits for Young People. 5 char
―――――. Great Caesar! In Durrell, D. Teen-Age Plays for Classroom Reading. 7 char; in Fontaine, R. Humorous Skits for Young People. 6 char
―――――. How the West was won. In Fontaine, R. Humorous Skits for Young People. 5 char
―――――. It's frightening! In Fontaine, R. Humorous Skits for Young People. 6 char
―――――. Let sleeping beauties lie. In Fontaine, R. Humorous Skits for Young People. 6 char
―――――. The loafer. In Fontaine, R. Humorous Skits for Young People. 4 char
―――――. Love seeks a way. In Fontaine, R. Humorous Skits for Young People. 4 char
―――――. Matter of taste. In Fontaine, R. Humorous Skits for Young People. 4 char
―――――. No starch in the collars. In Fontaine, R. Humorous Skits for Young People. 5 char
―――――. Oh, Medico! In Fontaine, R. Humorous Skits for Young People. 3 char
―――――. On you it looks good. In Fontaine, R. Humorous Skits for Young People. 5 char
―――――. Personality problem. In Fontaine, R. Humorous Skits for Young People. 4 char

FOOD

    ———. Ride your hobby. In Fontaine, R. Humorous Skits for Young People. 6 char
    ———. Supermarket blues. In Fontaine, R. Humorous Skits for Young People. 6 char
    ———. Sweetie-weeties! In Fontaine, R. Humorous Skits for Young People. 5 char
    ———. To the moon. In Fontaine, R. Humorous Skits for Young People. 6 char
    ———. United spies. In Fontaine, R. Humorous Skits for Young People. 5 char
    ———. Where banking is a pleasure. In Fontaine, R. Humorous Skits for Young People. 8 char
    ———. Who killed Doc Robin? In Fontaine, R. Humorous Skits for Young People. 8 char
    ———. The wurst student. In Fontaine, R. Humorous Skits for Young People. 5 char

FOOD see COOKING; RESTAURANTS; specific foods

Foolish Fred. Jarvis, S.

FOOLS

    Carlson, B. Seven Simons
    Corson, H. Fish in the forest
    Hale, L. Lady who put salt in her coffee
    Holmes, R. Wise men of Gotham
    Jarvis, S. Foolish Fred
    ———. Six wise travelers
    Martin, P. Invitation to supper
    ———. Little Ugo and the foolish ones
    Molière. Would-be gentleman
    Nolan, P. Courters
    Peterson, M. Old Four-legs
    Sanders, S. Three sillies
    Very, A. Three sillies
    Williams, G. Kettle of brains

Foot in the door. Howard, V.

FOOTBALL

    Dias, E. Ghost from Genoa
    ———. Landslide for Shakespeare

For the glory of Spain. Roberts, H.

FOREST FIRE PREVENTION

    Deming, D. Grey ghosts

Forgetful Easter rabbit. Miller, H.

FORTUNE

    Clapp, P. Girl whose fortune sought her
    Glass, G. Dick Whittington and his cat
    Holmes, R. Golden goose
    Molloy, L. Fortune of Merrylegs and Tawny-whiskers

Fortune of Merrylegs and Tawny-whiskers. Molloy, L.

Fortunes? Howard, V.

Foulk, C. W. and Doris P. Buck. Floating stone. In Burack, A. One Hundred Plays for Children. 10 char
417. Mayfield, J.
FOURTH OF JULY
    Slingluff, M. Naughty Susan
Fox, Damally U. Littlest month. In Kamerman, S. Little Plays for Little Players. 13 char
FRANCE
    Koon, H.   Pierre Patelin
    Love, S.   Madame Defarge
    Nicholson, M.   Price of eggs
    Nolan, P.   French cabinetmaker
    Orczy, B.   Scarlet Pimpernel
    Reines, B.   Turncoat
    Weik, M.   King's garden
    White, A.   Nice girls don't chase the boys
    ————. Sailor's return
    ————. Wonderous apple tree
    see also FRENCH REVOLUTION
FRANKLIN, BENJAMIN
    Boiko, C.   Melinda's incredible birthday
    Howard, H.   Ben Franklin, peace-maker
    Walsh, H.   Benjamin Franklin
Franklin reversal. Boiko, C.
FRAUD see CRIME
Fred and Lois. Howard, V.
Freddie proposes. Howard, V.
Free bacon. Jarvis, S. M.
FREEDOM
    Browne, T.   Natural man
    Clark, B.   Fires at Valley Forge
    Dias, E.   Express to Valley Forge
    Fisher, A.   Cavalcade of human rights
    Hansberry, L.   Raisin in the sun
    Jarvis, S. M.   Free bacon
    MacLellan, E.   Needle fights for freedom
    Miller, A.   Grandpa and the statue
    Miller, H.   Dolly saves the day
    Nolan, P.   Son of William Tell
    Roberts, H.   Test for William Tell
    Streacker, L.   Bob's armistice parade
    Suerken, E.   John Crown's legacy
    Very, A.   President Lincoln's children
    see also EQUALITY; HUMAN RIGHTS
French, Dawn and Marshall. Mud pack madness. In Burack, A. Skits, Comedies and Farces for Teen-agers. 5 char

French cabinetmaker. Nolan, P.
French doll's surprise. Bennett, R.
FRENCH REVOLUTION
    Love, S. Madame Defarge
    Orczy, B. Scarlet Pimpernel
Fresco for UNESCO. Fisher, A.
Freudenberger, Helen. Jack and Jill. In Burack, A. One Hundred Plays for Children. 7 char
Friday foursome packs a box. Barbee, L.
Fried onions and marshmallows. Jarvis, S. M.
Friendly as can be. Asbrand, K.
FRIENDSHIP
    Barr, J. Lion and the mouse
    Baum, L. Wizard of Oz
    Bellah, M. Blue toadstool
    Bradbury, R. The meadow
    Clapp, P. Other side of the wall
    Dias, E. The mantle
    Fisher, A. One-ring circus
    Hark, M. Good neighbors
    Holmes, R. King and the miller
    Howard, V. Children who found new friends
    Jarvis, S. Giant's cat
    _____. Who helped the lion?
    McArthur, J. Fiesta the first
    Miller, H. Friendship wheel
    _____. Mistletoe mystery
    Schwartz, E. Little Red Riding Hood
    Schwartz, M. All in favor
    Spyri, J. Heidi
    _____. Heidi finds the way
    Twain, M. Tom Sawyer, pirate
    Watts, F. Leprechaun's pot of gold
Friendship wheel. Miller, H.
Frog prince. Mahlmann, L.
Frog princess. Alexander, S.
FROGS AND TOADS
    Alexander, S. Frog princess
    Carlson, B. It had to be
    Local frog stages comeback
    Mahlmann, L. Frog prince
    Olfson, L. Once and future frog
    Tree toad loved a she-toad
    Twain, M. Celebrated jumping frog of Calaveras County
    Two frogs
From nine to five. McGee, C.

FUN 58

Fun with Hamlet and his friends. McGee, C.
Funny business. Howard, V.
Furman, Roger. To kill a devil. In Childress, A. Black Scenes. 2 char

- G -

Garden hold-up. Miller, H.
GARDEN OF EDEN
    Milton, J. Eve decides to eat the fruit of the tree of knowledge
GARDENING
    Miller, H. Garden hold-up
Gardner, Mercedes, and Jean Shannon Smith. King Midas. In Kamerman, S. Dramatized Folk Tales of the World. 5 char +
Garver, Juliet. Father hits the jackpot. In Kamerman, S. Fifty Plays for Junior Actors. 10 char
―――――. My fair Linda. In Durrell, D. Teen-Age Plays for Classroom Reading. 8 char
―――――. Turkey, anyone? In Kamerman, S. Fifty Plays for Holidays. 8 char
Gates of Dinkelsbuehl. Nolan, P.
Gathering sticks. Miller, H.
Geiger, Milton. In the fog. In Picozzi, R. Plays to Enjoy. 4 char
General returns. Miller, H.
GENERATION GAP
    Cable, H. Another man's family
    Furman, R. To kill a devil
    Miller, H. Man like Lincoln
    Nolan, P. This younger generation
    Ward, T. The daubers
    Wilder, T. Childhood
Gentle giant-killer. Miller, H.
GEORGE, SAINT
    Grahame, K. Reluctant dragon
George slept here, too. Martens, A.
GEORGIA
    Miller, H. Pink parasol
GERMANY
    Nolan P. Gates of Dinkelsbuehl
    Roberts, W. Musicians of Bremen Town
    Thane, A. Magic nutmeg-grater
    ―――――. Merry Tyll and the three rogues
    Watts, F. Crimson feather

Gertler, Luke. Punch and the heartless giant. In Philpott, A. Eight Plays for Hand Puppets. 8 char
Get on board, little children. Henderson, N.
Get-together dinner. Fisher, A.
Getting in line. Fisher, A.
GETTYSBURG, PA.
    Geiger, M. In the fog
Ghost from Genoa. Dias, E.
Ghost in the house. Miller, H.
Ghost town treasure. Bulla, C.
Ghost town treasure. Glass, G.
GHOST TOWNS
    Bulla, C. Ghost town treasure
    Cable, H. Last stop
Ghost walks tonight. Nicholson, J.
Ghosts. Carlson, B.
GHOSTS
    Bennett, R. Runaway pirate
    Blaine, B. Rosy-cheeked ghost
    Brydon, M. Reluctant ghost
    Carlson, B. Ghosts
    Chisholm, J. Shades of ransom
    Hark, M. House is haunted
    Irving, W. Legend of Sleepy Hollow
    Miller, H. Ghost in the house
    Stockton, F. Transferred ghost
    see also HALLOWEEN
Ghosts on guard. Fisher, A.
Giants. Hoff, S.
GIANTS
    Boylan, E. Jack the giant killer
    Hoff, S. Giants
    Jarvis, S. Giant's cat
    Lonely giant
    Mahlmann, L. Jack and the beanstalk
    Thane, A. Brave little tailor
    _____. Jack and the magic beanstalk
    Tichenor, T. Jack and the beanstalk
Giant's cat. Jarvis, S.
Gift for Hans Brinker. Thane, A.
Gift from Johnny Appleseed. Whittaker, H.
Gift of laughter. Dias, E.
Gift of the fairies. Very, A.
GIFTS
    Bennett, R. Piccola
    _____. Snowman who played Santa
    _____. Ye olden festival of Christmas

Miller, H.   Toy scout jamboree
Sagoff, S.   Hand-me-down Hildy
Gingerbread boy.   In Philpott, A.   Eight plays for Hand Puppets.   9 char
Girl from the sea.   Heiderstadt, D.
GIRL SCOUTS
   Miller, H.   Paper bag mystery
Girl talk.   Howard, V.
Girl who did very, very well.   Howard, V.
Girl whose fortune sought her.   Clapp, P.
GIRLS
   Baum, L.   Wizard of Oz
   Boiko, C.   All hands on deck
   Brydon, M.   May witch
   _____.   Reluctant ghost
   French, D.   Mud pack madness
   Glass, G.   Ellen's secret
   Greth, R.   Two masks
   Gross, N.   Mystery ring
   Hill, K.   Midnight burial
   McMeekin, I.   Runaway balloon
   Martens, A.   Thirteen
   Melchior, H.   Little Ki and the serpent
   Miller, S.   Dangerous game
   Neman, D.   Cinderella
   Nutter, C.   Red Riding Hood and the wolf
   Phillips, M.   Hat for mother
   St. Clair, R.   Miss Muffett's wish
   see also BROTHERS AND SISTERS; CHILDREN; SISTERS
Glass, Gerald G.   Dick Whittington and his cat.   In Glass, G.   From Plays into Reading.   12 char
_____.   Early life of George Washington Carver.   In Glass, G.   From Plays into Reading.   9 char
_____.   Ellen's secret.   In Glass, G.   From Plays into Reading.   8 char
_____.   Ghost town treasure.   In Glass, G.   From Plays into Reading.   9 char
_____.   Golden touch.   In Glass, G.   From Plays into Reading.   7 char
_____.   Henry and the night crawlers.   In Glass, G.   From Plays into Reading.   9 char
_____.   How to put out a dreadful dragon.   In Glass, G.   From Plays into Reading.   10 char
_____.   Lemonade trick.   In Glass, G.   From Plays into Reading.   9 char
_____.   Little witch.   In Glass, G.   From Plays into

GLASSES

Reading. 13 char
_____. Miss Pickerell goes to Mars. In Glass, G. From Plays into Reading. 7 char
_____. Mr. Popper's penguins. In Glass, G. From Plays into Reading. 10 char
_____. Pippi Longstocking. In Glass, G. From Plays into Reading. 7 char
_____. Princess Rosette. In Glass, G. From Plays into Reading. 24 char
_____. Saturdays. In Glass, G. From Plays into Reading. 13 char

GLASSES
    Miller, H. Country store cat
GLUE
    Slattery, M. King in the kitchen
GOATS
    Boylan, E. Three billy goats gruff
    Jarvis, S. M. !Trip-trap! trip-trap!
Goblin parade. Folmsbee, B.
GODS AND GODESSES
    Everyman's prayer
    Milton, J. Eve decides to eat the fruit of the tree of knowledge
    Roberts, H. Builder of the wall
Going steady. Nolan, P.
GOLD
    Bennett, R. Rainbow's end
    _____. Rumpelstiltskin
    Carlson, B. Why catch a Leprechaun?
    Felsheim, J. Ali Baba and the forty thieves
    Glass, G. Golden touch
    Jarvis, S. M. King's gold
    Spamer, C. Pot of gold
    Watts, F. Leprechaun's pot of gold
Gold detector. Taylor, L.
Gold mine at Jeremiah Flats. Anderson, R.
Golden bell for mother. Very, A.
Golden goose. Holmes, R.
Golden spike. Carson, B.
Golden tooth. Carlson, B.
Golden touch. Glass, G.
Golden voice of Little Erik. Nolan, P.
GOLDILOCKS
    Miller, H. Visit to Goldilocks
Goldsmith, Sophie L. Louisa Alcott's wish. In Burack, A. One Hundred Plays for Children. 7 char
Golf lesson. Howard, V.

Golfer. Howard, V.
GOOD AND EVIL
    Milton, J. Eve decides to eat the fruit of the tree of knowledge
    see also EVIL
Good health trolley. Lehman, J.
Good morning, Mr. Rabbit. Bennett, R.
Good morning, your honor. Fontaine, R.
Good neighbors. Hark, M.
Goodbye, Snikke-snak. Carlson, B.
Goom-bya, room-bya, zerko! Alexander, S.
GOSSIP
    Fontaine, R. Matter of taste
Gould, Jean. Seven little seeds. In Kamerman, S. Little Plays for Little Players. 10 char
    _____. Thanksgiving is for everybody. In Kamerman, S. Little Plays for Little Players. 7 char
GOVERNESSES
    Brontë, C. Jane Eyre
GOVERNMENT
    Oser, J. Running the country
GOVERNMENT--WORLD
    Fisher, A. Play without a name
Governor Bradford's scissors. DuBois, G.
Grabe, Mrs. Klaus. I know an old woman. In McGee, C. Drama for Fun. 7 char
GRADUATION
    Dias, E. The mantle
    Fisher, A. Caves of the earth
    Miller, H. Gathering sticks
Graduation address. Fontaine, R.
Graham, Manta S. Unusual flower. In Burack, A. One Hundred Plays for Children. 7 char
Grahame, Kenneth. Reluctant dragon. In Mahlmann, L. Puppet Plays for Young Players. 6 char; in Thane, A. Plays from Famous Stories and Fairy Tales. 4 char+
GRAMMAR
    Boiko, C. Wonderful circus of words
    Hall, M. Language shop
    _____. Trial of Billy Scott
    Hark, M. Mind your p's and q's
    Miller, H. Captain Castaway's captives
    _____. Gentle giant
Grandma crosses the street. Howard, V.
Grandpa and the statue. Miller, A.
Gransel and Hettal. McGee, C.
Great Caesar. Fontaine, R.

GREAT

Great Caesar's ghost! Olfson, L.
Great Samurai sword. Winther, B.
GREECE
    Cockrane, L. Karagiosis and the dragon
    Gardner, M. King Midas
    Homer. The Iliad
    Nolan, P. Skill of Pericles
    Welk, M. Moonlight
GREED
    Bealmear, J. Covetous councilman
    Browning, R. Pied piper of Hamlin
    Capell, L. Tongue-cut sparrow
    Carlson, B. Golden tooth
    Colbert, M. Salt in the sea
    Dickens, C. Christmas carol
    Dunsany, L. Jest of Hahalaba
    Feather, J. One wish too many
    Gardner, M. King Midas
    Glass, G. Golden touch
    ———. Princess Rosette
    Graham, M. Unusual flower
    Howard, H. What he deserves
    Howard, V. Strange tale of King Midas
    Howells, W. Christmas every day
    Jarvis, S. Dog's house
    Jarvis, S. M. King's gold
    Kennedy, L. Pied piper of Hamelin
    Love, S. Apache silver
    Mahlmann, L. Why the sea is salt
    Mills, G. Christmas comes to Hamelin
    Molière. Harpagon searches for his stolen money
    Rhodes, J. Crow and the corn
    Rowland, E. Precedent in pastries
    Shakespeare, W. Julius Caesar
    Spamer, C. Pot of gold
    Tichenor, T. Jack and the beanstalk
    Tolstoy, L. How much land does a man need?
    Watts, F. Crimson feather
    White, A. Lazarus
Green Leaf's lesson. Newman, D.
Gregg, Lisa. Miniature darzis. In Smith, M. 7 plays and How to Produce Them. 7 char
Greta and the prince. Cooper, E.
Greth, Roma. Two masks. In Durrell, D. Teen-Age Plays for Classroom Reading. 10 char
Grey ghosts. Deming, D.

GRIEF

Marlowe, C. Death of Zenocrate
Grimm, Brothers. Frog prince. In Mahlmann, L. Puppet Plays for Young Actors. 6 char
Gross, Nathalie F. Mystery ring. In Kamerman, S. Fifty Plays for Junior Actors. 8 char

GROUND-HOG DAY

Hark, M. Spring is here

GROWING UP

Miller, H. One to grow on
see also CHARACTER BUILDING
Guide for George Washington. Barbee, L.

GUILT

Ibsen, H. Aase searches for her son
―――――――. Peer Gynt leaves Solveig

GYPSIES

Heath, A. Gypsy look
White, A. Wraggle taggle gypsies
Gypsy look. Heath, A.

- H -

Hagy, Loleta. Fire in a paper. In Durrell, D. Thirty Plays for Classroom Reading. 6 char

HAIR

Pope, A. Belinda bemoans the loss of a lock of her hair
Hale, Edward Everett. Man without a country. In Olfson, L. Classics Adopted for Acting and Reading. 15 char+
Hale, Lucretia P. Lady who put salt in her coffee. In Smith, M. 7 Plays and How to Produce Them. 12 char

HALE, SARAH JOSEPHA

Fisher, A. Mother of Thanksgiving
Half-pint cowboy. Miller, H.
Hall, Holworthy, and Robert Middlemass. The valiant. In Maloney, H. Plays to Remember. 6 char
Hall, Margaret C. King Horn. In Kamerman, S. Dramatized Folk Tales of the World. 6 char
Hall, May Emery. Hearts of oak. In Burack, A. One Hundred Plays for Children. 6 char+
Hall, Mazie. Language shop. In Burack, A. One Hundred Plays for Children. 17 char
―――――――. Trial of Billy Scott. In Burack, A. One Hundred Plays for Children. 13 char

HALLOWEEN

Alderman, E. Wonderful witchware store
Bennett, R. Fire-face and the Indians

HALLUCINATIONS

    ———. In the witch's house
    ———. Scarecrow and the witch
    ———. Three terrors
Blaine, B. Rosy-cheeked ghost
Boiko, C. Scaredy cat
Cable, H. Reform of Sterling Silverheart
Cooper, E. Magic spell
    ———. Witch's pumpkin
Fisher, A. Ghosts on guard
    ———. On Halloween
Folmsbee, B. Goblin parade
Hark, M. House is haunted
    ———. Meet Mr. Witch
    ———. New Broom
Howard, H. Magic jack-o-lantern
Kingman, L. Magic pumpkin
Leuser, E. Little witch who tried
McGee, C. Witches and the crows
MacLellan, E. Test for a witch
Miller, H. Broken broomstick
    ———. Case of the giggling goblin
    ———. Curse of hag hollow
    ———. Ghost in the house
    ———. Haunts for hire
    ———. Miss Frankenstein
    ———. Spunky Punky
Molloy, L. Broom market day
Nicholson, J. Ghost walks tonight
Olfson, L. Equal rights
    ———. Happy hunting
Rybak, R. Election day in Spooksville
Thane, A. Saucy scarecrow
Watkins, M. Nobody believes in witches!
HALLUCINATIONS
    Saki. Open window
Hamelot. Alderman, E.
HAMILTON, ALEXANDER
    Walsh, H. Louisiana
HAMLET
    McGee, C. Fun with Hamlet and his friends
Hamlet. Shakespeare W.
Hamlet. Shakespeare, W. (Play title: To be or not to be)
Hammack, Beverly. Night before Christmas. <u>In</u> McGee, C.
    Drama for Fun. 5 char+
Hand-me-down Hildy. Sagoff, S.
Handwriting on the wall. Nicholson, J.
Hans, who made the princess laugh. Rowland, E.

HANSBERRY 66

Hansberry, Lorraine. Raisin in the sun. In Childress, A. Black Scenes. 6 char
Hansel and Gretel. McGee, C. (Play title: Gransel and Hettal)
Hansel and Gretel. Sanders, S.
Hansel and Gretal. Sayers, N. (Play title: Story of Gransel and Hettal)
Hansel and Gretel. Simonds, N.
Hansel and Gretel. Thane, A.
Happiest hat. Nolan, P.
HAPPINESS
    Arnold, E.   Make him smile
    Burtle, G.   Mystery of the gumdrop dragon
    Corson, H.   Dame Fortune and Don Money
    Hark, M.   Princess and the rose-colored glasses
    Jacob, E.   Crowded house
    Leuser, E.   Magic well
    Leuser, E. D.   Secret of the wishing well
    Muse, V.   Town mouse and his country cousin
    Nolan, P.   Going steady
    _____.   Happiest hat
    _____.   Trash and treasure
    _____.   View of the sea
    Spamer, C.   Shy prince
    Spyri, J.   Heidi
    _____.   Heidi finds the way
    Van Druten, J.   I remember Mama
Happy Christmas to all. Nolan, J.
Happy ending. Nolan, P.
Happy haunting. Olfson, L.
Happy hikers. Howard, V.
Happy holidays for little women. Howard, V.
Happy nesting. Carlson, B.
Happy prince. Wilde, O.
Hare and the tortoise. Bennett, R.
Hark, Mildred, and Noel McQueen. A B C for safety. In Hark, M. Junior Plays for All Occasions. 16 char
_____, _____. Bobby and the Lincoln speech. In Hark, M. Junior Plays for All Occasions. 6 char
_____, _____. Book revue. In Hark, M. Junior Plays for All Occasions. 33 char
_____, _____. Books a la mode. In Kamerman, S. Fifty Plays for Holidays. 13 char
_____, _____. Christmas eve news. In Hark, M. Junior Plays for All Occasions. 27 char+
_____, _____. Christmas in the woods. In Hark, M. Junior Plays for All Occasions. 7 char

———, ———. Christmas party. In Kamerman, S. Little Plays for Little Players. 12 char
———, ———. Christmas snowman. In Burack, A. Christmas Plays for Young Actors. 7 char
———, ———. Cupid's post office. In Hark, M. Junior Plays for All Occasions. 16 char+
———, ———. Cupies and hearts. In Hark, M. Junior Plays for All Occasions. 6 char
———, ———. Day for trees. In Hark, M. Junior Plays for All Occasions. 10 char
———, ———. Dish for the king. In Kamerman, S. Children's Plays from Favorite Stories. 18 char+
———, ———. Doctor Manners. In Hark, M. Junior Plays for All Occasions. 7 char; in Kamerman, S. Little Plays for Little Players. 7 char
———, ———. The dolls. In Hark, M. Junior Plays for All Occasions. 7 char
———, ———. Enter George Washington. In Hark, M. Junior Plays for All Occasions. 5 char
———, ———. Father keeps house. In Hark, M. Junior Plays for All Occasions. 9 char+
———, ———. Father's Easter hat. In Hark, M. Junior Plays for All Occasions. 6 char
———, ———. Five senses. In Hark, M. Junior Plays for All Occasions. 7 char
———, ———. Good neighbors. In Hark, M. Junior Plays for All Occasions. 8 char
———, ———. Hearts and flowers for Mother. In Hark, M. Junior Plays for All Occasions. 7 char
———, ———. House is haunted. In Durrell, D. Thirty Plays for Classroom Reading. 12 char; in Hark, M. Junior Plays for All Occasions. 11 char+
———, ———. In honor of Washington. In Hark, M. Junior Plays for All Occasions. 5 char+
———, ———. Johnnie Jump Up. In Hark, M. Junior Plays for All Occasions. 6 char
———, ———. Junction Santa Claus. In Hark, M. Junior Plays for All Occasions. 10 char
———, ———. Lincoln reminders. In Hark, M. Junior Plays for All Occasions. 17 char
———, ———. Magic egg. In Burack, A. One Hundred Plays for Children. 7 char
———, ———. Many thanks. In Hark, M. Junior Plays for All Occasions. 19 char
———, ———. Meet Mr. Witch. In Hark, M. Junior Plays for All Occasions. 14 char
———, ———. Mind your p's and q's. In Hark, M.

Junior Plays for All Occasions. 17 char
———, ———. New broom. In Hark, M. Junior Plays for All Occasions. 10 char
———, ———. New-fangled Thanksgiving. In Hark, M. Junior Plays for All Occasions. 7 char
———, ———. Not fit for man or beast. In Hark, M. Junior Plays for All Occasions. 7 char
———, ———. Nothing to be thankful for. In Hark, M. Junior Plays for All Occasions. 6 char
———, ———. Nursery rhyme diet. In Hark, M. Junior Plays for All Occasions. 14 char
———, ———. Off the shelf. In Burack, A. One Hundred Plays for Children. 8 char; in Hark, M. Junior Plays for All Occasions. 8 char
———, ———. Our own four walls. In Hark, M. Junior Plays for All Occasions. 6 char
———, ———. Pleasant dreams. In Hark, M. Junior Plays for All Occasions. 9 char
———, ———. Princess and the rose-colored glasses. In Hark, M. Junior Plays for All Occasions. 11 char
———, ———. Prize for Mother. In Hark, M. Junior Plays for All Occasions. 8 char
———, ———. Rainbow colors. In Hark, M. Junior Plays for All Occasions. 10 char
———, ———. Santa Claus parade. In Hark, M. Junior Plays for All Occasions. 2 char+
———, ———. See the parade. In Burack, A. One Hundred Plays for Children. 7 char
———, ———. Spring is here. In Hark, M. Junior Plays for All Occasions. 20 char
———, ———. Stuff of heroes. In Hark, M. Junior Plays for All Occasions. 5 char
———, ———. T for turkey. In Hark, M. Junior Plays for All Occasions. 8 char
———, ———. That Christmas feeling. In Kamerman, S. Fifty Plays for Holidays. 10 char+
———, ———. Three wishes for Mother. In Hark, M. Junior Plays for All Occasions. 8 char
———, ———. Too many kittens. In Durrell, D. Favorite Plays for Classroom Reading. 9 char; in Hark, M. Junior Plays for All Occasions. 8 char
———, ———. Visit of Johnny Appleseed. In Hark, M. Junior Plays for All Occasions. 6 char
———, ———. When do we eat? In Hark, M. Junior Plays for All Occasions. 8 char
see also McQueen, Mildred Hark

HARLEM

Childress, A. African garden
Harpagon searches for his stolen money. Molière
Harper, James M. First cat on Mars. In Burack, A.
Four-Star Plays for Boys. 9 char; in Durrell, D.
Favorite Plays for Classroom Reading. 11 char
Hartley, Carol. Children of the calendar. In Burack, A.
One Hundred Plays for Children. 13 char
Harvest for Lola. Henderson, N.
Hat for Mother. Phillips, M.
HATS
    Hark, M. Father's Easter hat
    Nolan, P. Happiest hat
    Phillips, M. Hat for Mother
Haunted bookshop. Nicholson, J.
Haunts for hire. Miller, H.
Hawthorne, Nathaniel. David Swan. In Gilfond, H. Plays for Reading. 17 char+
————. Dr. Heidegger's experiment. In Picozzi, R. Plays to Enjoy. 5 char
————. Feathertop. In Maloney, H. Plays to Remember. 10 char
Head, Faye E. Spouse for Suzie Mouse. In Kamerman, S. Dramatized Folk Tales of the World. 8 char
HEALTH
    Deming, D. First aid first
    Hark, M. Nursery rhyme diet
    ————. Pleasant dreams
    Kane, E. Piffle! It's only a sniffle!
    Lehman, J. Good health trolley
    Miller, H. Matter of health
    Parsons, M. Too much of a good thing
Healthy, wealthy, and wild. Murray, J.
Hearts and flowers for Mothers. Hark, M.
Hearts of oak. Hall, M.
Hearts, tarts and valentines. Fisher, A.
Heath, Anna Lenington. Gypsy look. In Kamerman, S. Fifty Plays for Junior Actors. 6 char
————. Much ado about ants. In Burack, A. One Hundred Plays for Children. 7 char
Heiderstadt, Dorothy. Girl from the sea. In Kamerman, S. Children's Plays from Favorite Stories. 6 char
Heidi. Spyri, J.
Heidi finds the way. Spyri, J.
Heine, Heinrich. Flying Dutchman. In Olfson, L. Classics adopted for Acting and Reading. 5 char

Heinzen, Barbara Brem. Miss Cast. In Burack, A. Skits, Comedies and Farces for Teen-agers. 8 char
Heir of Linne. Holmes, R.
Hello, little dog. Alexander, S.
Help wanted. Howard, V.
HELPING OTHERS see KINDNESS
Hen party. Olfson, L.
Henderson, Nancy. Automa. In Henderson, N. Walk Together: Five Plays on Human Rights. 16 char
_____. Get on board, little children. In Henderson, N. Walk Together: Five Plays on Human Rights. 31 char+
_____. Harvest for Lola. In Henderson, N. Walk Together: Five Plays on Human Rights. 18 char+
_____. Look behind the mask. In Henderson, N. Walk Together: Five Plays on Human Rights. 10 char
_____. The pledge. In Henderson, N. Walk Together: Five Plays on Human Rights. 21 char+
Henry, O. Last leaf. In Gilfond, H. Plays for Reading. 5 char
_____. Romance of a busy broker. In Gilfond, H. Plays for Reading. 5 char
Henry. McGee, C.
Henry and the night crawlers. Glass, G.
Henry Huggins. Cleary, B.
HEROES AND HEROINES
    Dias, E. Cleanest town in the West
    Glass, G. How to put out a dreadful dragon
    Hark, M. Stuff of heroes
    Love, S. Beowulf
    see also FOLK HEROES
Heroine of Wren. Colbo, E.
Harvey, Michael. Virtue is her own reward. In Burack, A. Skits, Comedies and Farces for Teen-agers. 12 char
Hester, Hal, Donald Driver, and Danny Apolinar. Your own thing. In Swortzell, L. All the World's a Stage. 10 char
Hi down there. Nolan, P.
High jumper. Howard, V.
Highland fling. Nolan, P.
HIKING
    Howard, V. Happy hikers
Hill, Kay. Midnight burial. In Burack, A. One Hundred Plays for Children. 8 char; in Durrell, D. Favorite Plays for Classroom Reading. 9 char
HILLBILLIES
    Olfson, L. Couple of right smart fellers
Hippie and the bard. Dias, E.

HIPPIES
 Cable, H. Way-out Cinderella
 Dias, E. Hippie and the bard
 Murray, J. National everything
 Nolan, P. What's zymurgy with you?
HIPPOPOTAMUSES
 Barrington, P. I had a hippopotamus
HISTORY--COMEDY
 Lawrence, J. Inside a kid's head
HISTORY--UNITED STATES see UNITED STATES--HISTORY
HOBBIES
 Fontaine, R. Ride your hobby
Hoff, Syd. Children on the moon. In Hoff, S. Giants and Other Plays for Kids. 4 char
_____. Family. In Hoff, S. Giants and Other Plays for Kids. 4 char
_____. Giants. In Hoff, S. Giants and Other Plays for Kids. 6 char
_____. Lion in the zoo. In Hoff, S. Giants and Other Plays for Kids. 6 char
_____. Wild flowers. In Hoff, S. Giants and Other Plays for Kids. 6 char
Hold back the redskins. Dias, E.
HOLIDAYS
 Boiko, C. Wayward witch
 Miller, H. Friendship wheel
 _____. S. O. S. from Santa
 see also specific holidays
HOLLAND
 Asbrand, K. Little hero of Holland
 Boiko, C. Search for the sky-blue princess
 MacLellan, E. Secret of the windmill
 _____. Small shoes and small tulips
 Nolan, P. Leak in the dike
 Thane, A. Gift for Hans Brinker
Hollingsworth, Leslie. Silent Night. In Burack, A. Christmas Plays for Young Actors. 9 char
Holly hangs high. Barbee L.
Holmes, Ruth Vickery. Golden goose. In Kamerman, S. Children's Plays from Favorite Stories. 21 char
_____. Heir of Linne. In Kamerman, S. Children's Plays from Favorite Stories. 8 char
_____. In the days of King Alfred. In Durrell, D. Thirty Plays for Classroom Reading. 4 char
_____. King and the miller. In Kamerman, S. Children's Plays from Favorite Stories. 8 char
_____. King John and the Abbot of Canterbury. In

Burack, A. Four-Star Plays for Boys. 7 char
___. Little Red Riding Hood. In Kamerman, S. Little Plays for Little People. 5 char
___. Wise men of Gotham. In Burack, A. One Hundred Plays for Children. 8 char+
HOME
   Sperling, L. Day Canary met Sparrow
Home cooking. Carlson, B.
Home, sweet home. Werner, S.
Homer. The Iliad. In Olfson, L. Dramatized Classics for Radio-Style Reading, Vol. II. 11 char
HONESTY
   Browning, R. Pied piper of Hamlin
   Collodi, C. Pinocchio
   Colson, J. Baron Barnaby's box
   Gross, N. Mystery ring
   Hark, M. Bobby and the Lincoln speech
   Leuser, E. Big stone
   Maupassant, G. The necklace
   Miller, H. Birthday pie
   ___. Mount Vernon cricket
   Peterson, M. Abe buys a barrel
   Rowland, E. Precedent in pastries
   Sealock, T. Lincoln coat
   Watts, F. Leprechaun's pot of gold
   see also TRUTH AND FALSEHOOD
Honey and dough. Jarvis, S. M.
HONOR
   Dumas, A. The duel
   Miller, H. Return of Bobby Shafto
   Winther, B. Great Samurai sword
Honorable cat's decision. Boiko, C.
Honored one. Leuser, E.
Hook and bait. Howard, V.
HOPE
   Asbrand, K. Pandora's box
   Fisher, A. Invasion from the stratosphere
   Hoppenstedt, Elbert M. Poet's nightmare. In Kamerman, S. Fifty Plays for Junior Actors. 8 char
   ___, and Helen E. Waite. Christmas house. In Burack, A. One Hundred Plays for Children. 10 char
   ___, ___. Naomi-of-the-inn. In Burack, A. Christmas Plays for Young Actors. 15 char+
   ___, ___. Not only the strong. In Burack, A. One Hundred Plays for Children. 11 char
Horn of plenty. Miller, H.

HORSES

Cochrane, L. Moon dragon
Hotel Oak. Boiko, C.
House is haunted. Hark, M.
Housework for hubby. Howard, V.
How? Howard, V.
How are you? Howard, V.
How I conquered worry. Howard, V.
How mothers came to be. Boiko, C.
How much land does a man need? Tolstoy, L.
How music made everyone happy. Howard, V.
How the west was won. Fontaine, R.
How to be successful. Howard, V.
How to choose a boy. Boiko, C.
How to hypnotize. Howard, V.
How to improve your memory. Howard, V.
How to live long. Taylor, L.
How to put out a dreadful dragon. Glass, G.
How we got our numbers. Kane, E.
Howard, Helen Littler. Ben Franklin, peace-maker. In Durrell, D. Thirty Plays for Classroom Reading. 5 char
——————. Christmas train. In Burack, A. Christmas Plays for Young Actors. 10 char+
——————. Doctor Know All. In Burack, A. Popular Plays for Classroom Reading. 13 char
——————. I'll share my fare. In Burack, A. One Hundred Plays for Children. 6 char
——————. Little circus donkey. In Burack, A. One Hundred Plays for Children. 10 char
——————. Magic jack-o-lantern. In Burack, A. One Hundred Plays for Children. 6 char+; in Kamerman, S. Little Plays for Little People. 6 char+
——————. Mother's gift. In Burack, A. One Hundred Plays for Children. 7 char
——————. Thankful indeed. In Durrell, D. Thirty Plays for Classroom Reading. 6 char
——————. Thanks to Sammy Scarecrow. In Burack, A. One Hundred Plays for Children. 4 char; in Kamerman, S. Little Plays for Little Players. 4 char
——————. What he deserves. In Durrell, D. Thirty Plays for Classroom Reading. 8 char
Howard, Vernon. All washed up. In Howard, V. Complete Book of Children's Theater. 1 char
——————. Arkwood two-four-two-four. In Howard, V. Complete Book of Children's Theater. 1 char
——————. Around the world. In Howard, V. Complete

HOWARD 74

    Book of Children's Theater. 1 char
―――――. The artist. In Howard, V. Complete Book of
Children's Theater. 1 char
―――――. Backward people. In Howard, V. Complete
Book of Children's Theater. 8 char+
―――――. Bible pantomimes. In Howard, V. Complete
Book of Children's Theater. 8 char+
―――――. Birthday surprises. In Howard, V. Complete
Book of Children's Theater. 1 char+
―――――. Boston tea party. In Howard, V. Complete
Book of Children's Theater. 6 char+
―――――. Box of chocolates. In Howard, V. Complete
Book of Children's Theater. 1 char
―――――. Building of the Panama Canal. In Howard, V.
Complete Book of Children's Theater. 9 char+
―――――. The bus. In Howard, V. Complete Book of
Children's Theater. 14 char+
―――――. Bus stop. In Howard, V. Complete Book of
Children's Theater. 2 char
―――――. But, Doctor. In Howard, V. Complete Book of
Children's Theater. 1 char
―――――. Cake bake. In Howard, V. Complete Book of
Children's Theater. 8 char+
―――――. California gold discovery. In Howard, V. Complete Book of Children's Theater. 5 char+
―――――. Call to a bride. In Howard, V. Complete Book
of Children's Theater. 1 char
―――――. Calling all cooks. In Howard, V. Complete
Book of Children's Theater. 1 char
―――――. Calling all spies. In Howard, V. Complete
Book of Children's Theater. 1 char
―――――. Children who found new friends. In Howard, V.
Complete Book of Children's Theater. 5 char+
―――――. The colonel. In Howard, V. Complete Book of
Children's Theater. 1 char
―――――. Columbus' discovery of America. In Howard, V.
Complete Book of Children's Theater. 6 char+
―――――. Comedy team. In Howard, V. Complete Book of
Children's Theater. 2 char
―――――. Complaint desk. In Howard, V. Complete Book
of Children's Theater. 1 char
―――――. Courtesy at the wheel. In Howard, V. Complete
Book of Children's Theater. 1 char
―――――. The dancers. In Howard, V. Complete Book
of Children's Theater. 6 char+
―――――. Daniel in the lion's den. In Howard, V. Com-

plete Book of Children's Theater. 5 char+
———. Daring sailormen. In Howard, V. Complete Book of Children's Theater. 11 char
———. David and Goliath. In Howard, V. Complete Book of Children's Theater. 12 char+
———. David's battle with Goliath. In Howard, V. Complete Book of Children's Theater. 5 char+
———. Dear Judy. In Howard, V. Complete Book of Children's Theater. 1 char
———. Dear Mr. Loveletter. In Howard, V. Complete Book of Children's Theater. 1 char
———. Directions. In Howard, V. Complete Book of Children's Theater. 2 char
———. Dizzy Dinners. In Howard, V. Complete Book of Children's Theater. 1 char
———. Don Quixote saves the day. In Howard, V. Complete Book of Children's Theater. 14 char
———. Drive in the country. In Howard, V. Complete Book of Children's Theater. 1 char
———. The experts. In Howard, V. Complete Book of Children's Theater. 4 char+
———. Explanations. In Howard, V. Complete Book of Children's Theater. 1 char
———. Famous words. In Howard, V. Complete Book of Children's Theater. 1 char
———. First flight of the Wright brothers. In Howard, V. Complete Book of Children's Theater. 5 char+
———. Fisherman. In Howard, V. Complete Book of Children's Theater. 1 char
———. Flight fifteen. In Howard, V. Complete Book of Children's Theater. 1 char
———. Foot in the door. In Howard, V. Complete Book of Children's Theater. 1 char
———. Fortunes? In Howard, V. Complete Book of Children's Theater. 1 char
———. Fred and Lois. In Howard, V. Complete Book of Children's Theater. 2 char
———. Freddie proposes. In Howard, V. Complete Book of Children's Theater. 1 char
———. Funny business. In Howard, V. Complete Book of Children's Theater. 2 char
———. Girl talk. In Howard, V. Complete Book of Children's Theater. 2 char
———. Girl who did very, very well. In Howard, V. Complete Book of Children's Theater. 1 char
———. Golf lesson. In Howard, V. Complete Book of

Children's Theater. 1 char
———. The golfer. In Howard, V. Complete Book of Children's Theater. 1 char
———. Grandma crosses the street. In Howard, V. Complete Book of Children's Theater. 1 char
———. Happy hikers. In Howard, V. Complete Book of Children's Theater. 3 char+
———. Happy holidays for little women. In Howard, V. Complete Book of Children's Theater. 10 char
———. Help wanted. In Howard, V. Complete Book of Children's Theater. 1 char
———. Help wanted. In Howard, V. Complete Book of Children's Theater. 2 char
———. High-jumper. In Howard, V. Complete Book of Children's Theater. 1 char
———. Hook and bait. In Howard, V. Complete Book of Children's Theater. 1 char
———. Housework for hubby. In Howard, V. Complete Book of Children's Theater. 1 char
———. How? In Howard, V. Complete Book of Children's Theater. 1 char
———. How are you? In Howard, V. Complete Book of Children's Theater. 1 char
———. How I conquered worry. In Howard, V. Complete Book of Children's Theater. 1 char
———. How music made everyone happy. In Howard, V. Complete Book of Children's Theater. 3 char+
———. How to be successful. In Howard, V. Complete Book of Children's Theater. 1 char
———. How to hypnotize. In Howard, V. Complete Book of Children's Theater. 1 char
———. How to improve your memory. In Howard, V. Complete Book of Children's Theater. 1 char
———. In the army. In Howard, V. Complete Book of Children's Theater. 7 char+
———. In the jungle. In Howard, V. Complete Book of Children's Theater. 2 char+
———. It's a mystery. In Howard, V. Complete Book of Children's Theater. 1 char
———. Johnny Appleseed in danger. In Howard, V. Complete Book of Children's Theater. 12 char+
———. The juggler. In Howard, V. Complete Book of Children's Theater. 1 char
———. Kiss me good night! In Howard, V. Complete Book of Children's Theater. 1 char
———. Larry's lesson. In Howard, V. Complete Book of Children's Theater. 1 char

HOWARD

_____. Left turn. In Howard, V. Complete Book of Children's Theater. 1 char
_____. The letter. In Howard, V. Complete Book of Children's Theater. 1 char
_____. Lincoln's Gettysburg Address. In Howard, V. Complete Book of Children's Theater. 14 char+
_____. Lincoln's middle name. In Howard, V. Complete Book of Children's Theater. 1 char
_____. Little known facts about birds. In Howard, V. Complete Book of Children's Theater. 1 char
_____. Look, George. In Howard, V. Complete Book of Children's Theater. 1 char
_____. Look here, boss. In Howard, V. Complete Book of Children's Theater. 1 char
_____. Lunch at Pierre's. In Howard, V. Complete Book of Children's Theater. 1 char
_____. Man who didn't like rain. In Howard, V. Complete Book of Children's Theater. 8 char+
_____. Mechanical man. In Howard, V. Complete Book of Children's Theater. 2 char
_____. Meet me in the moonlight. In Howard, V. Complete Book of Children's Theater. 1 char
_____. Men of Mars. In Howard, V. Complete Book of Children's Theater. 6 char
_____. Mirror stunt. In Howard, V. Complete Book of Children's Theater. 2 char
_____. My boy friend. In Howard, V. Complete Book of Children's Theater. 1 char
_____. My first football game. In Howard, V. Complete Book of Children's Theater. 1 char
_____. My vocal career. In Howard, V. Complete Book of Children's Theater. 1 char
_____. Newspaper dramatics. In Howard, V. Complete Book of Children's Theater. 3 char+
_____. Not exactly. In Howard, V. Complete Book of Children's Theater. 1 char
_____. Oliver Twist asks for more. In Howard, V. Complete Book of Children's Theater. 12 char+
_____. Our famous proverbs. In Howard, V. Complete Book of Children's Theater. 1 char
_____. Our national sports. In Howard, V. Complete Book of Children's Theater. 1 char
_____. Pantomime orchestra. In Howard, V. Complete Book of Children's Theater. 3 char+
_____. Party night. In Howard, V. Complete Book of Children's Theater. 1 char
_____. Pay and be gay. In Howard, V. Complete Book

of Children's Theater. 1 char
_____. Pep talk. In Howard, V. Complete Book of Children's Theater. 1 char
_____. Perfumes. In Howard, V. Complete Book of Children's Theater. 1 char
_____. Personality machine. In Howard, V. Complete Book of Children's Theater. 4 char+
_____. The picnic. In Howard, V. Complete Book of Children's Theater. 7 char+
_____. Pilgrim's first Thanksgiving. In Howard, V. Complete Book of Children's Theater. 10 char+
_____. Pony express. In Howard, V. Complete Book of Children's Theater. 4 char+
_____. Ranch romance. In Howard, V. Complete Book of Children's Theater. 2 char
_____. Return of Rip Van Winkle. In Howard, V. Complete Book of Children's Theater. 20 char+
_____. Ride of Paul Revere. In Howard, V. Complete Book of Children's Theater. 4 char+
_____. Roller coaster. In Howard, V. Complete Book of Children's Theater. 1 char
_____. Romantic facts for men. In Howard V. Complete Book of Children's Theater. 1 char
_____. Romantic facts for women. In Howard, V. Complete Book of Children's Theater. 1 char
_____. Salesman! In Howard, V. Complete Book of Children's Theater. 2 char+
_____. Saturday chatter. In Howard, V. Complete Book of Children's Theater. 2 char
_____. School daze. In Howard, V. Complete Book of Children's Theater. 1 char
_____. Schoolwork. In Howard, V. Complete Book of Children's Theater. 2 char
_____. Setting the table. In Howard, V. Complete Book of Children's Theater. 1 char
_____. The shopper. In Howard, V. Complete Book of Children's Theater. 1 char
_____. Sir Galahad and the maidens. In Howard, V. Complete Book of Children's Theater. 15 char+
_____. Size, please. In Howard, V. Complete Book of Children's Theater. 1 char
_____. Slow motion pantomime. In Howard, V. Complete Book of Children's Theater. 2 char+
_____. Sour notes. In Howard, V. Complete Book of Children's Theater. 8 char+
_____. Space talk. In Howard, V. Complete Book of Children's Theater. 1 char

———— . Staff of life. In Howard, V. Complete Book of Children's Theater. 1 char
———— . Stagecoach. In Howard, V. Complete Book of Children's Theater. 1 char
———— . Stagecoach stop. In Howard, V. Complete Book of Children's Theater. 6 char+
———— . Strange tale of King Midas. In Howard, V. Complete Book of Children's Theater. 12 char
———— . Strong man. In Howard, V. Complete Book of Children's Theater. 1 char
———— . Super sale. In Howard, V. Complete Book of Children's Theater. 8 char+
———— . Supper in silence. In Howard, V. Complete Book of Children's Theater. 1 char
———— . Take-turners. In Howard, V. Complete Book of Children's Theater. 10 char
———— . Telephone chuckles. In Howard, V. Complete Book of Children's Theater. 2 char
———— . Television tricks. In Howard, V. Complete Book of Children's Theater. 4 char+
———— . Tennis match. In Howard, V. Complete Book of Children's Theater. 2 char+
———— . Texas cowboy. In Howard, V. Complete Book of Children's Theater. 1 char
———— . Texas roundup. In Howard, V. Complete Book of Children's Theater. 1 char
———— . Time of my life. In Howard, V. Complete Book of Children's Theater. 1 char
———— . Treasure of Monte Cristo. In Howard, V. Complete Book of Children's Theater. 11 char+
———— . Valentines. In Howard, V. Complete Book of Children's Theater. 1 char
———— . Waiter! In Howard, V. Complete Book of Children's Theater. 2 char+
———— . Waiting for Grandma. In Howard, V. Complete Book of Children's Theater. 1 char
———— . Walking with Wilma. In Howard, V. Complete Book of Children's Theater. 1 char
———— . Washington at Valley Forge. In Howard, V. Complete Book of Children's Theater. 10 char+
———— . Wild dreams. In Howard, V. Complete Book of Children's Theater. 6 char
———— . Wild, wild west. In Howard, V. Complete Book of Children's Theater. 1 char
———— . The winners. In Howard, V. Complete Book of Children's Theater. 12 char+
———— . Wrist watch. In Howard, V. Complete Book of

Children's Theater. 1 char
_____. Yes, officer! In Howard, V. Complete Book of Children's Theater. 1 char
_____. You look lovely, dear. In Howard, V. Complete Book of Children's Theater. 1 char
_____. Your happy friend. In Howard, V. Complete Book of Children's Theater. 1 char
Howells, William Dean. Christmas every day. In Thane, A. Plays from Famous Stories and Fairy Tales. 9 char
Howling success. Garver, J.
Hubbub on the bookshelf. Woster, A.
Huff, Betty Tracy. Case of the missing masterpiece. In Burack, A. Popular Plays for Classroom Reading. 10 char
_____. Feast of the thousand lanters. In Kamerman, S. Fifty Plays for Junior Actors. 12 char+
_____. Ride the Gooberville stage! In Burack, A. Skits, Comedies and Farces for Teen-agers. 13 char
Hughes, Langston. Soul gone home. In Swortzell, L. All the World's a Stage. 4 char
Hughes, Ted. Beauty and the beast. In Hughes, T. Tiger's Bones and Other Plays for Children. 7 char
_____. Coming of the kings. In Hughes, T. Tiger's Bones and Other Plays for Children. 12 char
_____. Orpheus. In Tiger's Bones and Other Plays for Children. 9 char+
_____. Sean, the fool, the devil, and the cats. In Tiger's Bones and Other Plays for Children. 14 char
_____. Tiger's bones. In Hughes, T. Tiger's Bones and Other Plays for Children. 8 char+
Hugo, Victor. Bishop's candlesticks. In Olfson, L. Classics Adopted for Acting and Reading. 8 char

HUMAN NATURE
   Anderson, R. Trouble in outer space
   Pope, A. Belinda bemoans the loss of a lock of her hair
   Rostand, E. Nose speech
   Shore, M. Watch out for Aunt Hattie

HUMAN RIGHTS
   Barbour, F. Bird cage
   Fisher, A. Cavalcade of human rights
   Glass, G. Early life of George Washington Carver
   Hansberry, L. Raisin in the sun
   Henderson, N. Walk Together: Five Plays on Human Rights
   Mitchell, L. Land beyond the river

see also BLACK AMERICANS; EQUALITY; FREE-
DOM; MINORITIES
HUNGER
    Fisher, A. Empty bowls
    _____. Let there be bread
HUNT, ROBERT
    Walsh, H. Jamestown
Huntsberry, W. Minor developments. In Durrell, D.
    Teen-Age Plays for Classroom Reading. 14 char
HUSBAND AND WIFE
    Carlson, B. Shut the door!
    Fontaine, R. On you it looks good
HYGIENE
    Bennett, R. In the witch's house
    Fisher, A. King's toothache
    Miller, H. Matter of health

- I -

I had a hippopotamus. Barrington, P.
I know an old woman. Grabe, Mrs. Klaus
I remember Mama. Van Druten, J.
I think I know. Jarvis, S. M.
I want to report a murder. Murray, J.
Ibsen, Henrik. Aase searches for her son (Peer Gynt) In
    Kline, P. Theatre Student: Scenes to Perform. 1 char
    _____. Peer Gynt leaves Solveig (Peer Gynt) In Kline,
    P. Theatre Student: Scenes to Perform. 1 char
Ickler, Lyda M. Kitty hawk--1903. In Durrell, D. Thirty
    Plays for Classroom Reading. 7 char
Ideal husband. Wilde, O. (Play title: On being too frequent-
    ly proposed to)
If wishes were horses. Nathan, B.
The Iliad. Homer
I'll share my fare. Howard, H.
IMAGINATION
    Lawrence, J. Inside a kid's head
    Ward, M. Mr. Lazy Man's family
Importance of being earnest. Wilde, O.
Impossible room. Murray, J.
Impossible! unacceptable! preposterous! Carlson, B.
In a manger laid. Preston, C.
In Bibberley Town. White, A.
In-group. Nolan, P.
In honor of Washington. Hark, M.
In the army. Howard, V.

In the days of King Alfred.   Holmes, R.
In the dumps.   Carlson, B.
In the fog.   Geiger, M.
In the jungle.   Howard, V.
In the name of Miles Standish.   Ramsey, H.
In the witch's house.   Bennett, R.
Incredible housing shortage.   Olfson, L.
INDEPENDENCE [personal]
    Miller, H.   Gathering sticks
INDIA
    Cochrane, L.   Story of Rama and Sita
    Gregg, L.   Miniature darzis
    Love, S.   Clive of India
    Simon, S.   Tiger and the brahman
    Smith, G.   Tiger, the brahman, and the jackal
Indian boy without a name.   Vahl, R.
INDIANA
    Boiko, C.   Tall-tale tournament
INDIANS
    Boiko, C.   How mothers came to be
    Cable, H.   Peace, pilgrim
    Carlson, B.   Why the leaves of the aspen tree quake in a breeze
    Cooper, E.   Little white cloud
    Dias, E.   Hold back the redskins
    Henderson, N.   The pledge
    Miller, H.   Half-pint cowboy
    Roberts, H.   Pocahontas, the tomboy princess
    Vahl, R.   Indian boy without a name
    Waite, H.   Not only the strong
INDIVIDUALITY
    Driver, D.   Your own thing
INDONESIA
    Nolan, P.   Our sister, Sitya
Insatiable dragon.   Boiko, C.
Inside a kid's head.   Lawrence, J.
INSURANCE
    Fontaine, R.   To the moon
INTELLIGENCE
    Corson, H.   Triumph for two
Interview with Punchy McPugg.   McGee, C.
Invasion from the stratosphere.   Fisher, A.
INVENTIONS
    Newman, D.   Rebellious robots
Invisible dragon of Winn Sinn Tu.   Musil, R.
Invitation to supper.   Martin, P.

INVOLVEMENT
    Nolan, P. In-group
Ionesco, Eugene. The leader. In Maloney, H. Plays to
    Remember. 6 char
IRELAND
    Boiko, C. Cinder-riley
    Carlson, B. Ghosts
    _____. Why catch a leprechaun?
    Davis, L. St. Patrick and the last snake in Ireland
    Leuser, E. Courage piece
    Lynch, M. Finn McCool
    Malone, M. Last snake in Ireland
    Turnbull, L. Magic shoes
    Watts, F. Bridge to Killybog Fair
    _____. Leprechaun shoemakers
    _____. Leprechaun's pot of gold
IRONY
    Wilde, O. On being too frequently proposed to
Irving, Washington. Legend of Sleepy Hollow. In Picozzi, R. Plays to Enjoy. 14 char+
_____. Rip Van Winkle. In Boylan, E. How to be a Puppeteer. 10 char+
_____. Rip Van Winkle. In Olfson, L. Classics Adopted for Acting and Reading. 19 char
_____. Rip Van Winkle. In Sanders, S. Creating Plays with Children. 18 char+
_____. Rip Van Winkle. In Thane, A. Plays from Famous Stories and Fairy Tales. 17 char+
Is there life on other planets? Lane, M.
ISRAEL--ANCIENT
    Whitworth, V. King and the bee
It had to be. Carlson, B.
ITALY
    Leuser, E. Magic grapes
    Nolan, P. Courters
    Peterson, M. Magic box
    Weik, M. The rehearsal
It's a mystery. Howard, V.
It's frightening! Fontaine, R.

- J -

Jack and Jill. Freudenberger, H.
Jack and the beanstalk. Cable, H. (Play title: Little Jackie and the Beanstalk)
Jack and the beanstalk. Mahlmann, L.

JACK 84

Jack and the beanstalk. Tichenor, T.
Jack and the magic beanstalk. Thane, A.
Jack Jouette's ride. Boiko, C.
Jack the giant killer. Boylan, E.
JACKSON, ANDREW
    Walsh, H. Young Hickory
Jacob, Eva. Crowded house. In Kamerman, S. Children's Plays from Favorite Stories. 12 char+
_____. Robin Hood tricks the sheriff. In Kamerman, S. Children's Plays from Favorite Stories. 19 char+
_____. Snow White. In Kamerman, S. Children's Plays from Favorite Stories. 15 char
Jailer's daughter falls in love with a prince. Fletcher, J.
James, Henry. Washington Square. In Olfson, L. Dramatized Classics for Radio-Style Reading. 8 char
Jamestown. Walsh, H.
Jane Eyre. Brontë, C.
JAPAN
    Boiko, C. Honorable cat's decision
    _____. Small crimson parasol
    Foley, M. Emperor's new robes
    Mapp, F. Ogre who built a bridge
    Musil, R. Peach tree kingdom
    Nolan, P. Boshibari and the two thieves
    Winther, B. Great samurai sword
The jar. Pirandello, L.
Jarvis, Sally. Dog's house. In Martin, J. Little Plays for Little People. 5 char
_____. Foolish Fred. In Martin, J. Little Plays for Little People. 6 char
_____. Giant's cat. In Martin, J. Little Plays for Little People. 4 char
_____. Mr. Maybe. In Martin, J. Little Plays for Little People. 6 char
_____. Six wise travelers. In Martin, J. Little Plays for Little People. 7 char
_____. Sun and the wind. In Martin, J. Little Plays for Little People. 3 char
_____. Supper with the queen. In Martin, J. Little Plays for Little People. 4 char
_____. Who helped the lion? In Martin, J. Little Plays for Little People. 2 char
Jarvis, Sally Melcher. Fisherman and the elf. In Jarvis, S. Fried Onions and Marshmallows. 2 char
_____. Free bacon. In Jarvis, S. Fried Onions and Marshmallows. 3 char+
_____. Fried onions and marshmallows. In Jarvis, S.

Fried Onions and Marshmallows. 2 char
    ――――――. Honey and dough. In Jarvis, S. Fried Onions and Marshmallows. 6 char+
    ――――――. I think I know. In Jarvis, S. Fried Onions and Marshmallows. 3 char
    ――――――. King's gold. In Jarvis, S. Fried Onions and Marshmallows. 4 char
    ――――――. Lion and the birds. In Jarvis, S. Fried Onions and Marshmallows. 4 char
    ――――――. Lion and the mosquitoes. In Jarvis, S. Fried Onions and Marshmallows. 4 char+
    ――――――. Mitten tree. In Jarvis, S. Fried Onions and Marshmallows. 3 char
    ――――――. !Trip-trap! trip-trap! In Jarvis, S. Fried Onions and Marshmallows. 4 char
    ――――――. Turkeys are tricky. In Jarvis, S. Fried Onions and Marshmallows. 3 char
    ――――――. Two silly wolves. In Jarvis, S. Fried Onions and Marshmallows. 5 char
    ――――――. Why the turtle does not talk. In Jarvis, S. Fried Onions and Marshmallows. 3 char

JAVA
    Cochrane, L. Story of Rama and Sita

JEALOUSY
    Olfson, L. Hen party.

JEFFERSON, THOMAS
    Carlson, B. To build a federal city
    Pyle, M. Three royal r's
    Walsh, H. Louisiana

Jenny-by-the-day. Molloy, L.
Jest of Hahalaba. Dunsany, L.

JESTERS
    Whitman, C. School for jesters

JESUS CHRIST--NATIVITY
    DuBois, G. Two strangers from Nazareth
    DuBois, H. Perfect gift
    Hark, M. Christmas Eve news
    Hughes, T. Coming of the kings
    Newman, D. One night in Bethlehem
    Patterson, E. No room at the inn
    Preston, Carol. Born in a stable
    ――――――. In a manger laid
    ――――――. Old Christmas
    Ross, L. Three kings
    Waite, H. Naomi-of-the-inn

Jiminy Cinders. Miller, H.
Jingle bells. Pendleton, E.

Joan of Arc. Love, S.
JOAN OF ARC
    Love, S. Joan of Arc
John Crown's legacy. Suerken, E.
Johnnie Jump Up. Hark, M.
Johnny Appleseed. Nolan, P.
Johnny Appleseed in danger. Howard, V.
JOKES
    Carlson, B. It had to be
    ————. Let's fool someone
    ————. What is it?
Jonathan's Thanksgiving. Very, A.
Jones, David Cadwalader, and Lewis Mahlmann. Alice's adventures in Wonderland. In Mahlmann, L. Puppet Plays for Young Players. 17 char
————, ————. Frog prince. In Mahlmann, L. Puppet Plays for Young People. 6 char
————, ————. Jack and the beanstalk. In Mahlmann, L. Puppet Plays for Young Players. 10 char
————, ————. Magic mushrooms. In Mahlmann, L. Puppet Plays for Young Players. 3 char
————, ————. Magic shoes. In Mahlmann, L. Puppet Plays for Young Players. 9 char
————, ————. Pinocchio. In Mahlmann, L. Puppet Plays for Young Players. 13 char
————, ————. Princess and the pea. In Mahlmann, L. Puppet Plays for Young Players. 5 char
————, ————. Reluctant dragon. In Mahlmann, L. Puppet Plays for Young Players. 6 char
————, ————. Snow White and the seven dwarfs. In Mahlmann, L. Puppet Plays for Young Players. 14 char
————, ————. The tinderbox. In Mahlmann, L. Puppet Plays for Young Players. 11 char
————, ————. Why the sea is salt. In Mahlmann, L. Puppet Plays for Young Players. 9 char
————, ————. Wizard of Oz. In Mahlmann, L. Puppet Plays for Young Players. 13 char+
JOURNALISM
    Dias, E. Bow-wow blues
    Sayre, G. Final edition
The juggler. Howard, V.
Julius Caesar. Shakespeare, W.
JULY FOURTH
    Slingluff, M. Naughty Susan
Jump for Joy. Schaaf, A.
Junction Santa Claus. Hark, M.

JUNIOR

Junior prom. Wilde, C.
JUSTICE
 Cervantes, M. Don Quixote
 Dumas, A. Count of Monte Cristo
 Fisher, A. Cavalcade of human rights
 Henderson, N. Get on board, little children
 <u>   </u>. The pledge
 Holmes, R. Golden goose
 Howard, V. Sir Galahad and the maidens
 Huff, B. Feast of the thousand lanterns
 Koon, H. Pierre Patelin
 MacFarlan, E. The olive jar
 <u>   </u>. Tiger catcher
 Simon, S. Tiger and the Brahman
 Smith, G. Tiger, the brahman, and the jackal
 Stockton, F. Lady or the tiger?
 Thane, A. Baker's neighbor
 Twain, M. Prince and the pauper
Justice for all. Carlson, B.

- K -

KABUKI [Japanese drama]
 Winther, B. Great Samurai sword
Kane, Eleanora Bowling. Children of chocolate street. <u>In</u>
 Kamerman, S. Little Plays for Little Players. 10 char
<u>   </u>. Elves and the shoemaker. <u>In</u> Burack, A. Christmas Plays for Young Actors. 10 char+
<u>   </u>. How we got our numbers. <u>In</u> Burack, A. One Hundred Plays for Children. 9 char
Karagiosis and the dragon. Cochrane, L.
Katherina's obedience. Shakespeare, W.
Kaufman, Ted. Piffle! It's only a sniffle. <u>In</u> Burack, A.
 One Hundred Plays for Children. 10 char+
Kennedy, Lucy. Pied piper of Hamelin. <u>In</u> Burack, A.
 One Hundred Plays for Children. 12 char+
KENTUCKY--HISTORY
 Waite, H. Not only the strong
Kettle of brains. Williams, G.
Key to understanding. Biggs, L.
Kidnapped. Stevenson, R. (Play title: Kidnapping of David Balfour)
KIDNAPPING
 Boiko, C. All hands on deck
 Chisholm, J. Shades of ransom
 Stevenson, R. Kidnapping of David Balfour

KIDNAPPING 88

Kidnapping of David Balfour. Stevenson, R.
KINDNESS
 Arnold, E. Make him smile
 Asbrand, K. Adalmina's pearl
 ―――――. Friendly as can be
 Barr, J. Old Mother Hubbard
 Bennett, R. Lion and the mouse
 Burnett, F. Little princess
 Colbo, E. Heroine of Wren
 Collodi, C. Pinocchio
 Cooper, E. Greta and the prince
 Dickens, C. Magic fishbone
 Fisher, A. Christmas tree for kitty
 ―――――. One-ring circus
 Freudenberger, H. Jack and Jill
 Glass, G. Little witch
 Holmes, R. King and the miller
 Howard, H. Thankful indeed
 Huff, B. Feast of the thousand lanterns
 Hugo, V. Bishop's candlesticks
 Irving, W. Rip Van Winkle
 Jacob, E. Snow White
 Jarvis, S. Who helped the lion?
 Jarvis, S. M. Turkeys are tricky
 Kane, E. Children of chocolate street
 King, W. Snow White
 Kingman, L. Mr. Thanks has his day
 Leuser, E. Broth of Christkindli
 ―――――. Courage piece
 ―――――. Little clown who forgot how to laugh
 Lonely giant
 McCarty, E. Little cake
 McKay, H. Surprise for Mr. Winkle
 Mahlmann, L. Snow White and the seven dwarfs
 Miller, H. Peter Rabbit volunteers
 Newman, D. Cinderella
 ―――――. Plum Blossom and the dragon
 Nicholson, M. Price of eggs
 Nolan, P. Johnny Appleseed
 ―――――. Licha's birthday serenade
 ―――――. Whole city's down below
 Simon, S. Baking contest
 Simonds, N. Unhappy Santa
 Thane, A. Dick Whittington and his cat
 ―――――. Elves and the shoemaker
 ―――――. Gift for Hans Brinker
 ―――――. King Alfred and the cakes

KINDNESS

    _____. Three wishes
    _____. Twelve dancing princesses
Walker, B. Rabbit and the wolf
Weathers, W. Vision of the silver bell
Werner, S. Choosing of Easter Rabbit
Wilde, O. Happy prince
see also UNSELFISHNESS

KINDNESS TO ANIMALS
    Asbrand, K. Friendly as can be
King, Walter. Little Snow White. In Kamerman, S. Little Plays for Little Players. 10 char
_____. Snow White. In Durrell, D. Thirty Plays for Classroom Reading. 11 char
King Alfred and the cakes. Thane, A.
King and the bee. Whitworth, V.
King and the miller. Holmes, R.
King Arthur. Love, S.
KING ARTHUR see ARTHUR, KING
King Arthur and his knights. Morley, O.
King Horn. Hall, M.
King in the kitchen. Slattery, M.
King John and the Abbot of Canterbury. Holmes, R.
King Midas. Gardner, M.
King who couldn't be fooled. Elfenbein, J.
King who was bored. Thane, A.
King with the terrible temper. McGee, C.
Kingman, Lee. Magic pumpkin. In Burack, A. One Hundred Plays for Children. 16 char
_____. Mr. Thanks has his day. In Burack, A. One Hundred Plays for Children. 11 char

KINGS AND QUEENS
    Alexander, S. Goom-bya, room-bya, zerko!
    Bennett, R. King's holiday
    Carlson, B. Fit for a king
    Duvall, L. Valentine's Day
    Ferguson, D. Most special dragon
    Hark, M. Dish for the king
    Holmes, R. King John and the Abbot of Canterbury
    Lynch, M. Scheherazade
    Malory, T. Crowning of King Arthur
    Molloy, L. Stolen tarts
    Pyle, H. Apple of contentment
    Roberts, H. For the glory of Spain
    Shakespeare, W. Cleopatra's death scene
    _____. Hamlet
    Swintz, M. King's creampuffs
    _____. Posies for the potentate

Very, A. Tom Tit Tot
    Werner, S. King's bean soup
King's bean soup. Werner, S.
King's calendar. Oser, J.
King's creampuffs. Swintz, M.
King's garden. Weik, M.
King's gold. Jarvis, S. M.
King's holiday. Bennett, R.
King's toothache. Fisher, A.
Kiss me good night! Howard, V.
Kitty Hawk--1903. Ickler, L.
Knight, Lee. Flibber turns the tables. In Kamerman, S.
    Little Plays for Little Players. 4 char
KNIGHTS AND KNIGHTHOOD
    Howard, V. Sir Galahad and the maidens
    Love, S. King Arthur
KNIGHTS AND KNIGHTHOOD--SATIRE
    Cervantes, M. Don Quixote
    Howard, V. Don Quixote saves the day
KNOWING YOURSELF see SELF-KNOWLEDGE
Koon, Helene. Pierre Patelin. In Kamerman, S. Folk
    Tales of the World. 5 char
KOREA
    Head, F. Spouse for Susie Mouse

- L -

La farza del Miss Muffet. Olfson, L.
Lady Macbeth receives a letter from her husband. Shakespeare, W.
Lady Moon and the thief. Boiko, C.
Lady or the tiger? Stockton, F.
Lady who put salt in her coffee. Hale, L.
Land beyond the river. Mitchell, L.
Landslide for Shakespeare. Dias, E.
Lane, Marion. Is there life on other planets? In Burack,
    A. Skits, Comedies and Farces for Teen-agers. 6 char
Language shop. Hall, M.
Larry's lesson. Howard, V.
Last laugh. DuBois, G.
Last leaf. Henry, O.
Last snake in Ireland. Malone, M.
Last stop. Cable, H.
Last time I saw Paris. Olfson, L.
Laughing princess. Nicholson, M.

LAUGHTER

LAUGHTER
    Asbrand, K. Crystal flask
    Dias, E. Gift of laughter
    Holmes, R. Golden goose
    Leuser, E. Little clown who forgot how to laugh
    Martens, A. Roscoe the robot
    Melcher, M. Princess who would not smile
    Newman, D. Magic goose
    Nicholson, M. Laughing princess
    Rowland, E. Hans, who made the princess laugh
    Thane, A. Dummling and the golden goose
Lawrence, Jerome, and Robert E. Lee. Inside a kid's head.
   <u>In</u> Picozzi, R. Plays to Enjoy. 22 char+
<u>Lazarus</u>. White, A.
Lazy leprechaun. Taylor, J.
The leader. Ionesco, E.
Leader of the people. Steinbeck, J.
LEADERS
    Carlson, B. Follow-the-leader
    Ionesco, E. The leader
    Shakespeare, W. Julius Caesar
Leak in the dike. Nolan, P.
Lee, Robert E., and Jerome Lawrence. Inside a kid's head.
   <u>In</u> Picozzi, R. Plays to Enjoy. 22 char+
<u>Left turn</u>. Howard, V.
Legend of Sleepy Hollow. Irving, W.
Legend of the Christmas rose. Leuser, E.
LEGENDS
    Asbrand, K. Little hero of Holland
    Boiko, C. Honorable cat's decision
    <u>   </u>. How mothers came to be
    <u>   </u>. Pepe and the cornfield bandit
    <u>   </u>. Roman romance
    <u>Carlson</u>, B. Summer maker
    <u>   </u>. Why the leaves of the aspen tree quake in a <u>breeze</u>
    <u>   </u>. Why the nightingale sings gloriously
    <u>   </u>. Why the owl is sacred in Hawaii
    <u>Cochrane</u>, L. Karagiosis and the dragon
    <u>   </u>. Moon dragon
    <u>   </u>. Story of Rama and Sita
    <u>Faulk</u>, C. Floating stone
    Fitz-Adcock, I. Royal cloth of China
    Hagy, L. Fire in a paper
    Hark, M. Princess and the rose-colored glasses
    Heine, H. Flying Dutchman
    Jarvis, S. M. Why the turtle does not talk

Leuser, E. Legend of the Christmas rose
Love, S. Beowulf
Mahlmann, L. Why the sea is salt
Morley, O. King Arthur and his knights
Nicholson, M. Wise wife
Nolan, P. Double nine of Chih Yuan
───────. Stanislaw and the wolf
Winther, B. African trio
───────. Sleeping mountains
Lehman, John F. Biskie the snowman. In Kamerman, S. Little Plays for Little People. 9 char
───────. Good health trolley. In Kamerman, S. Little Plays for Little Players. 12 char
Lello, Elizabeth. Mystery at Tumble Inn. In Burack, A. Popular Plays for Classroom Reading. 10 char; in Burack, A. Skits, Comedies and Farces for Teen-agers. 9 char
Lemonade trick. Corbett, S.
Leprechaun shoemakers. Watts, F.
LEPRECHAUNS
 Carlson, B. Why catch a Leprechaun?
 Leuser, E. Courage piece
 Taylor, J. Lazy leprechaun
 Watts, F. Bridge to Killybog Fair
 ───────. Leprechaun shoemakers
 ───────. Leprechaun's pot of gold
 see also ELVES
Leprechaun's pot of gold. Watts, F.
Let her ride! Carlson, B.
Let sleeping beauties lie. Fontaine, R.
Let there be bread. Fisher, A.
Let's fool someone. Carlson, B.
The letter. Howard, V.
Letter to Lincoln. Barbee, L.
Leuser, Eleanor D. Magic grapes. In Kamerman, S. Dramatized Folk Tales of the World. 9 char
───────. Secret of the wishing well. In Kamerman, S. Dramatized Folk Tales of the World. 19 char+
───────. Thanksgiving scarecrow. In Kamerman, S. Fifty Plays for Holidays. 9 char
───────. Wise people of Gotham. In Kamerman, S. Dramatized Folk Tales of the World. 16 char
Leuser, Eleanore. Big stone. In Kamerman, S. Children's Plays from Favorite Stories. 12 char
───────. Broth of Christkindli. In Burack, A. Christmas Plays for Young Actors. 8 char+
───────. Courage piece. In Kamerman, S. Fifty Plays for

Junior Actors. 9 char
───── . Five brothers. In Durrell, D. Thirty Plays for Classroom Reading. 7 char
───── . Honored one. In Kamerman, S. Fifty Plays for Junior Actors. 13 char
───── . Legend of the Christmas rose. In Durrell, D. Favorite Plays for Classroom Reading. 11 char
───── . Little bird in the tree. In Kamerman, S. Little Plays for Little Players. 8 char+
───── . Little clown who forgot how to laugh. In Kamerman, S. Children's Plays from Favorite Stories. 10 char
───── . Little witch who tried. In Kamerman, S. Little Plays for Little Players. 8 char
───── . Magic well. In Kamerman, S. Children's Plays from Favorite Stories. 19 char+
───── . Mixing stick. In Burack, A. One Hundred Plays for Children. 11 char
───── . Tommy's adventure. In Burack, A. One Hundred Plays for Children. 11 char
LIBERTY
    Lipnik, E. Son of liberty
    see also FREEDOM
LIBERTY BELL
    Fisher, A. Voice of liberty
LIBRARY
    Chaloner, G. Bookworm
    Hark, M. Books a la mode
    Miller, H. Library circus
Licha's birthday serenade. Nolan, P.
LIFE
    Carter, S. One last look
    Conrad, E. Show boat
    Hansberry, L. Raisin in the sun
    Hark, M. Dish for the king
    Nolan, P. Anton Chekhov sort of evening
    ───── . In-group
    ───── . Moon's up there
    ───── . Take it from the beginning
    ───── . Trash and treasure
    ───── . Tree to the sky
    ───── . Whole city's down below
Lincoln, Abbey. Streak o' lean. In Childress, A. Black Scenes. 2 char
LINCOLN, ABRAHAM
    Bennett, R. Visitors for Nancy Hawks
    Boiko, C. Long table

LINCOLN 94

    _____. Young Abe's destiny
    Carlson, B. Where there are no snags
    Dias, E. Visitor to Gettysburg
    Fisher, A. Abe's winkin' eye
    _____. Young Abe Lincoln
    Hark, M. Bobby and the Lincoln speech
    _____. Lincoln reminders
    Howard, V. Lincoln's Gettysburg Address
    MacLellan, E. Birthday gift
    Miller, H. Ten pennies for Lincoln
    Newman, E. Looking for Lincoln
    Pendleton, E. Bobby and the Lincoln speech
    Peterson, M. Abe buys a barrel
    Ross, L. Young Abe wrestles Armstrong
    Sherwood, R. Abe Lincoln in Illinois
    Very, A. Gift of the fairies
    _____. President Lincoln's children
    Weik, M. River risin'!
Lincoln coat. Sealock, T.
Lincoln reminders. Hark, M.
LINCOLN'S BIRTHDAY
    Barbee, L. Letter to Lincoln
    Dias, E. Gift of laughter
    Fisher, A. Abe's winkin' eye
    Hark, M. Bobby and the Lincoln speech
    _____. Lincoln reminders
    MacLellan, E. Birthday gift
    Miller, H. Man like Lincoln
    _____. Ten pennies for Lincoln
    Ross, L. Young Abe wrestles Armstrong
    Sealock, T. Lincoln coat
    see also LINCOLN, ABRAHAM
Lincoln's Gettysburg address. Howard, V.
Lincoln's middle name. Howard, V.
Lindgrin, Astrid. Pippi Longstocking. In Glass, G. From
    Plays into Reading. 7 char
Lion and the birds. Jarvis, S. M.
Lion and the mosquitoes. Jarvis, S. M.
Lion and the mouse. Barr, J.
Lion and the mouse. Bennett, R.
Lion hunt. McGee, C.
Lion in the zoo. Hoff, S.
Lion to lamb. Boiko, C.
Lion's den. Walker, B.
Lipnik, Esther. Angel of mercy. In Kamerman, S. Fifty
    Plays for Junior Actors. 10 char
    _____. Son of liberty. In Burack, A. One Hundred

Plays for Children. 7 char
LITTER
 Boiko, C. Operation litterbug
 Carlson, B. Marked trail
 Hoff, S. Children on the moon
 Newman, D. Rebellious robots
 see also ECOLOGY; POLLUTION
Little bird in the tree. Leuser, E.
Little cake. McCarty, E.
Little circus donkey. Howard, H.
Little clown who forgot how to laugh. Leuser, E.
Little girls wiser than men. Tolstoy, L.
Little hero of Holland. Asbrand, K.
Little Jackie and the beanstalk. Cable, H.
Little Ki and the serpent. Melchior, H.
Little known facts about birds. Howard, V.
Little man who wasn't there. Dias, E.
Little princess. Burnett, F.
Little red hen. Boiko, C.
Little Red Riding Hood. Cable, H. (Play title: Big Red Riding Hood)
Little Red Riding Hood. Holmes, R.
Little Red Riding Hood. Schwartz, E.
Little Snow White. King, W.
Little Ugo and the foolish ones. Martin, P.
Little white cloud. Cooper, E.
Little witch. Bennett, A.
Little witch who tried. Leuser, E.
Little women. Alcott, L. (Play title: Spirit of Christmas, written by St. Clair, R.)
Littlest artist. Bennett, R.
Littlest fir. Colbo, E.
Littlest month. Faux, D.
Littlest month. Fox, D.
The loafer. Fontaine, R.
Local frog stages comeback. In McGee, C. Drama for Fun. 2 char+
LONDON
 Wilde, O. Importance of being earnest
LONELINESS
 Furman, R. To kill a devil
 Lonely giant
 Roberts, H. Lonely fir tree
Lonely fir tree. Roberts, H.
Lonely giant. In Philpott, A. Eight Plays for Hand Puppets. 6 char+
Long and short division. Nesbit, E.

LONG 96

Long live Christmas. Benson, I.
Long table. Boiko, C.
Look behind the mask. Henderson, N.
Look, George. Howard, V.
Look here, boss. Howard, V.
Looking for Lincoln. Newman, D.
Looking glass murder. Murray, J.
Lorca, Federico García. Billy-club puppets. In Swortzell,
    L. All the World's a Stage. 17 char+
Lord Foppington's day. Vanbrugh, John
Lost Christmas cards. Miller, H.
Louisa Alcott's wish. Goldsmith, S.
Louisiana. Walsh, H.
LOUISIANA TERRITORY
    Walsh, H. Louisiana
LOVE
    Andersen, H. The tinderbox
    Barr, J. Rapunzel
    Bennett, R. Child who was made of snow
    Blanton, C. Dulce man
    Boiko, C. Roman romance
    Brontë, C. Jane Eyre
    Brontë, E. Wuthering Heights
    Colbo, E. Heroine of Wren
    Dias, E. Dear Lottie
    Dickens, C. Martin Chuzzlewit
    Dumas, A. The duel
    Fisher, A. Hearts, tarts, and valentines
    ———. Three and the dragon
    Fletcher, J. Jailer's daughter falls in love with a prince
    Fontaine, R. Love seeks a way
    Foulk, C. Floating stone
    Heiderstadt, D. Girl from the sea
    Heine, H. Flying Dutchman
    Henry, O. Last leaf
    ———. Romance of a busy broker
    Howard, H. Mother's gift
    Howard, V. Don Quixote saves the day
    Hughes, T. Beauty and the beast
    ———. Orpheus
    Hugo, V. Bishop's candlesticks
    Ibsen, H. Aase searches for her son
    ———. Peer Gynt leaves Solveig
    Irving, W. Rip Van Winkle
    James, H. Washington Square
    McGee, C. Sofapillio

Mantle, M. Doctor for Lucinda
Marlowe, C. Death of Zenocrate
Melcher, M. Princess who would not smile
Molière. Would-be gentleman
Munro, H. Pom-pom
Murray, J. Mad about art
Nolan, P. French cabinetmaker
─────── . Johnny Appleseed
─────── . View of the sea
─────── . Whole city's down below
─────── . Wishing well or ill
─────── . Young man of considerable value
Shakespeare, W. Cleopatra's death scene
─────── . Katherina's obedience
─────── . Midsummer night's dream
─────── . Romeo and Juliet
─────── . The tempest
Sheridan, R. The rivals
Stevenson, R. Sire de Maletroit's door
Stockton, F. Lady or the tiger?
─────── . Transferred ghost
Streacker, L. No-mother land
Tennyson, A. Enoch Arden
Urban, C. Queen with a broken heart
Van Druten, J. I remember Mama
Weik, M. Moonlight
White, A. Bailiff's daughter of Islington
─────── . May I woo the lassie?
─────── . My son John
─────── . Willie's gane to Melville castle
Wilde, C. Comic strip antics
Wilde, O. Importance of being earnest
─────── . On being too frequently proposed to
Winther, B. Sleeping mountains
Love, Stewart, and William D. Cumming. Apache silver. In Love, S. Plays for Reading and Recording. 4 char
───────, ─────── . Beowulf. In Love, S. Plays for Reading and Recording. 11 char
───────, ─────── . Black idol. In Love, S. Plays for Reading and Recording. 5 char
───────, ─────── . Clive of India. In Love, S. Plays for Reading and Recording. 7 char
───────, ─────── . Fifth of November. In Love, S. Plays for Reading and Recording. 14 char
───────, ─────── . Joan of Arc. In Love, S. Plays for Reading and Recording. 7 char
───────, ─────── . King Arthur. In Love, S. Plays for

LOVE 98

    Reading and Recording. 11 char
   _____, _____. Madame Defarge. In Love, S. Plays for Reading and Recording. 3 char+
   _____, _____. Man who shot the president. In Love, S. Plays for Reading and Recording. 7 char
   _____, _____. Moby Dick. In Love, S. Plays for Reading and Recording. 12 char
   _____, _____. One-eyed giant. In Love, S. Plays for Reading and Recording. 6 char
Love seeks a way. Fontaine, R.
Lover's errand. McGee, C.
LOYALTY
    Dias, E. Express to Valley Forge
    _____. The mantle
    Felsheim, J. Ali Baba and the forty thieves
LUCIFER--SPOOF
    Nolan, P. Happy ending
LUCK
    Corson, H. Triumph for two
    Simon, S. Doctor farmer
Lunch at Pierre's. Howard, V.
Lynch, May. Finn McCool. In Kamerman, S. Dramatized Folk Tales of the World. 11 char
   _____. Scheherazade. In Durrell, D. Favorite Plays for Classroom Reading. 11 char

- M -

McArthur, Jean. Fiesta. In Kamerman, S. Fifty Plays for Holidays. 18 char+
McArthur, Jean A. Fiesta the first. In Kamerman, S. Fifty Plays for Junior Actors. 16 char+
Macbeth. Shakespeare, W.
Macbeth. Shakespeare, W. (Play title: Lady Macbeth receives a letter from her husband)
McCarty, E. Clayton. Little cake. In Burack, A. One Hundred Plays for Children. 8 char+
McCarty, Sara Sloane. Tree friends. In Kamerman, S. Fifty Plays for Holidays. 19 char
McCoy, Paul S. No garden this year. In Burack, A. Skits, Comedies and Farces for Teen-agers. 3 char
McFarlan, Ethel. Olive jar. In Kamerman, S. Dramatized Folk Tales of the World. 7 char
   _____. Pear tree. In Kamerman, S. Children's Plays from Favorite Stories. 6 char+
   _____. Tiger catcher. In Kamerman, S. Dramatized

Folk Tales of the World. 7 char+
McGee, Cecil. Can'tsee Poorsight. In McGee, C. Drama for Fun. 3 char
———. Dr. Quack's medicine show. In McGee, C. Drama for Fun. 10 char+
———. Fatal quest. In McGee, C. Drama for Fun. 6 char
———. Fun with Hamlet and his friends. In McGee, C. Drama for Fun. 1 char
———. Gransel and Hettal. In McGee, C. Drama for Fun. 5 char
———. Henry. In McGee, C. Drama for Fun. 1 char
———. Interview with Punchy McPugg. In McGree, C. Drama for Fun. 2 char
———. King with the terrible temper. In McGee, C. Drama for Fun. 7 char+
———. Lion hunt. In McGee, C. Drama for Fun. 1 char+
———. Lover's errand. In McGee, C. Drama for Fun. 2 char
———. Peanut butter. In McGee, C. Drama for fun. 1 char
———. Pure white. In McGee, C. Drama for Fun. 1 char
———. Romance of Minnie Martin or it shouldn't happen to a dog. In McGee, C. Drama for Fun. 6 char+
———. Russian quartet. In McGee, C. Drama for Fun. 5 char
———. Sofapillio. In McGee, C. Drama for Fun. 5 char
———. Spasm in three speeds. In McGee, C. Drama for Fun. 5 char
———. The stand-in. In McGee, C. Drama for Fun. 6 char+
———. Trip to Mexico. In McGee, C. Drama for Fun. 5 char
MacGregor, Ellen. Miss Pickerell goes to Mars. In Glass, G. From Plays into Reading. 7 char
McKay, Helen Rein. Surprise for Mr. Winkle. In Ross, L. Holiday Puppets. 2 char
McKee, Helen F. Witches and the crows. In McGee, C. Drama for Fun. 8 char+
MacLellan, Esther. Return of the Nina. In Durrell, D. Thirty Plays for Classroom Reading. 12 char
———. Test for a witch. In Kamerman, S. Fifty Plays for Holidays. 11 char+
———, and Catherine V. Schroll. Birthday gift. In

Kamerman, S. Little Plays for Little Players. 7 char
———, ———. Clock's secret. In Burack, A. One Hundred Plays for Children. 6 char
———, ———. Cross princess. In Kamerman, S. Fifty Plays for Junior Actors. 10 char
———, ———. Needle fights for freedom. In Durrell, D. Thirty Plays for Classroom Reading. 10 char; in Kamerman, S. Little Plays for Little Players. 9 char
———, ———. Return of the Nina. In Kamerman, S. Little Plays for Little Players. 11 char+
———, ———. Secret of the windmill. In Kamerman, S. Fifty Plays for Junior Actors. 9 char
———, ———. Small shoes and small tulips. In Durrell, D. Thirty Plays for Classroom Reading. 8 char
———, ———. Swiss mystery. In Durrell, D. Favorite Plays for Classroom Reading. 8 char
McMeekin, Isabel McLennan. Runaway balloon. In Durrell, D. Thirty Plays for Classroom Reading. 6 char
McNair, James Keith. Blown with the breeze. In McGee, C. Drama for Fun. 6 char
McQueen, Mildred Hark. Mother's choice. In Kamerman, S. Fifty Plays for Holidays. 5 char
McQueen, Noel see Hark, Mildred, and Noel McQueen
Mad about art. Murray, J.
Mad tea party. Worcester, N.
Madame Defarge. Love, S.
Madison Avenue merry-go-round. Dias, E.
MAGIC
    Asbrand, K. Silver coffeepot
    Barbee, L. Princess who couldn't dance
    Bennett, A. Little witch
    Bennett, H. Sleeping beauty
    Bennett, R. Rumpelstiltskin
    ———. What will the toys say?
    Browning, R. Pied piper of Hamlin
    Brydon, M. Dreadful dragon
    Colbert, M. Salt in the sea
    Corbett, S. Lemonade trick
    Corey, C. Dancing princesses
    Gregg, L. Miniature darzis
    Hawthorne, H. Dr. Heidegger's experiment
    ———. Feathertop
    Jarvis, S. M. Fried onions and marshmallows
    Lindgren, A. Pippi Longstocking
    Mahlmann, L. Frog prince
    ———. Jack and the beanstalk
    ———. Magic mushrooms

	Magic shoes
Miller, H.	Busy barbers
Molloy, L.	Broom market day
Munro, H.	Pom-pom
Musil, R.	Invisible dragon of Winn Sinn Tu
Newman, D.	Cinderella
Nolan, P.	Golden voice of Little Erik
Perrault, C.	Puss in boots
	Sleeping beauty
Pyle, M.	Clever Peter
Richards, L.	With all my heart
Shakespeare, W.	The tempest
Silver key	
Slattery, M.	Royal magic
Stockton, F.	Old Pipes
Swintz, M.	Three wishing bags
Thane, A.	Aladdin and his wonderful lamp
	Magic nutmeg-grater
	Rapunzel
	Rumpelstiltskin
	Twelve dancing princesses
Thomson, J.	Pepi and Sombrero
Tichenor, T.	Jack and the beanstalk
Whitworth, V.	Magic cloak

Magic bookshelf. Clapp, P.
Magic box. Peterson, M.
Magic cloak. Whitworth, V.
Magic cookie jar. Miller, H.
Magic egg. Hark, M.
Magic fishbone. Dickens, C.
Magic goose. Newman, D.
Magic grapes. Leuser, E. D.
Magic jack-o-lantern. Howard, H.
Magic mushrooms. Mahlmann, L.
Magic nutmeg-grater. Thane, A.
Magic of Salamanca. Nolan, P.
Magic pumpkin. Kingman, L.
Magic shoes. Mahlmann, L.
Magic shoes. Turnbull, L.
Magic spell. Cooper, E.
Magic weaver. Bennett, R.
Magic well. Leuser, E.

MAGICIANS
 Alexander, S. Goom-bya, room-bya, zerko!
Mahlmann, Lewis, and David Cadwalader Jones. Alice's adventures in Wonderland. In Mahlmann, L. Puppet Plays for Young Players. 17 char

———, ———. Frog prince. In Mahlmann, L. Puppet Plays for Young Players. 6 char
———, ———. Jack and the beanstalk. In Mahlmann, L. Puppet Plays for Young Players. 10 char
———, ———. Magic mushrooms. In Mahlmann, L. Puppet Plays for Young Players. 3 char
———, ———. Magic shoes. In Mahlmann, L. Puppet Plays for Young Players. 9 char
———, ———. Pinocchio. In Mahlmann, L. Puppet Plays for Young Players. 13 char
———, ———. Princess and the pea. In Mahlmann, L. Puppet Plays for Young Players. 5 char
———, ———. Reluctant dragon. In Mahlmann, L. Puppet Plays for Young Players. 6 char
———, ———. Snow White and the Seven Dwarfs. In Mahlmann, L. Puppet Plays for Young Players. 14 char
———, ———. The tinderbox. In Mahlmann, L. Puppet Plays for Young Players. 11 char
———, ———. Why the sea is salt. In Mahlmann, L. Puppet Plays for Young Players. 9 char
———, ———. Wizard of Oz. In Mahlmann, L. Puppet Plays for Young Players. 13 char+

MAIL
    McKay, H. Surprise for Mr. Winkle
    Miller, H. Lost Christmas cards
Make him smile. Arnold, E.
Make your own bed. Carlson, B.
Malone, Mary. Last snake in Ireland. In Kamerman, S. Fifty Plays for Holidays. 8 char+
Malory, Thomas. Crowning of King Arthur. In Olfson, L. Dramatized Classics for Radio-Style Reading. 15 char
Man in the red suit. Moessenger, B.
Man like Lincoln. Miller, H.
Man who didn't like rain. Howard, V.
Man who shot the president. Love, S.
Man with the heart in the highlands. Saroyan, W.
Man without a country. Hale, E.
Manning, Susan. Background for Nancy. In Burack, A. Skits, Comedies and Farces for Teen-agers. 7 char; in Durrell, D. Teen-Age Plays for Classroom Reading. 10 char
The mantle. Dias, E.
Mantle, Margaret. Doctor for Lucinda. In Kamerman, S. Fifty Plays for Junior Actors. 6 char
Many thanks. Hark, M.
Mapp, Frances. Ogre who built a bridge. In Kamerman,

S. Dramatized Folk Tales of the World. 10 char
MARDI GRAS
    Greth, R. Two masks
Marked trail. Carolson, B.
Marlowe, Christopher. Death of Zenocrate. In Kline, P.
    Theatre Student: Scenes to Perform. 1 char
MARRIAGE
    Head, F. Spouse for Susie Mouse
    Henry, O. Romance of a busy broker
    McCoy, P. No garden this year
    Mantle, M. Doctor for Lucinda
    Miller, H. Return of Bobby Shafto
    Nolan, P. Courters
    ――――――. Young man of considerable value
    Olfson, L. Bride of Gorse-bracken Hall
    Shakespeare, W. Midsummer night's dream
    ――――――. Taming of the shrew
    Sherwood, R. Abe Lincoln in Illinois
    White, A. In Bibberley Town
Martens, Anne Coulter. George slept here, too. In Kamerman, S. Fifty Plays for Holidays. 8 char
――――――. Roscoe the robot. In Burack, A. Skits, Comedies and Farces for Teen-agers. 8 char
――――――. Thirteen. In Burack, A. Popular Plays for Classroom Reading. 13 char; in Kamerman, S. Fifty Plays for Junior Actors. 13 char
Martha Washington's spy. Dias, E.
Martin Chuzzlewit. Dickens, S.
Martin, Patricia Miles. Invitation to supper. In Martin, P. Two Plays about Foolish People. 10 char
――――――. Little Ugo and the foolish ones. In Martin, P. Two Plays about Foolish People. 8 char
Marvelous time machine. Boiko, C.
Masque of the red death. Poe, E.
MASSACHUSETTS
    Boiko, C. All hands on deck
Matter of conscience. Coyle, R.
Matter of health. Miller, H.
Matter of taste. Fontaine, R.
MATURING see CHARACTER BUILDING; GROWING UP
Maupassant, Guy. The necklace. In Gilfond, R. Plays for Reading. 4 char
May basket fantasia. Boiko, C.
MAY DAY
    Boiko, C. May basket fantasia
    Brydon, M. May witch
    Miller, H. May Day for mother

May Day for mother. Miller, H.
May I woo the lassie? White, A.
May witch. Brydon, M.
Mayfield, Julian. 417. In Childress, A. Black Scenes.
    4 char
MAYFLOWER
        Carlson, B. Another way
        Walsh, H. Mutiny on the Mayflower
The meadow. Bradbury, R.
Mechanical maid. Whitworth, V.
Mechanical man. Howard, V.
Mechanical man. Murray, J.
MEDIAEVAL MIRACLE PLAYS
        White, A. Lazarus
MEEK, JOE
        Carlson, B. There's always a leader
Meet me in the moonlight. Howard, V.
Meet Miss Stone-age! Olfson, L.
Meet Mr. Witch. Hark, M.
Meet the pilgrims. Boiko, C.
Melcher, Marguerite F. Princess who would not smile.
    In Kamerman, S. Children's Plays from Favorite Stories. 9 char
Melchior, Hathaway Kale. Little Ki and the serpent. In Kamerman, S. Children's Plays from Favorite Stories. 12 char
———. Visit to the planets. In Kamerman, S. Fifty Plays for Junior Actors. 19 char
Melinda's incredible birthday. Boiko, C.
A mellerdrammer. Pylant, A.
MELODRAMA
        Anderson, R. Gold mine at Jeremiah Flats
        Boiko, C. Yes, yes, a thousand times yes!
        Boyd, J. Featherweight champ or tickled to death
        Cable, H. Deputy for Broken Bow
        ———. Reform of Sterling Silverheart
        ———. Way, way down south
        Dias, E. Cast up by the sea
        ———. Cleanest town in the West
        ———. Hold back the redskins
        Downing, R. Shop girl's revenge
        Fay, M. Saving the old homestead
        Hark, M. Not fit for man or beast
        Hervey, M. Virtue is her own reward
        Huff, B. Ride the Gooberville stage!
        Lorca, F. Billy-club puppets
        McNair, J. Blown with the breeze

Pylant, A. A mellerdrammer
Smith, F. The rhyme's the crime or the verse is yet to come
Stevenson, R. Sire de Maletroit's door
Stuart, M. Abigail stands fast
Tausheck, R. Saga of Davey Rocket
MEMORIAL DAY
Hark, M. See the parade
Miller, H. Part-time hero
———. Pink parasol
———. Teddy bear hero
Men of Mars. Howard, V.
Menotti, Gian-Carlo. Amahl and the night visitors. In
Swortzell, L. All the World's a Stage. 6 char+
MERMAIDS
Heiderstadt, D. Girl from the sea
Merry Christmas elf. Fisher, A.
Merry, merry, merry. Carroll, G.
Merry Tyll and the three rogues. Thane, A.
MEXICAN AMERICANS
Henderson, N. Harvest for Lola
MEXICO
Blanton, C. Dulce man
Boiko, C. Pepe and the cornfield bandit
Campbell, C. Bell of Dolores
Fisher, A. Story of a well
McArthur, J. Fiesta
Nolan, P. Licha's birthday serenade
Thane, A. King who was bored
Thomson, J. Pepi and Sombrero
Winther, B. Sleeping mountains
MICE
Bennett, R. City mouse and the country mouse
Blanton, C. Dulce man
Boiko, C. Who will bell the cat?
Head, F. Spouse for Susie Mouse
Jarvis, S. M. Free bacon
Muse, V. Town mouse and his country cousin
Thane, A. Dick Whittington and his cat
Tichenor, T. Jack and the beanstalk
Very, A. Golden bell for mother
Werner, S. Home, sweet home
Middlemass, Robert, and Holworthy Hall. The valiant. In
Maloney, H. Plays to Remember. 6 char
Midnight burial. Hill, K.
Midsummer night's dream. Shakespeare, E.

MIGRANT WORKERS
    Henderson, N. Harvest for Lola
Miller, Arthur. Grandpa and the statue. In Picozzi, R.
    Plays to Enjoy. 15 char
Miller, Helen Louise. All-American thank you. In Miller,
    H. Short Plays for Children. 9 char
_____. Birthday pie. In Miller, H. Short Plays for
    Children. 12 char
_____. Broadway turkey. In Miller, H. Modern Plays
    for Special Days. 7 char
_____. Broken broomstick. In Miller, H. First Plays
    for Children. 14 char+
_____. Busy barbers. In Miller, H. First Plays for
    Children. 37 char
_____. Call Washington 1 7 7 6. In Miller, H. Modern
    Plays for Special Days. 14 char
_____. Captain Castaway's captives. In Miller, H.
    Short Plays for Children. 17 char
_____. Case of the giggling goblin. In Miller, H. Short
    Plays for Children. 26 char
_____. Christmas peppermints. In Miller, H. Short
    Plays for Children. 14 char
_____. Circus daze. In Miller, H. Short Plays for Children. 15 char
_____. Country store cat. In Miller, H. First Plays
    for Children. 27 char
_____. Cupid in demand. In Miller, H. Short Plays for
    Children. 11 char
_____. Curse of hag hollow. In Miller, H. Modern
    Plays for Special Days. 6 char
_____. Damsels in distress. In Miller, H. Modern
    Plays for Special Days. 15 char
_____. Dial M for mother. In Miller, H. Modern Plays
    for Special Days. 8 char
_____. Dolly saves the day. In Burack, A. One Hundred Plays for Children. 6 char
_____. Forgetful Easter rabbit. In Miller, H. Short
    Plays for Children. 23 char
_____. Friendship wheel. In Miller, H. Short Plays for
    Children. 22 char
_____. Garden hold-up. In Miller, H. First Plays for
    Children. 18 char
_____. Gathering sticks. In Miller, H. Modern Plays
    for Special Days. 9 char
_____. The general returns. In Miller, H. Modern
    Plays for Special Days. 10 char

_____. Gentle giant-killer. In Miller, H. Short Plays for Children. 17 char
_____. Ghost in the house. In Burack, A. Popular Plays for Classroom Reading. 8 char
_____. Half-pint cowboy. In Miller, H. First Plays for Children. 23 char
_____. Haunts for hire. In Miller, H. Modern Plays for Special Days. 14 char
_____. Horn of plenty. In Miller, H. Modern Plays for Special Days. 10 char
_____. Jiminy Cinders. In Burack, A. Four-Star Plays for Boys. 8 char
_____. Library circus. In Miller, H. First Plays for Children. 25 char+
_____. Lost Christmas cards. In Miller, H. First Plays for Children. 21 char
_____. Magic cookie jar. In Burack, A. One Hundred Plays for Children. 4 char
_____. Man like Lincoln. In Miller, H. Modern Plays for Special Days. 9 char
_____. Matter of health. In Miller, H. Short Plays for Children. 15 char
_____. May Day for mother. In Miller, H. First Plays for Children. 20 char+
_____. Miss Frankenstein. In Burack, A. Skits, Comedies and Farces for Teen-agers. 19 char+
_____. Mistletoe mystery. In Miller, H. Modern Plays for Special Days. 9 char
_____. Mother beats the band. In Miller, H. Modern Plays for Special Days. 15 char+
_____. Mother Goose bakeshop. In Miller, H. First Plays for Children. 15 char+
_____. Mount Vernon cricket. In Miller, H. Short Plays for Children. 10 char
_____. Old Glory grows up. In Miller, H. First Plays for Children. 29 char
_____. One to grow on. In Miller, H. Short Plays for Children. 25 char
_____. Paper bag mystery. In Miller, H. Short Plays for Children. 13 char
_____. Part-time hero. In Miller, H. Modern Plays for Special Days. 6 char
_____. Peter Rabbit volunteers. In Miller, H. Short Plays for Children. 12 char
_____. Pink parasol. In Burack, A. One Hundred Plays for Children. 9 char
_____. Puppy love. In Burack, A. Christmas Plays

_____ for Young Actors. 7 char
_____. Rabbit who refused to run. In Miller, H. Short Plays for Children. 9 char
_____. Rabbits who changed their minds. In Miller, H. First Plays for Children. 19 char
_____. Real princess. In Miller, H. First Plays for Children. 18 char
_____. Red carpet Christmas. In Miller, H. Modern Plays for Special Days. 12 char
_____. Red flannel suit. In Miller, H. Modern Plays for Special Days. 12 char
_____. Return of Bobby Shafto. In Miller, H. Short Plays for Children. 9 char
_____. S. O. S. from Santa. In Miller, H. Short Plays for Children. 16 char
_____. Safety clinic. In Miller, H. First Plays for Children. 19 char
_____. Santa calls a conference. In Miller, H. Short Plays for Children. 38 char
_____. Shady shadows. In Burack, A. One Hundred Plays for Children. 6 char
_____. Shirley Holmes and the FBI. In Burack, A. Popular Plays for Classroom Reading. 16 char; in Miller, H. Short Plays for Children. 15 char
_____. Shower of hearts. In Miller, H. First Plays for Children. 20 char+
_____. Simple Simon's reward. In Miller, H. Short Plays for Children. 18 char
_____. Spunky Punky. In Miller, H. First Plays for Children. 2 char
_____. Teddy bear hero. In Miller, H. First Plays for Children. 13 char+
_____. Ten pennies for Lincoln. In Miller, H. First Plays for Children. 21 char
_____. Thankful's red beads. In Miller, H. First Plays for Children. 10 char
_____. Thanksgiving riddle. In Miller, H. First Plays for Children. 11 char
_____. Three little kittens. In Miller, H. First Plays for Children. 8 char+
_____. Tomboy and the dragon. In Miller, H. Short Plays for Children. 12 char
_____. Toy scout jamboree. In Miller, H. Short Plays for Children. 24 char+
_____. Trial of Mother Goose. In Miller, H. Short Plays for Children. 31 char
_____. Trouble in Tick-Tock Town. In Miller, H.

First Plays for Children. 25 char
———. Valentine for Kate. In Miller, H. Modern Plays for Special Days. 9 char
———. Visit to Goldilocks. In Miller, H. First Plays for Children. 9 char
———. Wait and see. In Miller, H. First Plays for Children. 13 char
———. Wake up, Santa Claus! In Miller, H. First Plays for Children. 16 char+
———. Weatherman on trial. In Miller, H. First Plays for Children. 13 char+
———. Wishing stream. In Miller, H. First Plays for Children. 8 char+
Miller, Stephanie. Dangerous game. In Burack, A. Popular Plays for Classroom Reading. 9 char
Mills, Grace Evelyn. Christmas comes to Hamelin. In Burack, A. One Hundred Plays for Children. 26 char+
Milton, John. Eve decides to eat the fruit of the tree of knowledge. In Kline, P. Theatre Student: Scenes to Perform. 1 char
MIME see PANTOMIME; SKITS--PANTOMIME
Mind your p's and q's. Hark, M.
Miniature darzis. Gregg, L.
Minor developments. Huntsberry, W.
MINORITIES
    Childress, A. Black Scenes
    Henderson, N. Walk together
    see also BLACK AMERICANS; MEXICAN AMERICANS; OPPRESSION
Mintier, Wilma. Othello. In McGee, C. Drama for Fun. 6 char+
MIRACLE PLAYS
    White, A. Lazarus
MIRACLES
    Bennett, R. Child who was made of snow
    ———. Piccola
    Leuser, E. Legend of the Christmas rose
Mirror stunt. Howard, V.
Miss Cast. Heinzen, B.
Miss Forsythe is missing. Murray, J.
Miss Frankenstein. Miller, H.
Miss Louisa and the outlaws. Watts, F.
Miss Muffet and the spider. Bennett, R.
Miss Muffet's wish. St. Clair, R.
Miss Pickerell goes to Mars. MacGregor, E.
MISSOURI
    Weik, M. River risin'!

MR. 110

Mr. Bates goes to the polls. Reay, N.
Mr. Lazy Man's family. Ward, M.
Mr. Longfellow observes book week. Moore, E.
Mr. Maybe. Jarvis, S.
Mr. Popper's penguins. Atwater, R.
Mr. Thanks has his day. Kingman, L.
Mistletoe mystery. Miller, H.
MISUNDERSTANDINGS
    Elfenbeim, J. Ten-penny tragedy
    Nolan, P. Wishing well or ill
Mitchell, Loften. Land beyond the river. In Childress, A.
    Black Scenes. 5 char
Mitten tree. Jarvis, S. M.
Mixing stick. Leuser, E.
Moby Dick. Love, S.
Moessenger, Bill. Man in the red suit. In Burack, A.
    Skits, Comedies and Farces for Teen-Agers. 20 char+
Molière. Harpagon searches for his stolen money. In
    Kline, P. Theatre Student. 1 char
_____. Would-be gentleman. In Olfson, L. Dramatized
    Classics for Radio-Style Reading, Vol. II. 9 char
Molloy, Lida Lisle. Broom market day. In Burack, A.
    One Hundred Plays for Children. 9 char
_____. Cat and the queen. In Kamerman, S. Children's
    Plays from Favorite Stories. 10 char
_____. Fortune of Merrylegs and Tawny-whiskers. In
    Burack, A. Four-Star Plays for Boys. 11 char
_____. Jenny-by-the-day. In Burack, A. One Hundred
    Plays for Children. 7 char
_____. Stolen tarts. In Kamerman, S. Dramatized
    Folk Tales of the World. 5 char+
MONEY
    Asbrand, K. What's a penny?
    Boiko, C. Penny wise
    Fisher, A. Best bargain in the world
    Graver, J. Father hits the jackpot
    Lincoln, A. Streak o' lean
    Molière. Harpagon searches for his stolen money
    Nolan, P. Young man of considerable value
    Taylor, L. $25,000
MONOLOGUES
    Howard, V. All washed up
    _____. Around the world
    _____. The artist
    _____. Box of chocolates
    _____. But, doctor
    _____. Call to a bride

MONOLOGUES

- Calling all cooks
- Calling all spies
- Complaint desk
- Courtesy at the wheel
- Dear Judy
- Dear Mr. Loveletter
- Explanations
- Famous words
- Flight fifteen
- Fortunes?
- Freddie proposes
- Golf lesson
- Housework for hubby
- How?
- How are you?
- How I conquered worry
- How to be successful
- How to improve your memory
- It's a mystery
- Kiss me good night!
- Larry's lesson
- Left turn
- Letter
- Lincoln's middle name
- Little known facts about birds
- Look, George
- Look here, boss
- Meet me in the moonlight
- My boy friend
- My first football game
- My vocal career
- Not exactly
- Our famous proverbs
- Our national sports
- Party night
- Pay and be gay
- Pep talk
- Roller coaster
- Romantic facts about women
- Romantic facts for men
- School daze
- The shopper
- Size please
- Space talk
- Staff of life
- Supper in silence
- Texas roundup

MONOLOGUES 112

    _____. Time of my life
    _____. Waiting for Grandma
    _____. Walking with Wilma
    _____. Your happy friend
MONOLOGUES--TWO CHARACTER [1 actor plays 2 parts.]
    Howard, V. Arkwood two-four-two-four
    _____. Drive in the country
    _____. Foot in the door
    _____. Girl who did very, very well
    _____. Help wanted
    _____. Hook and bait
    _____. How!
    _____. How to hypnotize
    _____. Lunch at Pierre's
    _____. Perfumes
    _____. Stagecoach
    _____. Valentines
    _____. Wild, wild west
    _____. Yes, officer!
    _____. You look lovely, dear
    Kline, P. Theatre Student: Scenes to Perform
MONROE, JAMES
    Walsh, H. Louisiana
MONSTERS
    Love, S. Beowulf
    Miller, H. Haunts for hire
MONTHS see CALENDAR; TIME; specific months
MOON
    Boiko, C. Lady Moon and the thief
    McMeekin, I. Runaway balloon
    Nolan, P. Moon's up there
Moon dragon. Cochrane, L.
Moonlight. Weik, M.
Moon's up there. Nolan, P.
MOORE, DR. CLEMENT CLARKE
    Nolan, J. Happy Christmas to all
Moore, Edna G. Mr. Longfellow observes book week. <u>In</u>
    Burack, A. One Hundred Plays for Children. 11 char
MORALITY PLAYS
    Everyman's prayer
Morley, Olive J. King Arthur and his knights. <u>In</u> Kamer-
    man, S. Dramatized Tales of the World. 29 char+
Morning maker. Campbell, C.
MOSQUITOES
    Burlingame, C. Yellow fever
    Jarvis, S. M. Lion and the mosquitoes
Most memorable voyage. Bakeless, K.

Most special dragon. Ferguson, D.
MOTELS
    Carlson, B. Make your own bed
Mother beats the band. Miller, H.
MOTHER GOOSE
    Barr, J. Old Mother Hubbard
    Boiko, C. Book that saved the earth
    ———. Mother Goose's Christmas surprise
    Miller, H. Mother Goose bakeshop
    ———. Trial of Mother Goose
Mother Goose bakeshop. Miller, H.
Mother Goose gives a dinner. Vandevere, J.
Mother Goose's Christmas surprise
Mother of Thanksgiving. Fisher, A.
MOTHERS
    Boiko, C. All about mothers
    ———. How mothers came to be
    Fisher, A. Mother's Day off and on
    Hark, M. Prize for mother
    Manning, S. Background for Nancy
    Miller, H. May Day for mother
    Streacker, L. No-mother land
Mother's choice
MOTHER'S DAY
    Barr, J. Present for mother
    Boiko, C. Care and feeding of mother
    Fisher, A. Mother's Day off and on
    ———. Time for Mom
    Hark, M. Hearts and flowers for mother
    ———. Prize for mother
    ———. Three wishes for mother
    Howard, H. Mother's gift
    McQueen, M. Mother's choice
    Miller, H. Dial M for mother
    ———. May Day for mother
    ———. Mother beats the band
    Phillips, M. Hat for mother
    Streacker, L. No-mother land
    Very, A. Golden bell for mother
Mother's Day off and on. Fisher, A.
Mother's gift. Howard, H.
Mount Vernon cricket. Miller, H.
MOVIES
    McGee, C. The stand-in
Mrs. Gibbs advertises. Pyle, M.
Mrs. Santa's Christmas gift. Newman, D.
Much ado about ants. Heath, A.

MUD 114

Mud pack madness. French, D.
Munro, H. H. see Saki
Munro, Helen Waite. Pom-pom. In Kamerman, S. Children's Plays from Favorite Stories. 9 char
MURDER
    Fletcher, L. Sorry, wrong number
    Fontaine, R. Who killed Doc Robin?
    Hall, H. The valiant
    Huff, B. Case of the missing masterpiece
    Love, S. Man who shot the president
    Murray, J. Case for two detectives
    ————. Looking glass murder
    ————. Miss Forsythe is missing
    ————. Scaredy cat
    ————. Sixth juror
    Poe, E. Cask of Amontillado
    Sanders, S. Tragedy in the graveyard
    Shakespeare, W. Hamlet
    ————. Julius Caesar
    ————. Lady Macbeth receives a letter from her husband
    ————. Macbeth
    Twain, M. Tom Sawyer and Injun Joe
MURILLO
    Myrick, N. Day is bright
Murky monster foiled again. Carlson, B.
Murphy, Helen A. Wise and clever maiden. In Kamerman, S. Children's Plays from Favorite Stories. 9 char+
Murray, John. Airport adventure. In Murray, J. Comedies and Mysteries for Young Actors. 15 char+
————. Case for two detectives. In Burack, A. Skits, Comedies and Farces for Teen-agers. 11 char
————. Case of mistaken identity. In Murray, J. Comedies and Mysteries for Young Actors. 9 char
————. Come to the fair! In Murray, J. Comedies and Mysteries for Young Actors. 15 char
————. Dead of night. In Murray, J. Comedies and Mysteries for Young Actors. 6 char
————. Healthy, wealthy, and wild. In Murray, J. Comedies and Mysteries for Young Actors. 14 char
————. I want to report a murder. In Murray, J. Comedies and Mysteries for Young Actors. 8 char
————. Impossible room. In Burack, A. Popular Plays for Classroom Reading. 9 char
————. Looking glass murder. In Durrell, D. Teen-Age Plays for Classroom Reading. 11 char; in Murray, J. Comedies and Mysteries for Young Actors. 10 char

MUSE

_____. Mad about art. In Murray, J. Comedies and Mysteries for Young Actors. 9 char
_____. Mechanical man. In Durrell, D. Favorite Plays for Classroom Reading. 13 char
_____. Miss Forsythe is missing. In Murray, J. Comedies and Mysteries for Young Actors. 6 char
_____. National everything. In Murray, J. Comedies and Mysteries for Young Actors. 15 char
_____. One in a million. In Murray, J. Comedies and Mysteries for Young Actors. 17 char+
_____. Publisher's choice. In Murray, J. Comedies and Mysteries for Young Actors. 12 char
_____. Scaredy cat. In Murray, J. Comedies and Mysteries for Young Actors. 8 char
_____. Sixth juror. In Murray, J. Comedies and Mysteries for Young Actors. 14 char+
_____. Spies and dolls. In Durrell, D. Teen-Age Plays for Classroom Reading. 10 char; in Murray, J. Comedies and Mysteries for Young Actors. 9 char
_____. Triumph for Trimbly. In Murray, J. Comedies and Mysteries for Young Actors. 13 char+
Muse, Violet. Town mouse and his country cousin. In Burack, A. One Hundred Plays for Children. 8 char
MUSHROOMS
    Mahlmann, L. Magic mushrooms
MUSIC
    Boiko, C. Song goes forth
    Howard, V. How music made everyone happy
_____. Take-turners
MUSICAL COMEDY
    Driver, D. Your own thing
    McGee, C. Dr. Quack's medicine show
_____. Romance of Minnie Martin or it shouldn't happen to a dog
MUSICAL PLAYS
    Mintier, W. Othello
MUSICAL TEAMS
    Boiko, C. Song goes forth
Musicians of Bremen. Boylan, E.
Musicians of Bremen Town. Roberts, W.
Musil, Rosemary G. Invisible dragon of Winn Sin Tu. In Kamerman, S. Fifty Plays for Junior Actors. 5 char
_____. Peach tree kingdom. In Kamerman, S. Dramatized Folk Tales of the World. 7 char
Mutiny on the Mayflower. Walsh, H.
My boy friend. Howard, V.
My fair Linda. Garver, J.

My first football game. Howard, V.
My last duchess. Browning, R.
My son John. White, A.
My son, the prince. Olfson, L.
My treasure. Carlson, B.
My vocal career. Howard, V.
Myrick, Norman. Day is bright. In Burack, A. One Hundred Plays for Children. 9 char
Mysterious stranger. Nicholson, J.

MYSTERY
    Bierce, A. Shipwreck
    Dias, E. Treasure at Bentley Inn
    Doyle, A. Sherlock Holmes and the red-headed league
    ———————. Sherlock Holmes and the stockbroker's clerk
    Fletcher, L. Sorry, wrong number
    Hill, K. Midnight burial
    Huff, B. Case of the missing masterpiece
    Irving, W. Legend of Sleepy Hollow
    Lello, E. Mystery at Tumble Inn
    MacLellan, E. Clock's secret
    ———————. Secret of the windmill
    ———————. Swiss mystery
    Miller, H. Shirley Holmes and the FBI
    Murray, J. Airport adventure
    ———————. Case for two detectives
    ———————. Case of mistaken identity
    ———————. Dead of night
    ———————. I want to report a murder
    ———————. Impossible room
    ———————. Looking glass murder
    ———————. Miss Forsythe is missing
    ———————. Scaredy cat
    ———————. Sixth juror
    Nicholson, J. Mysterious stranger
Mystery at Tumble Inn. Lello, E.
Mystery of the gumdrop dragon. Burtle, G.
Mystery ring. Gross, N.

MYTHOLOGY
    Asbrand, K. Pandora's box
    Fisher, A. Of gods and men
    Glass, G. Golden touch
    Howard, V. Strange tale of King Midas
    Hughes, T. Orpheus
    Olfson, L. Last time I saw Paris

MYTHOLOGY--SPOOF
 Nightingale, E. Ariadne exposed

- N -

Naomi-of-the-inn. Hoppenstedt, E.
NAPOLEON BONAPARTE
 Walsh, H. Louisiana
Nathan, Bertha. If wishes were horses. In Burack, A. One Hundred Plays for Children. 8 char
National everything. Murray, J.
Natural man. Browne, T.
NATURE
 Boiko, C. Crocus who couldn't bloom
 _____. Exterior decorator
 Hark, M. Five senses
 Hoff, S. Wild flowers
 Nolan, P. View of the sea
Naughty Susan. Slingluff, M.
The necklace, Maupassant, G.
Needle fights for freedom. MacLellan, E.
NEGROES see BLACK AMERICANS
NEIGHBORS
 Miller, H. Red Carpet Christmas
Nesbit, E. Long and short division. In Smith, M. 7 Plays and How to Produce Them. 8 char +
NETHERLANDS see HOLLAND
New broom. Hark, M.
New hearts for old. Fisher, A.
NEW YEAR
 Bennett, R. On New Year's Eve
 _____. Out of the clock
 Boiko, C. Clean sweep
NEW YORK (CITY)
 Miller, A. Grandpa and the statue
NEWBERY AWARD BOOKS
 Moore, E. Mr. Longfellow observes book week
New-fangled Thanksgiving. Hark, M.
Newman, Deborah. Cinderella. In Kamerman, S. Children's Plays from Favorite Stories. 15 char
 _____. Green Leaf's lesson. In Kamerman, S. Little Plays for Little Players. 7 char
 _____. Looking for Lincoln. In Kamerman, S. Fifty Plays for Holidays. 14 char
 _____. Magic goose. In Durrell, D. Thirty Plays for Classroom Reading. 18 char

NEWSPAPER 118

    _____. Mrs. Santa's Christmas gift. In Burack, A. Christmas Plays for Young Actors. 2 char+
    _____. One night in Bethlehem. In Kamerman, S. Fifty Plays for Holidays. 18 char
    _____. Plum Blossom and the dragon. In Kamerman, S. Dramatized Folk Tales of the World. 11 char+
    _____. Rebellious robots. In Kamerman, S. Fifty Plays for Junior Actors. 16 char
    _____. Yankee-doodle kitten. In Kamerman, S. Fifty Plays for Holidays. 15 char+
Newspaper dramatics. Howard, V.
NEWSPAPERS
    Fisher, A. Special edition
    Sayre, G. Final edition
NEWSPAPERS--SCHOOL
    Dias, E. Bow-wow blues
Next stop--spring! Boiko, C.
Nice girls don't chase the boys. White, A.
Nicholson, Jessie. Ghost walks tonight. In Durrell, D. Favorite Plays for Classroom Reading. 13 char
    _____. Handwriting on the wall. In Kamerman, S. Fifty Plays for Holidays. 8 char
    _____. Haunted bookshop. In Kamerman, S. Fifty Plays for Holidays. 13 char+
    _____. Mysterious stranger. In Kamerman, S. Fifty Plays for Junior Actors. 7 char
    _____. Teapot trouble. In Kamerman, S. Fifty Plays for Junior Actors. 8 char
    _____. Valentine stardust. In Kamerman, S. Fifty Plays for Holidays. 11 char
Nicholson, Mary Ann. Crying clown. In Burack, A. Four-Star Plays for Boys. 4 char
    _____. Laughing princess. In Kamerman, S. Children's Plays from Favorite Stories. 8 char+
    _____. Price of eggs. In Kamerman, S. Dramatized Folk Tales of the World. 4 char
    _____. Princess Nimble-wit. In Kamerman, S. Children's Plays from Favorite Stories. 9 char
    _____. Wise wife. In Kamerman, S. Children's Plays from Favorite Stories. 7 char
Nickel and a dime. Fisher, A.
Night before Christmas. McGee, C.
NIGHT BEFORE CHRISTMAS
    Nolan, J. Happy Christmas to all
Nightingale, E. M. Ariadne exposed. In Burack, A. Skits, Comedies and Farces for Teen-agers. 5 char

NIGHTINGALE, FLORENCE
    Lipnik, E. Angel of mercy
No braver soldier. Bierling, J.
No garden this year. McCoy, P.
No-mother land. Streacker, L.
No room at the inn. Patterson, E.
No starch in the collars. Fontaine, R.
Nobility. Bowers, E.
Nobody believes in witches! Watkins, M.
Nolan, Jeannette Covert. Happy Christmas to all. In Burack, A. Christmas Plays for Young Actors. 6 char; in Burack, A. One Hundred Plays for Children. 6 char
Nolan, Paul T. America is a song. In Kamerman, S. Fifty Plays for Holidays. 14 char; in Nolan, P. Round-the-World Plays for Young People. 14 char+
_____. And Christmas is its name. In Nolan, P. Round-the-World Plays for Young People. 25 char
_____. Anton Chekhov sort of evening. In Nolan, P. Drama Workshop Plays for Young People. 7 char
_____. Boshibari and the two thieves. In Nolan, P. Round-the-World Plays for Young People. 3 char
_____. Courters. In Nolan, P. Round-the-World Plays for Young People. 6 char
_____. Double nine of Chih Yuan. In Nolan, P. Round-the-World Plays for Young People. 5 char
_____. French cabinetmaker. In Nolan, P. Round-the-World Plays for Young People. 8 char
_____. Gates of Dinkelsbuehl. In Nolan, P. Round-the-World Plays for Young People. 8 char+
_____. Going steady. In Nolan, P. Drama Workshop Plays for Young People. 8 char
_____. Golden voice of Little Erik. In Nolan, P. Round-the-World Plays for Young People. 9 char+
_____. Happiest hat. In Nolan, P. Drama Workshop Plays for Young People. 10 char
_____. Happy ending. In Nolan, P. Drama Workshop Plays for Young People. 11 char
_____. Hi down there. In Nolan, P. Drama Workshop Plays for Young People. 8 char
_____. Highland fling. In Nolan, P. Round-the-World Plays for Young People. 8 char+
_____. In-group. In Nolan, P. Drama Workshop Plays for Young People. 12 char
_____. Johnny Appleseed. In Nolan, P. Round-the-World Plays for Young People. 9 char
_____. Leak in the dike. In Nolan, P. Round-the-World Plays for Young People. 8 char

NONSENSE   120

———. Licha's birthday serenade. In Nolan, P. Round-the-World Plays for Young People. 14 char+
———. Magic of Salamanca. In Nolan, P. Round-the-World Plays for Young People. 6 char
———. Moon's up there. In Nolan, P. Drama Workshop Plays for Young People. 10 char
———. Our sister, Sitya. In Nolan, P. Round-the-World Plays for Young People. 8 char
———. Robin Hood and the match at Nottingham. In Nolan, P. Round-the-World Plays for Young People. 10 char+
———. Skill of Pericles. In Nolan, P. Round-the-World Plays for Young People. 10 char+
———. Son of William Tell. In Nolan, P. Round-the-World Plays for Young People. 11 char
———. Stanislaw and the wolf. In Nolan, P. Round-the-World Plays for Young People. 9 char
———. Take it from the beginning. In Nolan, P. Drama Workshop Plays for Young People. 9 char
———. Trash and treasure. In Nolan, P. Drama Workshop Plays for Young People. 10 char
———. Tree to the sky. In Nolan, P. Drama Workshop Plays for Young People. 8 char
———. View of the sea. In Nolan, P. Drama Workshop Plays for Young People. 9 char
———. What's zymurgy with you? In Nolan, P. Drama Workshop Plays for Young People. 8 char
———. Whole city's down below. In Nolan, P. Drama Workshop Plays for Young People. 10 char
———. Wishing well or ill. In Nolan, P. Drama Workshop Plays for Young People. 7 char
———. Young man of considerable value. In Nolan, P. Drama Workshop Plays for Young People. 10 char
———. Younger generation. In Nolan, P. Drama Workshop Plays for Young People. 11 char

NONSENSE
    Carroll, L. Alice's adventures in Wonderland
    ———. Through the looking glass
    Worcester, N. Mad tea party

NORWAY
    Nolan, P. Golden voice of Little Erik
    Roberts, H. Builder of the wall.
Nose speech. Rostand, E.
Not exactly. Howard, V.
Not fit for man or beast. Hark, M.
Not for one sandwich. Taylor, L.
Not on the menu. Pyle, M.

Not only the strong. Hoppenstedt, E.
Nothing! Carlson, B.
Nothing to be thankful for. Hark, M.
Number one Apple Tree Lane. Boiko, C.
NUMBERS see COUNTING
NUMBERS--HISTORY
 Kane, E. How we got our numbers
Nursery rhyme diet. Hark, M.
NURSERY RHYMES
 Barr, J. Three little kittens
 Fisher, A. Once upon a time
 Freudenberger, H. Jack and Jill
 Gingerbread boy
 Hark, M. Nursery rhyme diet
 Holmes, R. Wise men of Gotham
 Miller, H. Mother Goose bakeshop
 _____. Simple Simon's reward
 _____. Three little kittens
 Molloy, L. Jenny-by-the-day
 Olfson, L. La farza del Miss Muffet
 Spamer, C. Pop-up books
 Vandevere, J. Mother Goose gives a dinner
 see also MOTHER GOOSE
NURSERY RHYMES--FARCE
 Olfson, L. Incredible housing shortage
NURSES
 Lipnik, E. Angel of mercy
Nutter, Carolyn, F. Red Riding Hood and the wolf. In
 Kamerman, S. Children's Plays from Favorite Stories.
 9 char+

- O -

O little town. Carlson, B.
OBEDIENCE
 Shakespeare, W. Katherina's obedience
O'Casey, Sean. End of the beginning. In Swortzell, L. All
 the World's a Stage. 3 char
OCEAN
 Nolan, P. View of the sea
OCEAN VOYAGE
 Bakeless, K. Most memorable voyage
 MacLellan, E. Return of the Nina
 Peterson, M. Beyond mutiny
ODYSSEUS
 Love, S. One-eyed giant

Of gods and men. Fisher, A.
Off the shelf. Hark, M.
Ogre who built a bridge. Mapp, F.
Oh, Medico! Fontaine, R.
OKLAHOMA
    Glass, G. Mr. Popper's penguins
OLD AGE
    Hawthorne, N. Dr. Heidegger's experiment
    Steinbeck, J. Leader of the people
Old Christmas. Preston, C.
Old Four-legs. Peterson, M.
Old Glory grows up. Miller, H.
Old man river. Deming, D.
OLD MEN
    Dickens, C. Christmas carol
    _____. Martin Chuzzlewit
    Hark, M. Christmas snowman
    Irving, W. Rip Van Winkle
    On being a senior adult
    Saroyan, William. Man with the heart in the highlands
    Spyri, J. Heidi
    _____. Heidi finds the way
    Taylor, L. How to live long
Old Mother Hubbard. Barr, J.
Old Pipes. Stockton, F.
OLD WOMEN
    Grabe, Mrs. Klaus. I know an old woman
    On being a senior adult
Olfson, Lewy. Avon calling! In Olfson, L. Skits and Short Farces for Young Actors. 4 char
_____. Bride of Gorse-bracken Hall. In Olfson, L. Skits and Short Farces for Young Actors. 5 char
_____. Cinderella revisited. In Olfson, L. Skits and Short Farces for Young Actors. 5 char
_____. Couple of right smart fellers. In Olfson, L. Skits and Short Farces for Young Actors. 4 char
_____. Equal rights. In Olfson, L. Skits and Short Farces for Young Actors. 16 char+
_____. La farza del Miss Muffett. In Olfson, L. Skits and Short Farces for Young Actors. 4 char+
_____. Great Caesar's ghost! In Olfson, L. Skits and Short Farces for Young Actors. 4 char
_____. Happy haunting! In Olfson, L. Skits and Short Farces for Young Actors. 6 char
_____. Hen party. In Olfson, L. Skits and short farces for Young Actors. 5 char

———. Incredible housing shortage. In Olfson, L.
Skits and Short Farces for Young Actors. 4 char
———. Last time I saw Paris. In Olfson, L. Skits
and Short Farces for Young Actors. 4 char
———. Meet Miss Stone-Age! In Olfson, L. Skits and
Short Farces for Young Actors. 5 char
———. My son, the prince. In Olfson, L. Skits and
Short Farces for Young Actors. 5 char
———. Once and future frog. In Olfson, L. Skits and
Short Farces for Young Actors. 4 char
———. Sail on! sail on! In Olfson, L. Skits and Short
Farces for Young Actors. 6 char
———. Spying high. In Olfson, L. Skits and Short
Farces for Young Actors. 4 char
———. Ten-year-old detective. In Olfson, L. Skits
and Short Farces for Young Actors. 4 char
———. Three swine of most small stature. In Olfson,
L. Skits and Short Farces for Young Actors. 5 char
———. Try data-date! In Olfson, L. Skits and Short
Farces for Young Actors. 5 char
Olive jar. McFarlan, E.
Oliver Twist. Dickens, C.
Oliver Twist asks for more. Howard, V.
On being a senior adult. In McGee, C. Drama for fun. 7 char+
On being too frequently proposed to. Wilde, O.
On camera, Noah Webster! Boiko, C.
On Halloween. Fisher, A.
On myself. Carlson, B.
On New Year's Eve. Bennett, R.
On strike. Fisher, A.
On the fence. Beach, M.
On you it looks good. Fontaine, R.
Once and future frog. Olfson, L.
Once upon a time. Fisher, A.
One-eyed giant. Love, S.
One hundred words. Boiko, C.
One in a million. Murray, J.
One last look. Carter, S.
One night in Bethlehem. Newman, D.
One-ring circus. Fisher, A.
One to grow on. Miller, H.
One wish too many. Feather, J.
Open window. Saki
OPERA--FARCE
    Olfson, L. La farza del Miss Muffet
Operation litterbug. Boiko, C.

Operation satellite. Carlson, B.
OPPRESSION
    Davis, O. Purlie Victorious
    Ward, D. Day of absence
    Ward, T. The daubers
    see also MINORITIES
OPTIMISM
    Nolan, P. Tree to the sky
Or make pot holders. Carlson, B.
Orczy, Baroness. Scarlet Pimpernel. In Burack, A. Popular Plays for Classroom Reading. 18 char
OREGON--HISTORY
    Carlson, B. There's always a leader
ORPHANS
    Dickens, C. Oliver Twist
    Mills, G. Christmas comes to Hamelin
Orpheus. Hughes, T.
Oser, Janice Auritt. King's calendar. In Kamerman, S. Fifty Plays for Junior Actors. 12 char
    ———. Running the country. In Kamerman, S. Fifty Plays for Holidays. 11 char
    ———. Weeping willow's happy day. In Kamerman, S. Fifty Plays for Holidays. 18 char
Othello. Mintier, W.
Other side of the wall. Clapp, P.
Our famous proverbs. Howard, V.
Our national sports. Howard, V.
Our own four walls. Hark, M.
Our sister, Sitya. Nolan, P.
Out of the clock. Bennett, R.
Owl's birthday. Pantopuck

- P -

PAINTING
    Beach, M. On the fence
    Hark, M. Our own four walls
PAINTINGS
    Huff, B. Case of the missing masterpiece
PANAMA CANAL
    Howard, V. Building of the Panama Canal
PAN-AMERICAN DAY
    Campbell, C. Bell of Dolores
    McArthur, J. Fiesta
    ———. Fiesta the first

PANCAKES
    Boylan, E. Runaway pancake
Pandora's box. Asbrand, K.
Pandora's perilous predicament. Boiko, C.
Panic in the palace. Swintz, M.
PANTOMIME
    Chermak, S. Peter and the wolf
    Howard, V. Pantomime orchestra
    see also SKITS--PANTOMIME
Pantomime orchestra. Howard, V.
Pantopuck the Puppetman. Owl's birthday. In Philpott, A. Eight Plays for Hand Puppets. 6 char
Paper bag mystery. Miller, H.
Paradis, Marjorie B. Santa goes to town. In Burack, A. Christmas Plays for Young Actors. 10 char
PARENT AND CHILD
    Bullins, E. Son come home
    Collodi, C. Pinocchio goes to school
    Furman, R. To kill a devil
    Ibsen, H. Aase searches for her son
    MacLellan, E. Return of the Nina
    Miller, H. Man like Lincoln
    Nolan, P. This younger generation
    White, A. Prodigal son
Parsons, Margaret. Too much of a good thing. In Kamerman, S. Little Plays for Little Players. 9 char+
Part-time hero. Miller, H.
Party night. Howard, V.
Patchwork princess. Slattery, M.
PATRICK, SAINT
    Malone, M. Last snake in Ireland
    see also SAINT PATRICK'S DAY
Patterson, Emma L. No room at the inn. In Burack, A. Christmas Plays for Young Actors. 16 char; in One Hundred Plays for Children. 16 char+
Pay and be gay. Howard, V.
PEACE
    Hark, M. See the parade
    see also GOVERNMENT--WORLD; UNITY
Peace, pilgrim. Cable, H.
Peach tree kingdom. Musil, R.
Peanut butter. McGee, C.
PEANUTS
    Blumenfeld, L. Another way to weigh an elephant
Pear tree. McFarlan, E.
Pedro and the burro. Peterson, M.
Peer Gynt leaves Solveig. Ibsen, H.

Pendleton, Edrie. Bobby and the Lincoln speech. In Durrell, D. Favorite Plays for Classroom Reading. 7 char
———. Jingle bells. In Burack, A. Christmas Plays for Young Actors. 7 char
PENGUINS
    Glass, G. Mr. Popper's penguins
PENN, WILLIAM
    Carlson, B. Let her ride!
PENNSYLVANIA
    Dias, E. Express to Valley Forge
    see also GETTYSBURG
Penny wise. Boiko, C.
Pep talk. Howard, V.
Pepe and the cornfield bandit. Boiko, C.
Pepi and Sombrero. Thomson, J.
Perambulating pie. Pyle, M.
PERCY, GEORGE
    Walsh, H. Jamestown
Perfect gift. DuBois, H.
Perfumes. Howard, V.
Perrault, Charles. Puss in boots. In Thane, A. Plays from Famous Stories and Fairy Tales. 11 char
———. Sleeping beauty. In Thane, A. Plays from Famous Stories and Fairy Tales. 18 char
PERSIA
    Carlson, B. My treasure
    McFarlan, E. Olive jar
Personality machine. Howard, V.
Personality problem. Fontaine, R.
PERU
    Thane, A. Baker's neighbor
Peter and the wolf. Chermak, S.
Peter, Peter, Peter! Boiko, C.
Peter Rabbit. Simonds, N.
Peter Rabbit volunteers. Miller, H.
Peterson, Mary Nygaard. Abe buys a barrel. In Kamerman S. Fifty Plays for Junior Actors. 10 char
———. Beyond mutiny. In Kamerman, S. Fifty Plays for Holidays. 10 char+
———. Magic box. In Kamerman, S. Dramatized Folk Tales of the World. 14 char
———. Old Four-legs. In Kamerman, S. Children's Plays from Favorite Stories. 6 char
———. Pedro and the burro. In Kamerman, S. Dramatized Folk Tales of the World. 9 char+
———. Simple Olaf. In Kamerman, S. Dramatized Folk Tales of the World. 7 char+

_____. Stone soup. In Kamerman, S. Children's Plays from Favorite Stories. 11 char
PETS
    Boiko, C. How to choose a boy
    Miller, H. Peter Rabbit volunteers
Phillips, Ernestine. Aesop, man of fables. In Kamerman, S. Fifty Plays for Junior Actors. 8 char+
Phillips, Marguerite Kreger. Hat for mother. In Durrell, D. Favorite Plays for Classroom Reading. 7 char; in Kamerman, S. Fifty Plays for Holidays. 6 char
Philpott, Violet, M. The egg. In Philpott, A. Eight Plays for Hand Puppets. 5 char
Phonograph record. Howard, V.
PHYSICS
    Boiko, C. Franklin reversal
PIANO
    Carlson, B. To play the piano
Piccola. Bennett, R.
The picnic. Howard, V.
PIE
    Bennett, R. Christmas pie
    Miller, H. Simple Simon's reward
    Pyle, M. Perambulating pie
Pied piper of Hamelin. Kennedy, L.
Pied piper of Hamlin. Browning, R.
Pierre Patelin. Koon, H.
Piffle! It's only a sniffle! Kaufman, T.
Pilgrim painting. Rawls, J.
PILGRIMS
    Bennett, R. Beaded moccasins
    Boiko, C. Meet the pilgrims
    Cable, H. Peace, pilgrim
    Carlson, B. Another way
    DuBois, G. Governor Bradford's scissors
    Miller, H. Thankful's red beads
    _____. Thanksgiving riddle
    Ramsey, H. In the name of Miles Standish
    Rawls, J. Pilgrim painting
    Very, A. Jonathan's Thanksgiving
    Walsh, H. Mutiny on the Mayflower
Pilgrim's first Thanksgiving. Howard, V.
Pink parasol. Miller, H.
Pink roses for Christmas. Campbell, J.
Pinocchio. Collodi, C.
Pinocchio goes to school. Collodi, C.
PIONEERS
    Boiko, C. All points west

Carlson, B. There's always a leader
Nolan, P. America is a song
see also UNITED STATES--HISTORY; THE WEST
Pippi Longstocking. Lindgrin, A.
Pirandello, Luigi. The jar. In Swortzell, L. Modern Plays for Young People. 11 char
Pirates. Carlson, B.
PIRATES
    Bennett, R. Runaway pirate
    Boiko, C. All hands on deck
    Carlson, B. Golden tooth
    _____. Pirates
    Miller, H. Captain Castaway's captives
    Slattery, M. Royal magic
    Stevenson, R. Treasure Island
    Twain, M. Tom Sawyer, pirate
Pixie in a trap. Bennett, R.
PLANETS
    Melchior, H. Visit to the planets
    Rittenhouse, C. Children of the sun
PLAY WITHIN A PLAY
    Conrad, E. Show boat
    Nolan, P. Take it from the beginning
    Weik, M. River risin'!
Play without a name. Fisher, A.
PLAYS IN VERSE see VERSE PLAYS
Pleasant dreams. Hark, M.
The pledge. Henderson, N.
The plot. Bennett, R.
Plum Blossom and the dragon. Newman, D.
Pocahontas, the tomboy princess. Roberts, H.
Poe, Edgar Allan. Cask of Amontillado. In Gilfond, H. Plays for Reading. 4 char
_____. Masque of the red death. In Olfson, L. Dramatized Classics for Radio-Style Reading, Vol. II. 13 char+
Poetry. Taylor, L.
POETRY
    Hoppenstedt, E. Poet's nightmare
    see also VERSE PLAYS
Poet's nightmare. Hoppenstedt, E.
POISON
    Hill, K. Midnight burial
POLAND
    Nolan, P. Stanislaw and the wolf
POLLUTION
    Boiko, C. Beware the genies!

    ————. What ever happened to Mother Nature?
    Carlson, B. Marked trail
    ————. Murky monster foiled again
    Hoff, S. Children on the moon
    Shore, M. Catastrophe Clarence
    see also ECOLOGY; LITTER
Pom-pom. Munro, H.
Pony express. Howard, V.
PONY EXPRESS
    Howard, V. Pony express
POOR see POVERTY
Pop-up books. Spamer, C.
Pope, Alexander. Belinda bemoans the loss of a lock of her hair. In Kline, P. Theatre Student: Scenes to Perform. 1 char
Posies for the potentate. Swintz, M.
POST OFFICE
    Miller, H. Lost Christmas cards
Pot of gold. Spamer, C.
POTATOES
    Carlson, B. Fit for a king
POVERTY
    Carlson, B. O little town
    Davis, O. Purlie Victorious
    Hughes, L. Soul gone home
    Lincoln, A. Streak o' lean
    Maupassant, G. The necklace
    Mayfield, J. 417
    Saroyan, William. Man with the heart in the highlands
    Shine, T. Shoes
POWER
    Browning, R. My last duchess
    Shakespeare, W. Julius Caesar
PRACTICAL JOKES
    DuBois, G. Last laugh
PRAYER
    Everyman's prayer
Precedent in pastries. Rowland, E.
Present for mother. Barr, J.
President Lincoln's children. Very, A.
Preston, Carol. Born in a stable. In Preston, C. Trilogy of Christmas Plays for Children. 38 char+
    ————. In a manger laid. In Preston, C. Trilogy of Christmas Plays for Children. 38 char+
    ————. Old Christmas. In Preston, C. Trilogy of Christmas Plays for Children. 49 char+

PRETENDING
    Hoff, S. Giants
Price of eggs. Nicholson, M.

PRIDE
    Browning, R. My last duchess
    Chekhov, A. The upheaval
    Cooper, E. Greta and the prince
    Milton, J. Eve decides to eat the fruit of the tree of knowledge
    Rostand, E. Nose speech
    Stevenson, R. Sire de Maletroit's door
    White, A. Lazarus
    _____. Prodigal son
Prince and the dragon. Boylan, E.
Prince and the pauper. Twain, M.
Prince is where you find him. Chisholm, J.
Prince of hearts. Bennett, R.

PRINCES AND PRINCESSES
    Alexander, S. Frog princess
    Andersen, H. Princess and the pea
    _____. The swineherd
    Bennett, R. Prince of hearts
    _____. Snow-white and Rose-red
    Boiko, C. Ah See and the six-colored heaven
    _____. All hands on deck
    Burnett, F. Little princess
    Burtle, G. Mystery of the gumdrop dragon
    Carlson, B. Who will be king?
    Chisholm, J. Prince is where you find him
    Cooper, E. Greta and the prince
    Corey, C. Dancing princesses
    Draper, C. Emperor's daughters
    Elfenbien, J. King who couldn't be fooled
    Hark, M. Princess and the rose-colored glasses
    Leuser, E. Little bird in the tree
    McGee, C. Fatal quest
    MacLellan, E. Cross princess
    Miller, H. Princess and the pea
    _____. Tomboy and the dragon
    Nesbit, E. Long and short division
    Nicholson, M. Laughing princess
    Perrault, C. Sleeping beauty
    Pyle, M. Clever Peter
    Richards, L. With all my heart
    Rowland, E. Three aunts
    Simon, S. Baking contest
    Slattery, M. Patchwork princess

Stockton, F. Lady or the tiger?
Thane, A. Aladdin and his wonderful lamp
———. Cinderella
———. Rapunzel
———. Rumpelstiltskin
———. Twelve dancing princesses
Twain, M. Prince and the pauper
Watkins, M. Nobody believes in witches!
White, A. Wonderous apple tree
Princess and the pea. Andersen, H.
Princess and the pea. Miller, H.
Princess and the rose-colored glasses. Hark, M.
Princess Nimble-wit. Nicholson, M.
Princess Rosette. D'Aulnoy, Mme.
Princess who couldn't dance. Barbee, L.
Princess who would not smile. Melcher, M.
PRINCESSES see PRINCES AND PRINCESSES
Printer's devil. Dias, E.
PRISONERS
    Hall, H. The valiant
    Hugo, V. Bishop's candlesticks
Prize for mother. Hark, M.
PRIZES
    Murray, J. One in a million
Prodigal son. White, A.
Professor Countdown takes off. Bradley, P.
PROMPTNESS
    Hark, M. Johnnie Jump Up
PROSPECTORS
    Love, S. Apache silver
PUBLISHERS
    Murray, J. Publisher's choice
Publisher's choice. Murray, J.
Pudding-bag string. Bennett, R.
PUNCH AND JUDY
    Gertler, L. Punch and the heartless giant
Punch and the heartless giant. Gertler, L.
PUNCTUATION
    Boiko, C. Punctuation proclamation
Punctuation proclamation. Boiko, C.
PUPPET PLAYS
    Boylan, E. How to be a puppeteer
    Canadian fairy tale
    Carlson, B. Golden spike
    ———. Happy nesting
    ———. Robin Hood meets Little John
    ———. Trailing arbutus

PUPPETS

    _____. Turn south at Voorhees' farm
    _____. Who will be king?
Cochrane, L. Shadow puppets in color
Gertler, L. Punch and the heartless giant
Gingerbread boy
Lonely giant
Lorca, F. Billy-club puppets
Pantopuck. Owl's birthday
Philpott, V. The egg
Ross, L. Holiday Puppets
Silver key
Thomson, J. Pepi and Sombrero
Tichenor, T. Jack and the beanstalk
PUPPETS
    Collodi, C. Pinocchio
Puppy love. Miller, H.
Pure white. McGee, C.
PURIM
    Zeligs, D. Queen Esther saves her people
Purlie Victorious. Davis, O.
Puss-in-boots. Elfenbein, J.
Puss-in-boots. Very, A.
Pylant, Agnes. A mellerdrammer. In McGee, C. Drama for Fun. 5 char
    _____. Starring you. In McGee, C. Drama for Fun. 2 char
Pyle, Howard. Apple of contentment. In Thane, A. Plays from Famous Stories and Fairy Tales. 9 char
Pyle, Mary Thurman. Clever Peter. In Kamerman, S. Children's Plays from Favorite Stories. 15 char+
    _____. Mrs. Gibbs advertises. In Kamerman, S. Fifty Plays for Junior Actors. 12 char+
    _____. Not on the menu. In Burack, A. One Hundred Plays for Children. 8 char
    _____. Perambulating pie. In Burack, A. Christmas Plays for Young Actors. 10 char
    _____. Three royal r's. In Kamerman, S. Fifty Plays for Holidays. 14 char+

- Q -

Queen Esther saves her people. Zeligs, D.
Queen with the broken heart. Urban, C.
QUEENS see KINGS AND QUEENS
Queen's mirror. Slattery, M.
Quick-witted Jack. Feather, J.

QUILTS
    Slattery, M. Patchwork princess

- R -

Rabbit and the wolf. Walker, B.
Rabbit who refused to run. Miller, H.
RABBITS
    Baher, C.   Cinder-rabbit
    Bennett, R.   School for scamperers
    Boiko, C.   Wild rabbit chase
    Knight, L.   Flibber turns the tables
    Miller, H.   Forgetful Easter rabbit
    _____. Peter Rabbit volunteers
    _____. Rabbit who refused to run
    Simonds, N.   Peter Rabbit
    Spamer, C.   Bunnyland brigade
    Werner, S.   Choosing of Easter Rabbit
Rabbits who changed their minds. Miller, H.
Rabe, Olive see Fisher, Aileen, and Olive Rabe
RADIO PLAYS
    Bierce, A.   Shipwreck
    Burack, A.   Popular Plays for Classroom Reading
    Carroll, L.   Through the looking glass
    Dickens, C.   Christmas carol
    Dumas, A.   Count of Monte Cristo
    _____. The duel
    Fisher, A.   Mother of Thanksgiving
    _____. Skills to share
    _____. Story of a well
    Hale, E.   Man without a country
    Henry, O.   Last leaf
    Irving, W.   Legend of Sleepy Hollow
    James, H.   Washington Square
    Kane, E.   Elves and the shoemaker
    Lawrence, J.   Inside a kid's head
    Love, S.   Plays for Reading and Recording
    Maupassant, G.   The necklace
    Miller, A.   Grandpa and the statue
    Poe, E.   Cask of Amontillado
    St. Clair, R.   Spirit of Christmas
    Stevenson, R.   Kidnapping of David Balfour
    Verne, J.   Around the world in eighty days
    Weathers, W.   Vision of the silver bell
    Wyss, J.   Swiss family Robinson

RAIN
    Howard, V. Man who didn't like rain
    Miller, H. Weatherman on trial
RAINBOW
    Spamer, C. Pot of gold
Rainbow colors. Hark, M.
Rainbow's end. Bennett, R.
Raisin in the sun. Hansberry, L.
Ramsey, Helen. In the name of Miles Standish. In Kamerman, S. Fifty Plays for Holidays. 11 char+
Ranch romance. Howard, V.
Rapunzel. Barr, J.
Rapunzel. Thane, A.
Rawls, James. Pilgrim painting. In Durrell, D. Favorite Plays for Classroom Reading. 8 char; in Kamerman, S. Fifty Plays for Holidays. 9 char
Real princess. Miller, H.
Reay, Nina Butler. Mr. Bates goes to the polls. In Kamerman, S. Little Plays for Little Players. 4 char+
Rebecca of Sunnybrook Farm. Carlson, B.
Rebellious robots. Newman, D.
RECREATION
    Hark, M. Good neighbors
Red carpet Christmas. Miller, H.
RED CROSS
    Deming, D. Old man river
Red flannel suit. Miller, H.
Red Riding Hood and the wolf. Nutter, C.
REED, WALTER
    Burlingame, C. Yellow fever
Reform of Sterling Silverheart. Cable, H.
The rehearsal. Weik, M.
Reines, Bernard, J. Turncoat. In Durrell, D. Thirty Plays for Classroom Reading. 8 char
Reluctant Columbus. Cable, H.
Reluctant dragon. Grahame, K.
Reluctant ghost. Brydon, M.
Remember the Christmas tree. Carlson, B.
REPENTANCE
    White, A. Prodigal son
RESPONSIBILITY
    Glass, G. Henry and the night crawlers
    Leuser, E. Tommy's adventure
    Nicholson, J. Teapot trouble
    see also CHARACTER BUILDING
RESTAURANTS
    Alexander, S. What's in my soup?

  Carlson, B. Home cooking
Return of Bobby Shafto. Miller, H.
Return of Rip Van Winkle. Howard, V.
Return of the Nina. MacLellan, E.
REVENGE
  Poe, E. Cask of Amontillado
  Shakespeare, W. Hamlet
REVERE, PAUL
  Howard, V. Ride of Paul Revere
  Lipnick, E. Son of liberty
REVOLUTIONARY WAR [American]
  Barbee, L. Guide for George Washington
  Bierling, J. No braver soldier
  Boiko, C. Jack Jouette's ride
  _____. Tale of two drummers
  Carlson, B. Remember the Christmas tree
  Clark, B. Fires at Valley Forge
  Colbo, E. Heroine of Wren
  Davis, L. Turtle, a flute, and the general's birthday
  Dias, E. Express to Valley Forge
  _____. Martha Washington's spy
  Howard, V. Boston tea party
  Lipnick, E. Son of liberty
  MacLellan, E. Needle fights for freedom
  Miller, H. Dolly saves the day
  Walsh, H. The spy
  _____. Young Hickory
  Willment, F. Whites of their eyes
Rhodes, James. Crow and the corn. <u>In</u> Martin, J. Little Plays for Little People. 3 char
The rhyme's the crime or the verse is yet to come. Smith, F.
Richard alone. Shakespeare, W.
Richard Brown and the dragon. Bright, R.
Richards, Laura E. Chop-chin and the golden dragon. <u>In</u> Smith, M. 7 Plays and How to Produce Them. 30 char+
  _____. With all my heart. <u>In</u> Smith, M. 7 Plays and How to Produce Them. 5 char+
RIDDLES
  Taylor, L. Say, Dad
  Williams, G. Kettle of brains
Ride of Paul Revere. Howard, V.
Ride the Gooberville stage! Huff, B.
Ride your hobby. Fontaine, R.

RINGS
    Gross, N. Mystery ring
Rip Van Winkle. Irving, W.
Rittenhouse, Charles. Children of the sun. In Burack, A. One Hundred Plays for Children. 23 char
The rivals. Sheridan, R.
River risin'! Weik, M.
Roberts, Helen. Builder of the wall. In Kamerman, S. Dramatized Folk Tales of the World. 9 char
   _____. For the glory of Spain. In Kamerman, S. Fifty Plays for Holidays. 6 char
   _____. Test for William Tell. In Kamerman, S. Dramatized Folk Tales of the World. 16 char+
Roberts, Helen M. Lonely fir tree. In Kamerman, S. Little Plays for Little Players. 10 char
   _____. Pocahontas, the tomboy princess. In Kamerman, S. Fifty Plays for Junior Actors. 16 char+
   _____. Washington's sacrifice. In Kamerman, S. Little Plays for Little Players. 6 char
Roberts, Walter. Musicians of Bremen Town. In Kamerman, S. Dramatized Folk Tales of the World. 10 char

ROBIN HOOD
    Baher, C. Robin Hood outwits the sheriff
    Carlson, B. Robin Hood meets Little John
    Colson, J. Message from Robin Hood
    _____. Robin Hood in Sherwood Forest
    Jacob, E. Robin Hood tricks the sheriff
    Nolan, P. Robin Hood and the match at Nottingham
Robin Hood and the match at Nottingham. Nolan, P.
Robin Hood in Sherwood Forest. Colson, J.
Robin Hood meets Little John. Carlson, B.
Robin Hood outwits the sheriff. Baher, C.
Robin Hood tricks the sheriff. Jacob, E.
Robinson, Christina. Boat club dance. In Durrell, D. Teen-Age Plays for Classroom Reading. 10 char

ROBOTS
    Boiko, C. Big shoo
    Martens, A. Roscoe the robot
    Newman, D. Rebellious robots
    Whitworth, V. Mechanical maid

ROCK MUSIC PLAYS
    Driver, D. Your own thing
Rock the baby, Granny. Carlson, B.
Roller coaster. Howard, V.
Roman romance. Boiko, C.
Romance of a busy broker. Henry, O.
Romance of Minnie Martin or it shouldn't happen to a dog. McGee, C.

Romantic facts for men. Howard, V.
Romantic facts for women. Howard, V.
ROME
    Shakespeare, W. Julius Caesar
Romeo and Juliet. Shakespeare, W.
Roscoe the robot. Martens, A.
ROSS, BETSY
    MacLellan, E. Needle fights for freedom
Ross, Laura. Admiral and the feathered pilots. In Ross, L. Holiday Puppets. 4 char+
————. Three kings. In Ross, L. Holiday Puppets. 5 char+
————. Washington and the first flight in America. In Ross, L. Holiday Puppets. 3 char+
————. Young Abe wrestles Armstrong. In Ross, L. Holiday Puppets. 4 char+
Rostand, Edmond. Nose speech. In Kline, P. Theatre Student: Scenes to Perform. 1 char
Rosy-cheeked ghost. Blaine, B.
Rowland, Elsi. Hans, who made the princess laugh. In Burack, A. One Hundred Plays for Children. 13 char+
————. Precedent in pastries. In Burack, A. One Hundred Plays for Children. 19 char+
————. Three aunts. In Burack, A. One Hundred Plays for Children. 15 char+
Royal cloth of China. Fitz-Adcock, I.
Royal magic. Slattery, M.
RULERS
    Shakespeare, W. Julius Caesar
    see also KINGS AND QUEENS
Rumpelstiltskin. Bennett, H.
Rumpelstiltskin. Bennett, R.
Rumpelstiltskin. Thane, A.
Runaway balloon. McMeekin, I.
Runaway bookmobile. Boiko, C.
Runaway pancake. Boylan, E.
Runaway pirate. Bennett, R.
Running the country. Oser, J.
RUSSIA
    Boiko, C. Snowflake
    Chekhov, A. The upheaval
    Chermak, S. Peter and the wolf
    Corson, H. Fish in the forest
    Schwartz, E. Little Red Riding Hood
    Tolstoy, L. How much land does a man need?
    ————. Little girls wiser than men
Russian quartet. McGee, C.

Rybak, Rose Kacherian. Day the moonmen landed. In
 Kamerman, S. Fifty Plays for Junior Actors. 16 char+
 ———. Election day in Spooksville. In Burack, A.
 Skits, Comedies and Farces for Teen-agers. 19 char+

- S -

S. O. S. from Santa. Miller, H.
SAFETY
    Hark, M. ABC for safety
    Miller, H. Safety clinic
    Woster, A. All houses are haunted
Safety clinic. Miller, H.
Saga of Davey Rocket
Sagoff, Sara E. Hand-me-down Hildy. In Kamerman, S.
    Fifty Plays for Holidays. 14 char
Sail on! sail on! Olfson, L.
SAILORS
    Dias, E. Cast up by the sea
    Heine, H. Flying Dutchman
    Howard, V. Daring sailormen
    Miller, H. Return of Bobby Shafto
    White, A. Eight bells
    ———. Sailor's return
    ———. Saucy sailor
Sailor's return. White, A.
St. Clair, Robert. Miss Muffet's wish. In Durrell, D.
    Thirty Plays for Classroom Reading. 5 char
———. Spirit of Christmas. In Burack, A. Christmas
    Plays for Young Actors. 8 char
St. Patrick and the last snake in Ireland. Davis, L.
St. Patrick saves the day. DuBois, G.
SAINT PATRICK'S DAY
    Burlingame, C. Three wishes
    Carlson, B. Why catch a leprechaun?
    Davis, L. St. Patrick and the last snake in Ireland
    DuBois, G. St. Patrick saves the day
    Taylor, J. Lazy leprechaun
    Watts, F. Bridge to Killybog Fair
    ———. Leprechaun shoemakers
    ———. Leprechaun's pot of gold
    see also PATRICK, SAINT
Saki. Open window. In Gilfond, H. Plays for Reading. 6
    char
Salesman! Howard, V.

SALT
    Carlson, B. Salt in the soup
    Colbert, M. Salt in the sea
    Mahlmann, L. Why the sea is salt
Salt in the sea. Colbert, M.
Salt in the soup. Carlson, B.
Sanderlin, Owenita. Follow the North Star. In Kamerman, S. Little Plays for Little Players. 7 char
Sanders, Sandra. Hansel and Gretel. In Sanders, S. Creating Plays with Children. 7 char
_____. Julius Caesar. In Sanders, S. Creating Plays with Children. 18 char+
_____. Rip Van Winkle. In Sanders, S. Creating Plays with Children. 18 char+
_____. Three sillies. In Sanders, S. Creating Plays with Children. 19 char+
_____. Tragedy in the graveyard. In Sanders, S. Creating Plays with Children. 8 char+
_____. Wizard of Oz. In Sanders, S. Creating Plays with Children. 13 char+

SANITATION
    Lipnik, E. Angel of mercy
Santa and the efficiency expert. Watts, F.
Santa calls a conference. Miller, H.

SANTA CLAUS
    Bennett, R. Santa's send-off
    McGee, C. Night before Christmas
    Miller, H. Christmas peppermints
    _____. S. O. S. from Santa
    _____. Wake up, Santa Claus!
    Paradis, M. Santa goes to town
    Spamer, C. Candy canes
    Thane, A. Brownie who found Christmas
    Watts, F. Santa and the efficiency expert
Santa Claus parade. Hark, M.
Santa goes to town. Paradis, M.
Santa's send-off. Bennett, R.
Saroyan, William. Man with the heart in the highlands. In Swortzell, W. All the World's a Stage. 25 char

SATIRE
    Dias, E. Hippie and the bard
    Ionesco, E. The leader
    Pope, A. Belinda bemoans the loss of a lock of her hair
    Swintz, M. King's creampuffs
    Vanbrugh, Sir L. Lord Foppington's day
    Wilde, O. On being too frequently proposed to

Saturday chatter. Howard, V.
The Saturdays. Enright, E.
Saucy sailor. White, A.
Saucy scarecrow. Thane, A.
Saving the old homestead. Fay, M.
Say, Dad. Taylor, L.
Sayers, Nancy James. Story of Gransel and Hettal. In McGee, C. Drama for Fun. 5 char
Sayre, George Wallace. Final edition. In Burack, A. Four-Star Plays for Boys. 8 char
SCANDINAVIA
    Feather, J. Quick-witted Jack
    Peterson, M. Simple Olaf
    Whitworth, V. Magic cloak
Scarecrow and the witch. Bennett, R.
SCARECROWS
    Bennett, R. Scarecrow and the witch
    Boiko, C. Big shoo
    Folmsbee, B. Goblin parade
    Howard, H. Thanks to Sammy Scarecrow
    Leuser, E. D. Thanksgiving scarecrow
    Thane, A. Saucy scarecrow
Scaredy cat. Boiko, C.
Scaredy cat. Murray, J.
Scarlet Pimpernel. Orczy, B.
Schaaf, Albert. Jump for Joy. In Burack, A. Skits, Comedies and Farces for Teen-agers. 14 char; in Durrell, D. Teen-Age Plays for Classroom Reading. 15 char
Scheherazade. Lynch, M.
SCHOOL
    Boiko, C. Terrible Terry's surprise
    Dias, E. The mantle
    ————. Printer's devil
    Elfenbein, J. Ten-penny tragedy
    Leuser, E. Tommy's adventure
    Pyle, M. Three royal r's
    Watts, F. Miss Louisa and the outlaws
School daze. Howard, V.
School for jesters. Whitman, C.
School for scamperers. Bennett, R.
Schoolwork. Howard, V.
Schroll, Catherine V. see MacLellan, Esther, and Catherine V. Schroll
Schwartz, Eugene. Little Red Riding Hood. In Swortzell, L. All the World's a Stage. 14 char+
Schwartz, Morton K. All in favor. In Burack, A. One

Hundred Plays for Children. 5 char
SCIENCE
    Boiko, C.   Franklin reversal
    Foulk, C.   Floating stone
SCIENCE FICTION
    Boiko, C.   Book that saved the earth
    _____. Pandora's perilous predicament
    _____. Take me to your marshal
    Dias, E.   Little man who wasn't there
    Harper, J.   First cat on Mars
    see also   FANTASY
SCIENTISTS
    Bradley, P.   Professor Countdown takes off
    Glass, G.   Early life of George Washington Carver
SCOTLAND
    Hall, M.   King Horn
    Nolan, P.   Highland fling
    Shakespeare, W.   Macbeth
    White, A.   Willie's gane to Melville castle
SCULPTURE   see   ART
SEA
    Nolan, P.   View of the sea
Sealock, Thelma W.   Lincoln coat.   In Burack, A.   One Hundred Plays for Children.   8 char+
Sean, the fool, the devil, and the cats.   Hughes, T.
Search for the sky-blue princess.   Boiko, C.
SEASONS
    Boiko, C.   Exterior decorator
    _____. Snowman who overstayed
    see also   specific seasons
Secret of the windmill.   MacLellan, E.
Secret of the wishing well.   Leuser, E. D.
SECRETARIES
    Dias, E.   Dear Lottie
SECRETS
    Cleary, B.   Ellen's secret
    Sanders, S.   Tragedy in the graveyard
See the parade.   Hark, M.
SELF-CONFIDENCE
    Dias, E.   Ballad for the shy
    Garver, J.   My fair Linda
    Miller, H.   Dial M for mother
    Nolan, P.   Hi down there
    _____. What's zymurgy with you?
SELF-INTEREST
    Boiko, C.   Star bright
    Browning, R.   My last duchess

SELF-INTEREST

_____. Pied piper of Hamlin
Capell, L. Tongue-cut sparrow
Carlson, B. Fit for a king
Collodi, C. Pinocchio
Conrad, E. Show boat
Dias, E. Christmas spirit
Dickens, C. Magic fishbone
_____. Martin Chuzzlewit
_____. Oliver Twist
Dunsany, L. Jest of Hahalaba
Ferguson, D. Most special dragon
Fisher, A. Ghosts on guard
_____. Way to Norwich
Garver, J. Father hits the jackpot
Graham, M. Unusual flower
Hagy, L. Fire in a paper
Hark, M. Christmas snowman
Holmes, R. Golden goose
_____. Heir of Linne
Ibsen, H. Peer Gynt leaves Solveig
Jacob, E. Snow White
James, H. Washington Square
Jarvis, S. M. I think I know
Kennedy, L. Pied piper of Hamelin
Leuser, E. D. Magic grapes
McCarty, E. Little cake
Mahlmann, L. Frog prince
_____. Snow White and the seven dwarfs
Miller, H. Mother beats the band
_____. Shady shadows
_____. Wishing stream
Mills, G. Christmas comes to Hamelin
Molloy, L. Cat and the queen
Murphy, H. Wise and clever maiden
Newman, D. Cinderella
_____. Magic goose
Nolan, P. In-group
_____. Stanislaw and the wolf
Peterson, M. Pedro and the burro
Poe, E. Masque of the red death
Pope, A. Belinda bemoans the loss of a lock of her hair
Pyle, H. Apple of contentment
Shakespeare, W. Macbeth
_____. The tempest
Shore, M. Watch out for Aunt Hattie
Simon, S. Baking contest

———. Tiger and the Brahman
Slattery, M. Queen's mirror
———. Royal magic
Thane, A. Dummling and the golden goose
Tichenor, T. Jack and the beanstalk
Vanbrugh, Sir J. Lord Foppington's day
Waite, H. Christmas house
Wilde, O. Happy prince

SELF-KNOWLEDGE
    Browne, T. Natural man
    Bullins, E. Son come home
    Carter, S. One last look
    Childress, A. African garden
    Conrad, E. Show boat
    Dias, E. Dear Lottie
    Hawthorne, N. Feathertop
    Henderson, N. Look behind the mask
    Ibsen, H. Peer Gynt leaves Solveig
    Martens, A. Roscoe the robot
    Nolan, P. Moon's up there
    Slattery, M. Queen's mirror
    Steinbeck, J. Leader of the people
    White, A. Wraggle taggle gypsies
    Wilde, C. Susan goes Hollywood

SELF-PITY
    Nolan, P. Whole city's down below
    Shakespeare, W. Richard alone

SENSES
    Hark, M. Five senses

SERVANTS
    Whitworth, V. Mechanical maid
Setting the table. Howard, V.
Seven little seeds. Gould, J.
Seven Simons. Carlson, B.

SEWING
    Rowland, E. Three aunts
Shades of ransom. Chisholm, J.

SHADOWS
    Miller, H. Shady shadows
Shady shadows. Miller, H.
Shakespeare, William. Cleopatra's death scene. In Kline,
    P. Theatre Student. 1 char
———. Comedy of errors. In Cullum, A. Shake Hands
    with Shakespeare. 16 char+
———. Hamlet. In Cullum, A. Shake Hands with Shakespeare. 14 char
———. Julius Caesar. In Cullum, A. Shake Hands with

SHAKESPEARE

Shakespeare. 9 char+; in Sanders, S. Creating Plays with Children. 18 char+
____. Katherina's obedience. In Kline, P. Theatre Student. 1 char
____. Lady Macbeth receives a letter from her husband. In Kline, P. Theatre Student. 1 char
____. Macbeth. In Cullum, A. Shake Hands with Shakespeare. 22 char+
____. Midsummer night's dream. In Cullum, A. Shake Hands with Shakespeare. 21 char+
____. Richard alone. In Kline, P. Theatre Student. 1 char
____. Romeo and Juliet. In Cullum, A. Shake Hands with Shakespeare. 12 char+
____. Taming of the shrew. In Cullum, A. Shake Hands with Shakespeare. 12 char+
____. The tempest. In Cullum, A. Shake Hands with Shakespeare. 14 char+
____. To be or not to be. In Kline, P. Theatre Student. 1 char

SHAKESPEARE, WILLIAM
    Boiko, C. Christmas revel
    Dias, E. Landslide for Shakespeare
    Dorand, J. Teen and twenty

SHAKESPEARE, WILLIAM--SPOOF
    Nolan, P. Happy ending
    Olfson, L. Avon calling!

SHAKESPEARE'S PLAYS
    Barbee, L. Enter Juliet
    Driver, D. Your own thing
    Mintier, W. Othello

SHARING
    Barr, J. Present for mother

SHEEP
    Jarvis, S. M. Honey and dough

Sheridan, Richard Brinsley. The rivals. In Olfson, L. Classics Adopted for Acting and Reading. 8 char
Sherlock Holmes and the red-headed league. Doyle, A.
Sherlock Holmes and the stockbroker's clerk. Doyle, A.
Sherwood, Robert E. Abe Lincoln in Illinois. In Maloney, H. Plays to Remember. 5 char
Shine, Ted. Shoes. In Childress, A. Black Scenes. 4 char
Ship like this. Carlson, B.

SHIPS
    Carlson, B. Ship like this

Shipwreck. Bierce, A.

Shirley Holmes and the FBI
Shoemaker and the elves. Bennett, R.
SHOEMAKERS
    Bennett, R. Shoemaker and the elves
    Thane, A. Elves and the shoemaker
    ———. Twelve dancing princesses
Shoes. Shine, T.
SHOES
    Carlson, B. In the dumps
    Kane, E. Elves and the shoemaker
    Mahlmann, L. Magic shoes
    Taylor, J. Lazy leprechaun
    Turnbull, L. Magic shoes
Shop girl's revenge. Downing, R.
Shore, Maxine. Catastrophe Clarence. In Burack, A. Four-Star Plays for Boys. 6 char; in Durrell, D. Favorite Plays for Classroom Reading. 7 char
——— . Watch out for Aunt Hattie. In Durrell, D. Teen-Age Plays for Classroom Reading. 5 char
Show boat. Conrad, E.
Shower of hearts. Miller, H.
Shut the door! Carlson, B.
Shy prince. Spamer, C.
SICILY
    Pirandello, L. The jar
Silent night. Hollingsworth, L.
SILENT NIGHT (SONG)
    Hollingsworth, L. Silent night
SILK
    Fitz-Adcock, I. Royal cloth of China
SILLIES see FOOLS
SILVER
    Love, S. Apache silver
Silver coffeepot. Asbrand, K.
Silver key. In Philpott, A. Eight Plays for Hand Puppets. 9 char
Simon, Shirley. Baking contest. In Kamerman, S. Fifty Plays for Junior Actors. 9 char
——— . Doctor farmer. In Kamerman, S. Children's Plays from Favorite Stories. 14 char
——— . Tiger and the brahman. In Kamerman, S. Children's Plays from Favorite Stories. 5 char
Simonds, Natalie. Hansel and Gretel. In Burack, A. One Hundred Plays for Children. 5 char; in Durrell, D. Thirty Plays for Classroom Reading. 6 char
——— . Peter Rabbit. In Burack, A. One Hundred Plays for Children. 6 char

SIMPLE

    _____. Unhappy Santa. In Burack, A. Christmas Plays for Young Actors. 3 char
Simple Olaf. Peterson, M.
Simple Simon's reward. Miller, H.
SIMPLICITY
    Hark, M. Dish for the king
SINGING see SONGS
Sir Galahad and the maidens. Howard, V.
Sire de Maletroit's door. Stevenson, R.
SISTERS
    Bennett, R. Fire-face and the Indians
    Carlson, B. Why the leaves of the aspen tree quake in a breeze
    Sherwood, R. Abe Lincoln in Illinois
    Thane, A. Cinderella
    see also BROTHERS AND SISTERS
Six wise travelers. Jarvis, S.
Sixth juror. Murray, J.
Size, please. Howard, V.
Skill of Pericles. Nolan, P.
Skills to share. Fisher, A.
SKITS
    Bowers, E. Nobility
    Bradley, P. Professor Countdown takes off
    Carlson, B. All about animals
    _____. Follow the leader
    _____. Home cooking
    _____. Impossible! unacceptable! preposterous!
    _____. In the dumps
    _____. It had to be
    _____. Let's fool someone
    _____. Make your own bed
    _____. Marked trail
    _____. Murkey monster foiled again
    _____. Nothing!
    _____. On myself
    _____. Operation satellite
    _____. Or make pot holders
    _____. Rock the baby, Granny
    _____. Salt in the soup
    _____. Ship like this
    _____. Smithtown, U.S.A.
    _____. The $10,000 dog
    _____. To play the piano
    _____. Touch one
    _____. Where there are no snags
    _____. Why don't you?

Cheatham, V. Snow White and friends
Fisher, A. On Halloween
Fontaine, R. Humorous Skits for Young People
Hammack, B. Night before Christmas
Lane, M. Is there life on other planets?
McCoy, P. No garden this year
McGee, C. Can'tsee Poorsight
————. Fatal quest
————. Fun with Hamlet and his friends
————. Gransel and Hettal
————. Henry
————. Interview with Punch McPugg
————. King with the terrible temper
————. Lover's errand
————. Peanut butter
————. Pure white
————. Russian quartet
————. Sofapillio
————. Spasm in three speeds
————. Stand-in
————. The story
————. Trip to Mexico
————. Witches and the crows
Moessenger, B. Man in the red suit
Nightingale, E. Ariadne exposed
Pylant, A. Starring you
Sayers, N. Story of Gransel and Hettal
Taylor, L. Stunts and Skits
Wallace, R. Case of the frustrated corpse
Willment, F. Whites of their eyes
Young, R. From nine to five
   see also AUDIENCE PARTICIPATION SKITS; SKITS
--PANTOMIME
SKITS--AUDIENCE PARTICIPATION see AUDIENCE PAR-
   TICIPATION SKITS
SKITS--PANTOMIME
   Howard, V. Backward people
————. Bible pantomimes
————. Birthday surprises
————. Boston tea party
————. Building of the Panama canal
————. The bus
————. Cake bake
————. California gold discovery
————. Children who found new friends
————. The colonel
————. Columbus' discovery of America

- The dancers
- Daniel in the lion's den
- Daring sailormen
- David's battle with Goliath
- Directions
- Dizzy dinners
- Experts
- First flight of the Wright brothers
- The fisherman
- The golfer
- Grandma crosses the street
- Happy hikers
- High jumper
- How music made everyone happy
- In the army
- In the jungle
- The juggler
- Lincoln's Gettysburg Address
- Man who didn't like rain
- Men of Mars
- Mirror stunt
- Newspaper dramatics
- Pantomime orchestra
- Personality machine
- Phonograph record
- The picnic
- Pilgrim's first Thanksgiving
- Pony express
- Ride of Paul Revere
- Salesman!
- Setting the table
- Slow-motion pantomime
- Sour notes
- Stagecoach stop
- Strong man
- Super sale
- Take-turners
- Telephone chuckles
- Television tricks
- Tennis match
- Texas cowboy
- Waiter!
- Washington at Valley Forge
- Wild dreams
- The winners
- Wrist watch

Slattery, Margaret E. King in the kitchen. In Kamerman,

S. Children's Plays from Favorite Stories. 8 char
———. Patchwork princess. In Kamerman, S. Children's Plays from Favorite Stories. 7 char
———. Queen's mirror. In Kamerman, S. Fifty Plays for Junior Actors. 10 char
———. Royal magic. In Kamerman, S. Children's Plays from Favorite Stories. 7 char

SLAVERY
 Barbee, L. Letter to Lincoln
 Henderson, N. Get on board, little children

SLEEP
 Bennett, H. Sleeping beauty
 Boylan, E. Rip Van Winkle
 Howard, V. Return of Rip Van Winkle
 Irving, W. Rip Van Winkle
 MacLellan, E. Cross princess

Sleeping beauty. Bennett, H.
Sleeping beauty. Perrault, C.
Sleeping mountains. Winther, B.
Slingluff, Mary O. Naughty Susan. In Kamerman, S. Little Plays for Little People. 7 char
Slow-motion pantomime. Howard, V.
Small crimson parasol. Boiko, C.
Small shoes and small tulips. MacLellan, E.
Smith, Frank Hart. Rhyme's the crime or the verse is yet to come. In McGee, C. Drama for Fun. 7 char
Smith, Gladys V. Star Light and the sandman. In Kamerman, S. Little Plays for Little Players. 17 char
———. The tiger, the brahman, and the jackal. In Kamerman, S. Dramatized Folk Tales of the World. 9 char
Smith, Jean Shannon, and Mercedes Gardner. King Midas. In Kamerman, S. Dramatized Folk Tales of the World. 5 char+

SMITH, JOHN
 Roberts, H. Pocahontas, the tomboy princess
 Walsh, H. Jamestown

Smith, Mary. Best gift of all. In Burack, A. Christmas Plays for Young Actors. 5 char+
Smithtown U.S.A. Carlson, B.

SMOG
 Shore, M. Catastrophe Clarence

SMUGGLING
 Howard, V. Treasure of Monte Cristo

SNAKES
 Malone, M. Last snake in Ireland

SNOBBERY
    Martin, P. Invitation to supper
    Pope, A. Belinda bemoans the loss of a lock of her hair
    Vanbrugh, Sir J. Lord Foppington's day
Snow White. Cable, H. (Play title: Fairest pitcher of them all)
Snow White. Jacob, E.
Snow White. King, W.
Snow White and friends. Cheatham, V.
Snow-white and Rose-Red. Bennett, R.
Snow White and the seven dwarfs. Mahlmann, L.
Snowflake. Boiko, C.
Snowman who overstayed. Boiko, C.
Snowman who played Santa. Bennett, R.
SOCIETY
    Nolan, P. In-group
Sofapillio. McGee, C.
SOLAR SYSTEM
    Melchior, H. Visit to the planets
    Rittenhouse, C. Children of the sun
SOLDIERS
    Anderson, H. The tinderbox
    Dumas, A. The duel
    Stevenson, R. Sire de Maletroit's door
SOLOMON, KING
    Whitworth, V. King and the bee
Son come home. Bullins, E.
Son of liberty. Lipnik, E.
Son of William Tell. Nolan, P.
Song goes forth. Boiko, C.
SONGS
    Boiko, C. Song goes forth
    Hollingsworth, L. Silent night
    Nolan, P. America is a song
    _____. Golden voice of Little Erik
    _____. Highland fling
SORROW
    Hale, E. Man without a country
Sorry, wrong number. Fletcher, L.
Soul gone home. Hughes, L.
SOUP
    Alexander, S. What's in my soup?
    Buechler, J. Stone soup
    Leuser, E. Mixing stick
    Peterson, M. Soup stone
Soup stone. Peterson, M.

Sour notes. Howard, V.
THE SOUTH
    Ward, D. Day of absence
    see also APPALACHIA
SPACE
    Lane, M. Is there life on other planets?
    see also SOLAR SYSTEM
SPACE FANTASY
    Boiko, C. Book that saved the earth
    ———————. Pandora's perilous predicament
    ———————. Take me to your marshal
    Dias, E. Little man who wasn't there
SPACE FLIGHT
    Anderson, R. Trouble in outer space
    Boiko, C. Spaceship Santa Maria
    Harper, J. First cat on Mars
    MacGregor, E. Miss Pickerell goes to Mars
Space talk. Howard, V.
Spaceship Santa Maria. Boiko, C.
SPAIN
    Bennett, R. The plot
    Corson, H. Dame Fortune and Don Money
    Lorca, F. Billy-club puppets
    MacLellan, E. Return of the Nina
    Myrick, N. Day is bright
    Nolan, P. Magic of Salamanca
    Roberts, H. For the glory of Spain
Spamer, Claribel. Bunnyland brigade. In Kamerman, S. Little Plays for Little People. 8 char
———————. Candy canes. In Burack, A. Christmas Plays for Young Actors. 5 char
———————. Dwarfs' beards. In Kamerman, S. Children's Plays from Favorite Stories. 5 char
———————. Pop-up books. In Kamerman, S. Little Plays for Little Players. 14 char
———————. Pot of gold. In Burack, A. One Hundred Plays for Children. 9 char
———————. Shy prince. In Kamerman, S. Little Plays for Little Players. 8 char
Spasm in three speeds. McGee, C.
Special edition. Fisher, A.
Sperling, Louise. Baby bird. In Martin, J. Little Plays for Little People. 2 char
———————. Day Canary met Sparrow. In Martin, J. Little Plays for Little People. 2 char
SPIDERS
    Bennett, R. Magic weaver

SPIES

   _____. Miss Muffet and the spider
   St. Clair, R. Miss Muffet's wish
SPIES
   Fontaine, R. United spies
   Murray, J. Airport adventure
   Olfson, L. Spying high
   Walsh, H. The spy
SPIES--INDUSTRIAL
   Dias, E. Madison Avenue merry-go-round
   Murray, J. Spies and dolls
Spies and dolls. Murray, J.
SPINNING
   Very, A. Tom Tit Tot
Spirit of Christmas. Fisher, A.
Spirit of Christmas. St. Clair, R.
SPORTS
   Cable, H. Best of sports
Spouse for Susie Mouse. Head, F.
SPRING
   Bennett, R. Magic weaver
   _____. School for scamperers
   _____. Waking the daffodil
   Boiko, C. Crocus who couldn't bloom
   _____. May basket fantasia
   _____. Next stop--spring!
   _____. Number one Apple Tree Lane
   _____. Snowman who overstayed
   _____. Sun up!
   Carlson, B. Happy nesting
   _____. Trailing arbutus
   Gould, J. Seven little seeds
   Hark, M. Rainbow colors
   _____. Spring is here
   _____. Visit of Johnny Appleseed
   Wilson, M. First flowers
Spring is here. Hark, M.
Spunky Punky. Miller, H.
The spy. Walsh, H.
Spying high. Olfson, L.
Spyri, Johanna. Heidi. In Thane, A. Plays from Famous
  Stories and Fairy Tales. 11 char
   _____. Heidi finds the way. In Durrell, D. Favorite
   Plays for Classroom Reading. 11 char
Staff of life. Howard, V.
Stagecoach. Howard, V.
Stagecoach stop. Howard, V.
Stand-in. McGee, C.

STANDISH, MILES
    Ramsey, H. In the name of Miles Standish
Stanislaw and the wolf. Nolan, P.
Star bright. Boiko, C.
Star light and the sandman. Smith, G.
Starring you. Pylant, A.
STARS
    Sanderlin, O. Follow the North Star
STATUE OF LIBERTY
    Miller, A. Grandpa and the statue
STEALING see THIEVES
Steinbeck, John. Leader of the people. In Maloney, H. Plays to Remember. 6 char
Stevenson, Robert Lewis. Kidnapping of David Balfour. In Olfson, L. Classics Adopted for Acting and Reading. 10 char
_____. Sire de Maletroit's door. In Gilfond, H. Plays for Reading. 5 char
_____. Treasure Island. In Burack, A. Popular Plays for Classroom Reading. 10 char
Stockton, Frank. Lady or the tiger? In Gilfond, H. Plays for Reading. 8 char; in Olfson, L. Dramatized Classics for Radio-Style Reading, Vol. II. 11 char
Stockton, Frank R. Old Pipes. In Smith, M. 7 Plays and How to Produce Them. 12 char+
_____. Transferred ghost. In Olfson, L. Classics Adopted for Acting and Reading. 5 char
Stolen tarts. Molloy, L.
Stone soup. Buechler, J.
Stone soup. Peterson, M. (Play title: Soup stone)
Story of a well. Fisher, A.
Story of Gransel and Hettal. Sayers, N.
Story of Rama and Sita. Cochrane, L.
Strange tale of King Midas. Howard, V.
Streacker, Lucille. Bob's armistice parade. In Burack, A. One Hundred Plays for Children. 12 char+
_____. No-mother land. In Kamerman, S. Little Plays for Little Players. 8 char
Streak o' lean. Lincoln, A.
STRENGTH
    Jarvis, S. Sun and the wind
Strong man. Howard, V.
Stuart, Mike. Abigail stands fast. In McGee, C. Drama for Fun. 5 char
STUDENTS
    Fontaine, R. Carefree high school orchestra
    _____. Graduation address

STUFF 154

  see also SCHOOL
Stuff of heroes. Hark, M.
Suerken, Ernst H. John Crown's legacy. In Burack, A.
 Four-Star Plays for Boys. 26 char
SUICIDE
  Shakespeare, W. Cleopatra's death scene
  ————. To be or not to be
SUMMER
  Bennett, R. French doll's surprise
  ————. King's holiday
  ————. Miss Muffet and the spider
  Carlson, B. Summer maker
Summer maker. Carlson, B.
Sun and the wind. Jarvis, S.
Sun up! Boiko, C.
Super sale. Howard, V.
Supermarket blues. Fontaine, R.
SUPERNATURAL
  Bierce, A. Shipwreck
  Dunsany, L. Jest of Hahalaba
  Geiger, M. In the fog
  see also FANTASY
SUPERSTITION
  Martens, A. Thirteen
Supper in silence. Howard, V.
Supper with the queen. Jarvis, S.
Surprise for Mr. Winkle. McKay, H.
Surprise party. Dorand, J.
SURPRISES
  Barbee, L. Holly hangs high
  Dias, E. Treasure at Bentley Inn
  McKay, H. Surprise for Mr. Winkle
  Nolan, P. Anton Chekhov sort of evening
Susan goes to Hollywood. Wilde, C.
SUSPENSE
  Chisholm, J. Enchanted I'm sure
  D'Aulnoy, Mme. Princess Rosette
  Fletcher, L. Sorry, wrong number
  Hill, K. Midnight burial
  Lello, E. Mystery at Tumble Inn
  Miller, S. Dangerous game
  Murray, J. Case of mistaken identity
  Stevenson, R. Treasure Island
  Stockton, F. Lady or the tiger?
Sweetie-weeties! Fontaine, R.
The swineherd. Andersen, H.
Swintz, Martha. King's creampuffs. In Burack, A. One

Hundred Plays for Children. 9 char
   _____. Panic in the palace. In Kamerman, S. Children's Plays from Favorite Stories. 13 char+
   _____. Posies for the potentate. In Kamerman, S. Fifty Plays for Junior Actors. 7 char+
   _____. Three wishing bags. In Kamerman, S. Children's Plays from Favorite Stories. 9 char+
Swiss family Robinson. Wyss, J.
Swiss mystery. MacLellan, E.
SWITZERLAND
    MacLellan, E. Swiss mystery
    Nolan, P. Son of William Tell
    Roberts, H. Test for William Tell
    Spyri, J. Heidi
    _____. Heidi finds the way
    Stockton, F. Old pipes
    White, A. May I woo the lassie?

- T -

T for turkey. Hark, M.
The "T" party. Boiko, C.
TAILORS
    Gregg, L. Miniature darzis
    Thane, A. Brave little tailor
Take it from the beginning. Nolan, P.
Take me to your marshal. Boiko, C.
The take-overs. Howard, V.
Tale of two drummers. Boiko, C.
Talent tree. Brown, T.
TALKING
    Nicholson, M. Princess Nimblewit
Tall-tale tournament. Boiko, C.
Tamburlaine the Great. Marlowe, C. (Play title: Death of Zenocrate)
Taming of the shrew. Shakespeare, W.
Taming of the shrew. Shakespeare, W. (Play title: Katherina's obedience)
Tausheck, Ruthe Massion. Saga of Davey Rocket. In Kamerman, S. Fifty Plays for Junior Actors. 7 char
TAX EVASION
    Weik, M. The bridge
Taylor, Jill. Lazy leprechaun. In Ross, L. Holiday Puppets. 6 char+
Taylor, Loren E. Baseball. In Taylor, L. Stunts and Skits. 3 char

TEACHERS   156

    ————. Comedy skit. In Taylor, L. Stunts and Skits.
2 char
    ————. Doctor's office. In Taylor, L. Stunts and Skits.
3 char
    ————. Don't be afraid. In Taylor, L. Stunts and Skits.
5 char
    ————. Gold detector. In Taylor, L. Stunts and Skits.
6 char
    ————. How to live long. In Taylor, L. Stunts and
Skits. 4 char
    ————. Not for one sandwich. In Taylor, L. Stunts and
Skits. 3 char
    ————. Poetry. In Taylor, L. Stunts and Skits. 2 char
    ————. Say, Dad. In Taylor, L. Stunts and Skits. 2
char
    ————. The telephone. In Taylor, L. Stunts and Skits.
3 char
    ————. $25,000. In Taylor, L. Stunts and Skits. 2
char

TEACHERS
    Hark, M. When do we eat?
    Leuser, E. Honored one
Teapot trouble. Nicholson, J.
Teddy bear hero. Miller, H.
Teen and twenty. Dorand, J.

TEENAGERS
    Cable, H. Best of sports
    ————. Last stop
    Dias, E. Ballad for the sky
    ————. Landslide for Shakespeare
    ————. Little man who wasn't there
    ————. Madison Avenue merry-go-round
    ————. The mantle
    ————. Printer's devil
    Dorand, J. Teen and twenty
    French, D. Mud pack madness
    Heinzen, B. Miss Cast
    Lello, E. Mystery at Tumble Inn
    Manning, S. Background for Nancy
    Nolan, P. Going steady
    ————. Hi down there
    ————. What's zymurgy with you?
    Ward, M. Family affair
    Wilde, C. Junior prom
    see also YOUNG MEN; YOUNG WOMEN

TEETH
    Fisher, A. King's toothache

The telephone. Taylor, L.
Telephone chuckles. Howard, V.
TELEVISION
    Dias, E. Hippie and the bard
    ───────. Video Christmas
    Fontaine, R. It's frightening!
    ───────. Sweetie-weeties!
Television tricks. Howard, V.
TELL, WILLIAM
    Nolan, P. Son of William Tell
    Roberts, H. Test for William Tell
TEMPER
    Howard, H. Ben Franklin, peace-maker
    Shakespeare, W. Taming of the shrew
The tempest. Shakespeare, W.
Ten pennies for Lincoln. Miller, H.
Ten-penny tragedy. Elfenbeim, J.
The $10,000 dog. Carlson, B.
The ten-year-old detective. Olfson, L.
TENNIS
    Chisholm, J. Prince is where you find him
    Howard, V. Tennis match
Tennis match. Howard, V.
Tennyson, Alfred. Enoch Arden. In Olfson, L. Classics Adopted for Acting and Reading. 6 char
TERRELL, MARY CHURCH
    Branch, W. To follow the phoenix
Terrible Terry's surprise. Boiko, C.
The test. Tobey, L.
Test for a witch. MacLellan, E.
Test for William Tell. Roberts, H.
TEXAS
    Carlson, B. Ghosts
Texas cowboy. Howard, V.
Texas roundup. Howard, V.
Thane, Adele. Aladdin and his wonderful lamp. In Thane, A. Plays from Famous Stories and Fairy Tales. 11 char
───────. Baker's neighbor. In Kamerman, S. Dramatized Folk Tales of the World. 10 char+
───────. Big Paul Bunyan. In Kamerman, S. Dramatized Folk Tales of the World. 12 char+
───────. Brave little tailor. In Thane, A. Plays from Famous Stories and Fairy Tales. 19 char+
───────. Brownie who found Christmas. In Kamerman, S. Fifty Plays for Holidays. 11 char+
───────. Cinderella. In Thane, A. Plays from Famous

THANKFUL 158

  Stories and Fairy Tales. 15 char+
 _____. Dick Whittington and his cat. In Thane, A.
Plays from Famous Stories and Fairy Tales. 9 char+
 _____. Dummling and the golden goose. In Thane, A.
Plays from Famous Stories and Fairy Tales. 28 char+
 _____. Elves and the shoemaker. In Thane, A. Plays from Famous Stories and Fairy Tales. 16 char
 _____. Gift for Hans Brinker. In Kamerman, S. Dramatized Folk Tales of the World. 15 char
 _____. Hansel and Gretel. In Thane, A. Plays from Famous Stories and Fairy Tales. 7 char+
 _____. Jack and the magic beanstalk. In Thane, A. Plays from Famous Stories and Fairy Tales. 10 char+
 _____. King Alfred and the cakes. In Thane, A. Plays from Famous Stories and Fairy Tales. 9 char
 _____. King who was bored. In Kamerman, S. Dramatized Folk Tales of the World. 12 char
 _____. Magic nutmeg-grater. In Durrell, D. Favorite Plays for Classroom Reading. 13 char; in Thane, A. Plays from Famous Stories and Fairy Tales. 9 char+
 _____. Merry Tyll and the three rogues. In Kamerman, S. Dramatized Folk Tales of the World. 24 char+
 _____. Rapunzel. In Thane, A. Plays from Famous Stories and Fairy Tales. 10 char
 _____. Rumpelstiltskin. In Thane, A. Plays from Famous Stories and Fairy Tales. 11 char
 _____. Saucy scarecrow. In Thane, A. Plays from Famous Stories and Fairy Tales. 14 char+
 _____. Three wishes. In Thane, A. Plays from Famous Stories and Fairy Tales. 8 char
 _____. Twelve dancing princesses. In Thane, A. Plays from Famous Stories and Fairy Tales. 17 char
Thankful indeed. Howard, H.
Thankful's red beads. Miller, H.
Thanks a million. Fisher, A.
Thanks to Sammy Scarecrow. Howard, H.
THANKSGIVING
  Bennett, R. Beaded moccasins
  _____. Fire-face and the Indians
  _____. Thanksgiving pageant
  Boiko, C. Long table
  _____. Meet the pilgrims
  Cable, H. Peace, pilgrim
  Cooper, E. Little white cloud
  DuBois, G. Governor Bradford's scissors
  Fisher, A. Mother of Thanksgiving
  _____. Unexpected guests

THANKSGIVING

Garver, J. Turkey, anyone?
Gould, J. Thanksgiving is for everybody
Hark, M. Many thanks
———. Newfangled Thanksgiving
———. Nothing to be thankful for
———. T for turkey
Howard, H. I'll share my fare
———. Thanks to Sammy Scarecrow
Howard, V. Pilgrims' first Thanksgiving
Kingman, L. Mr. Thanks has his day
Leuser, E. D. Thanksgiving scarecrow
Miller, H. All-American thank you
———. Broadway turkey
———. Horn of plenty
———. Thankful's red beads
———. Thanksgiving riddle
Ramsey, H. In the name of Miles Standish
Rawls, J. Pilgrim painting
Very, A. Jonathan's Thanksgiving
Thanksgiving is for everybody. Gould, J.
Thanksgiving pageant. Bennett, R.
Thanksgiving riddle. Miller, H.
Thanksgiving scarecrow. Leuser, E. D.

THEATER
Nolan, P. Take it from the beginning
Schaaf, A. Jump for Joy
There's always a leader. Carlson, B.

THIEVES
Asbrand, A. China comes to you
Boiko, C. Lady Moon and the thief
Carlson, B. Justice for all
———. Shut the door
Chekhov, A. The upheaval
Colson, J. Message from Robin Hood
Dias, E. Cleanest town in the west
Dickens, C. Martin Chuzzlewit
———. Oliver Twist
Doyle, A. Sherlock Holmes and the red-headed league
Felsheim, J. Ali Baba and the forty thieves
Greth, R. Two masks
Huff, B. Case of the missing masterpiece
Lello, E. Mystery at Tumble Inn
MacFarlan, E. Olive jar
Miller, H. Paper bag mystery
———. Shirley Holmes and the FBI
Murray, J. I want to report a murder
———. Impossible room

THIRTEEN

    Nolan, P. Boshibari and the two thieves
Thirteen. Martens, A.
Thomson, Joyce. Pepi and Sombrero. In Philpott, A. Eight Plays for Hand Puppets. 5 char
Three and the dragon. Fisher, A.
Three aunts. Rowland, E.
Three billy goats gruff. Boylan, E.
Three kings. Ross, L.
Three little kittens. Barr, J.
Three little kittens. Miller, H.
Three little pigs. Olfson, L. (Play title: Three swine of most small stature)
Three royal r's. Pyle, M.
Three sillies. Sanders, S.
Three sillies. Very, A.
Three swine of most small stature. Olfson, L.
Three terrors. Bennett, R.
Three wishes. Burlingame, C.
Three wishes. Thane, A.
Three wishes for mother. Hark, M.
Three wishing bags. Swintz, M.

THRIFT

    Asbrand, K. What's a penny?
    Boiko, C. Penny wise
Through the looking glass. Carroll, L.
Tichenor, Tom. Jack and the beanstalk. In Tichenor, T. Tom Tichenor's Puppets. 11 char
Tiger and the brahman. Simon, S.
Tiger catcher. McFarlan, E.
Tiger, the brahman, and the jackal. Smith, G.
Tiger's bones. Hughes, T.

TIME

    Boiko, C. Marvelous time machine
    _____. Peter, Peter, Peter!
    Faux, D. Littlest month
    Fox, D. Littlest month
    Hark, M. Johnnie Jump Up
    Miller, H. Real princess
    _____. Trouble in Tick Tock Town
    Oser, J. King's calendar
Time for Mom. Fisher, A.
Time of my life. Howard, V.
Time out for Christmas. Fisher, A.
The tinderbox. Andersen, H.
Tiniest heart. Watts, F.
To be or not to be. Shakespeare, W.
To build a federal city. Carlson, B.

To follow the phoenix. Branch, W.
To kill a devil. Furman, R.
To play the piano. Carlson, B.
To the moon. Fontaine, R.
TOADS see FROGS AND TOADS
Tobey, Loretta Capell. The test. In Burack, A. One Hundred Plays for Children. 11 char+
Toles, Myriam. We, the people. In Kamerman, S. Fifty Plays for Holidays. 22 char+
Tolstoy, Leo. How much land does a man need? In Burack, A. Popular Plays for Classroom Reading. 8 char
———. Little girls wiser than men. In Gilfond, H. Plays for Reading. 12 char
Tom Sawyer. Twain, M. (Play title: Tragedy in the graveyard)
Tom Sawyer and Injun Joe. Twain, M.
Tom Sawyer, pirate. Twain, M.
Tom Tit Tot. Very, A.
Tomboy and the dragon. Miller, H.
Tommy's adventure. Leuser, E.
Tongue-cut sparrow. Cappell, L.
Too many kittens. Hark, M.
Too much of a good thing. Parsons, M.
Top of the bill. Colson, J.
Touch one. Carlson, B.
TOURISTS
 Cable, H. Bailey, go home
Town mouse and his country cousin. Muse, V.
Toy scout jamboree. Miller, H.
TOYS
 Arnold, E. Make him smile
 Bennett, R. French doll's surprise
 ———. What will the toys say?
 Fisher, A. Time out for Christmas
 Hark, M. Christmas party
 ———. Santa Claus parade
 Howard, H. Christmas train
 Miller, H. Christmas peppermints
TRADITIONS
 Dias, E. The mantle
TRAGEDY
 Brontë, E. Wuthering Heights
 Homer. The Iliad
 Hughes, L. Soul gone home
 Love, S. Moby Dick
 Shakespeare, W. Hamlet
 ———. Julius Caesar

TRAGEDY 162

    _____. Macbeth
    _____. Romeo and Juliet
    Tennyson, A. Enoch Arden
Tragedy in the graveyard. Sanders, S.
Trailing arbutus. Carlson, B.
TRAINS
    Carlson, B. Golden spike
    Howard, H. Christmas train
Transferred ghost. Stockton, F.
TRANSPORTATION
    Boiko, C. Anywhere and everywhere
TRASH
    Carlson, B. Marked trail
    Nolan, P. Trash and treasure
Trash and treasure. Nolan, P.
TREASON
    Colson, J. Message from Robin Hood
    Hale, E. Man without a country
    Love, S. Fifth of November
    Reines, B. Turncoat
    Shakespeare, W. Julius Caesar
    _____. Macbeth
TREASURE
    Carlson, B. My treasure
    Dias, E. Treasure at Bentley Inn
    Glass, G. Ghost town treasure
    Howard, V. Treasure of Monte Cristo
    MacLellan, E. Swiss mystery
    Stevenson, R. Treasure Island
Treasure at Bentley Inn. Dias, E.
Treasure hunt. Fisher, A.
Treasure in the Smith house. Barnett, G.
Treasure Island. Stevenson, R.
Treasure of Monte Cristo. Howard, V.
Tree to the sky. Nolan, P.
Tree toad loved a she-toad. In McGee, C. Drama for Fun.
    2 char+
TREES
    Boiko, C. Hotel Oak
    _____. Trouble in tree-land
    Hark, M. Day for trees
    McCarty, S. Tree friends
    Oser, J. Weeping willow's happy day
Trial of Billy Scott. Hall, M.
Trial of Mother Goose. Miller, H.
TRIALS
    Murray, J. Sixth juror

TRICKERY

    Boiko, C. Christmas revel
    Carlson, B. Why catch a leprechaun?
    D'Aulnoy, Mme. Princess Rosette
    Dias, E. Dear Lottie
    ———— . Treasure at Bentley Inn
    Elfenbeim, J. King who couldn't be fooled
    ———— . Puss-in-boots
    Felsheim, J. Ali Baba and the forty thieves
    Foley, M. Emperor's new robes
    Hall, M. King Horn
    Howard, H. Magic jack-o-lantern
    Jacob, E. Robin Hood tricks the sheriff
    Jarvis, S. M. Fisherman and the elf
    ———— . Honey and dough
    ———— . Mitten tree
    ———— . Two silly wolves
    Leuser, E. D. Wise people of Gotham
    Love, S. One-eyed giant
    McFarlan, E. Pear tree
    McGee, C. Can'tsee Poorsight
    Malone, M. Last snake in Ireland
    Nolan, P. Boshibari and the two thieves
    ———— . Magic of Salamanca
    ———— . Robin Hood and the match at Nottingham
    ———— . Young man of considerable value
    Peterson, M. Soup stone
    Smith, G. Tiger, the brahman, and the jackal
    Stevenson, R. Kidnapping of David Balfour
    Thane, A. Brave little tailor
    ———— . Merry Tyll and the three rogues
    Very, A. Puss-in-boots
    Walker, B. Rabbit and the wolf
    ———— . Which piece is mine?
    Weik, M. The bridge
    Whitman, C. School for jesters
    Wilde, O. Importance of being earnest
Trip to Mexico. McGee, C.
!Trip-trap! trip-trap! Jarvis, S. M.
Triumph for Trimbly. Murray, J.
Triumph for two. Corson, H.

TROJAN WAR

    Homer. The Iliad.

TROLLS

    Jarvis, S. M. !Trip-trap! trip-trap!
Trouble in outer space. Anderson, R.
Trouble in Tick-tock Town. Miller, H.

Trouble in tree-land. Boiko, C.
TRUTH AND FALSEHOOD
    Andersen, H. The swineherd
    Carter, S. One last look
    Cervantes, M. Don Quixote
    Collodi, C. Pinocchio
    _____. Pinocchio goes to school
    Dias, E. Hippie and the bard
    Foley, M. Emperor's new robes
    Hansberry, L. Raisin in the sun
    Hughes, T. Tiger's bones
    Ibsen, H. Peer Gynt leaves Solveig
    Ionesco, E. The leader
    Leuser, E. Honored one
    Miller, H. Birthday pie
    _____. Magic cookie jar
    _____. Mount Vernon cricket
    Musil, R. Peach tree kingdom
    Reines, B. Turncoat
    Saki. Open Window
    Ward, M. Mr. Lazy Man's family
    see also HONESTY
Try data-date! Olfson, L.
TURKEY [nation]
    Bealmear, J. Covetous councilman
Turkey anyone? Garver, J.
Turkeys are tricky. Jarvis, S. M.
Turn south at Voorhee's farm. Carlson, B.
Turnbull, Lucia. Magic shoes. In Kamerman, S. Children's Plays from Favorite Stories. 7 char
Turncoat. Reines, B.
Turning the tables. Fisher, A.
A turtle, a flute, and the general's birthday. Davis, L.
TURTLES
    Jarvis, S. M. Why the turtle does not talk
Twain, Mark. Celebrated jumping frog of Calaveras County. In Gilfond, H. Plays for Reading. 6 char
_____. Prince and the pauper. In Durrell, D. Favorite Plays for Classroom Reading. 22 char
_____. Tragedy in the graveyard. In Sanders, S. Creating Plays with Children. 8 char+
_____. Tom Sawyer and Injun Joe. In Olfson, L. Dramatized Classics for Radio-Style Reading, Vol. II. 13 char+
_____. Tom Sawyer, pirate. In Burack, A. Popular Plays for Classroom Reading. 13 char; in Thane, A. Plays from Famous Stories and Fairy Tales. 12 char

TWELFTH NIGHT--ROCK VERSION
    Driver, D. Your own thing
Twelve dancing princesses. Thane, A.
$25,000. Taylor, L.
Twin cousins. Schwartz, M.
TWINS
    Schwartz, M. Twin cousins
    Shakespeare, W. Comedy of errors
Two frogs. In McGee, C. Drama for Fun. 2 char+
Two masks. Greth, R.
Two noble kinsmen. Fletcher, J. (Play title: Jailer's daughter falls in love with a prince)
Two silly wolves. Jarvis, S. M.
Two strangers from Nazareth. DuBois, G.

- U -

ULYSSES
    Love, S. One-eyed giant
Unexpected guests. Fisher, A.
UNHAPPINESS
    Ibsen, H. Aase searches for her son
Unhappy Santa. Simonds, N.
UNITED NATIONS
    Biggs, L. Key to understanding
    Fisher, A. Play without a name
    _____. Three and the dragon
    _____. United Nations Plays and Programs
United spies. Fontaine, R.
UNITED STATES
    Rybak, R. Day the moonmen landed
    Thane, A. Big Paul Bunyan
    Whittaker, H. Gift from Johnny Appleseed
UNITED STATES--HISTORY
    Barbee, L. Flag of the United States
    Carlson, B. Golden spike
    _____. Impossible! unacceptable! preposterous!
    _____. Turn south at Voorhees' farm
    Fisher, A. Mother of Thanksgiving
    Hall, M. Hearts of oak
    Miller, H. Old Glory grows up
    Nolan, P. America is a song
    Suerken, E. John Crown's legacy
    Walsh, H. Six Plays in American History
    see also particular events, people in U.S. history

UNITY

    Biggs, L.   Key to understanding
    Fisher, A. Caves of the earth
    _____. Invasion from the stratosphere
    Rybak, R. Day the moonmen landed

UNSELFISHNESS

    Barbee, L. Friday foursome packs a box
    Brontë, C. Jane Eyre
    Carroll, G. Merry, merry, merry
    Dias, E. Landslide for Shakespeare
    Fisher, A. Angel in the looking-glass
    _____. Merry Christmas elf
    Hark, M. Magic egg
    Howard, H. Mother's gift
    Leuser, E. Big stone
    _____. Magic well
    Miller, S. Dangerous game
    Nathan, B. If wishes were horses
    Nicholson, M. Wise wife
    Nolan, P. Johnny Appleseed
    _____. Leak in the dike
    _____. Licha's birthday present
    _____. Our sister, Sitya
    _____. Skill of Pericles
    Paradis, M. Santa goes to town
    Pyle, M. Perambulating pie
    St. Clair, R. Spirit of Christmas
    Smith, M. Best gift of all
    Tennyson, A. Enoch Arden
    Walsh, H. Benjamin Franklin
    _____. The spy
    see also KINDNESS

Unusual flower. Graham, M.
The upheaval. Chekhov, A.
Urban, Catherine. Queen with the broken heart. In Burack, A. One Hundred Plays for Children. 6 char; in Kamerman, S. Little Plays for Little Players. 6 char
    _____. Who started the fire? In Durrell, D. Thirty Plays for Classroom Reading. 9 char

- V -

Vahl, Rod. Indian boy without a name. In Kamerman, S. Dramatized Folk Tales of the World. 8 char
Valentine for Kate. Miller, H.
Valentine for Mary. Bennett, R.

Valentine stardust. Nicholson, J.
Valentine tree. Barrows, M.
Valentines. Howard, V.
Valentine's day. Duvall, L.
VALENTINE'S DAY
    Barrows, M. Valentine tree
    Bennett, R. Littlest artist
    ――――――. Prince of hearts
    ――――――. Valentine for Mary
    Duvall, L. Valentine's day
    Fisher, A. Hearts, tarts, and valentines
    ――――――. New hearts for old
    Hark, M. Cupid's post office
    McKay, H. Surprise for Mr. Winkle
    Miller, H. Cupid in demand
    ――――――. Shower of hearts
    ――――――. Valentine for Kate
    Nicholson, J. Valentine stardust
    Urban, C. Queen with the broken heart
    Very, A. What happened to the cakes
    Watts, F. Tiniest heart
The valiant. Hall, H.
Vanbrugh, John. Lord Foppington's day (The relapse) In
    Kline, P. Theatre Student: Scenes to Perform. 1 char
Vandevere, J. Lilian. Mother Goose gives a dinner. In
    Kamerman, S. Little Plays for Little Players. 10 char
Van Druten, John. I remember Mama. In Picozzi, R.
    Plays to Enjoy. 9 char
Van Dyke, Mary, and Edna Conrad. Show boat. In Conrad,
    E. History on the Stage. 21 char+
VANITY
    Asbrand, K. Adalmina's pearl
    Leuser, E. Five brothers
Verne, Jules. Around the world in eighty days. In Olfson,
    L. Classics Adopted for Acting and Reading. 19 char
――――――. Five weeks in a balloon. In Olfson, L. Drama-
    tized Classics for Radio-Style Reading. 8 char
VERSE PLAYS
    Asbrand, K. What's a penny?
    Barbee, L. Columbus sails the sea
    ――――――. Princess who couldn't dance
    Barr, J. Cinderella
    ――――――. Lion and the mouse
    ――――――. Old Mother Hubbard
    ――――――. Rapunzel
    ――――――. Three little kittens
    Bellah, M. Blue toadstool

VERSE   168

Bennett, R.   Beaded moccasins
    _____.   Christmas pie
    _____.   City mouse and the country mouse
    _____.   Fire-face and the Indians
    _____.   First Easter eggs
    _____.   French doll's surprise
    _____.   Hare and the tortoise
    _____.   Lion and the mouse
    _____.   Littlest artist
    _____.   Miss Muffett and the spider
    _____.   On New Year's Eve
    _____.   Out of the clock
    _____.   Pixie in a trap
    _____.   Prince of hearts
    _____.   Pudding-bag string
    _____.   Rainbow's end
    _____.   Runaway pirate
    _____.   Santa's send-off
    _____.   Scarecrow and the witch
    _____.   Snowman who played Santa
    _____.   Three terrors
    _____.   Waking the daffodil
    _____.   Ye olden festival of Christmas
Boiko, C.   Anywhere and everywhere
    _____.   Lion to lamb
    _____.   Sun up!
Browning, R. My last duchess
Colbo, E.   Littlest fir
Everyman's prayer
Fisher, A.   Christmas cake
    _____.   Ghosts on guard
    _____.   Mother's Day off and on
    _____.   New hearts for old
    _____.   On Halloween
    _____.   Spirit of Christmas
    _____.   Three and the dragon
    _____.   Treasure hunt
    _____.   Unexpected guests
    _____.   Way to Norwich
Fletcher, J. Jailer's daughter falls in love with a prince
Hark, M.   Cupid's post office
    _____.   Five senses
    _____.   Nursery rhyme diet
    _____.   Pleasant dreams
    _____.   Rainbow colors
    _____.   Santa Claus parade

_____. Visit of Johnny Appleseed
Hughes, T. Coming of the kings
_____. Orpheus
Kane, E. Elves and the shoemaker
McGee, C. Romance of Minnie Martin or it shouldn't happen to a dog
Marlowe, C. Death of Zenocrate
Menotti, G. Amahl and the night visitors
Miller, H. Busy barbers
Milton, J. Eve decides to eat the fruit of the tree of knowledge
Newman, D. Green Leaf's lesson
_____. Mrs. Santa's Christmas gift
Nutter, C. Red Riding Hood and the wolf
Pope, A. Belinda bemoans the loss of a lock of her hair
Preston, C. Born in a stable
Richards, L. With all my heart
Rostand, E. Nose speech
Shakespeare, W. Cleopatra's death scene
_____. Katherina's obedience
_____. Lady Macbeth receives a letter from her husband
_____. Richard alone
_____. To be or not to be
Smith, F. Rhyme's the crime or the verse is yet to come
Vandevere, J. Mother Goose gives a dinner
Very, A. Boy who could not tell a lie
_____. Everywhere Christmas
_____. Gift of the fairies
_____. Golden bell for mother
_____. Three sillies
_____. What happened to the cakes
Woster, A. All houses are haunted
Very, Alice. Boy who could not tell a lie. In Kamerman, S. Little Plays for Little Players. 6 char+
_____. Everywhere Christmas. In Burack, A. Christmas Plays for Young Actors. 24 char+
_____. Gift of the fairies. In Kamerman, S. Little Plays for Little Players. 18 char
_____. Golden bell for mother. In Burack, A. One Hundred Plays for Children. 14 char
_____. Jonathan's Thanksgiving. In Burack, A. One Hundred Plays for Children. 11 char
_____. President Lincoln's children. In Kamerman, S. Little Plays for Little Players. 6 char

VETERAN'S 170

    _____. Puss-in-boots. In Burack, A. One Hundred Plays for Children. 11 char
    _____. Three sillies. In Burack, A. One Hundred Plays for Children. 10 char+
    _____. Tom Tit Tot. In Kamerman, S. Children's Plays from Favorite Stories. 8 char+
    _____. What happened to the cakes? In Burack, A. One Hundred Plays for Children. 8 char+
VETERAN'S DAY
    Miller, H. Part-time hero
    Suerken, E. John Crown's legacy
Video Christmas. Dias, E.
View of the sea. Nolan, P.
VILLAINS
    Dias, E. Cast up by the sea
    Miller, H. Magic cookie jar
VIRGINIA
    Boiko, C. Jack Jouette's ride
VIRGINIA--HISTORY
    Walsh, H. Jamestown
Virtue is her own reward. Hervey, M.
Vision of the silver bell. Weathers, W.
Visit of Johnny Appleseed. Hark, M.
Visit to Goldilocks. Miller, H.
Visit to the planets. Melchior, H.
Visitor to Gettysburg. Dias, E.
Visitors for Nancy Hawks. Bennett, R.
VOCABULARY see WORDS
Voice of liberty. Fisher, A.
VOTING
    Fisher, A. Voice of liberty
    Murray, J. Mechanical man
    Reay N. Mr. Bates goes to the polls

- W -

WAGERS
    Twain, M. Celebrated jumping frog of Calaveras County
    Verne, J. Around the world in eighty days
Wait and see. Miller, H.
Waite, Helen E. see Hoppenstedt, Elbert M., and Helen E. Waite
Waiter! Howard, V.
Waiting for Grandma. Howard, V.
Wake up, Santa Claus! Miller, H.

Waking the daffodil. Bennett, R.
WALES
    Colson, J. Baron Barnaby's box
Walker, Barbara. Lion's den. In Martin, J. Little Plays for Little People. 4 char
─────. Rabbit and the wolf. In Martin, J. Little Plays for Little People. 3 char
─────. Which piece is mine? In Martin, J. Little Plays for Little People. 3 char
Walking with Wilma. Howard, V.
Wallace, Ruth. Case of the frustrated corpse. In Burack, A. Skits, Comedies and Farces for Teen-agers. 4 char
WALLPAPER
    Carlson, B. On myself
Walsh, Henry H. Benjamin Franklin. In Walsh, H. Six Plays in American History. 19 char+
─────. Jamestown. In Walsh, H. Six Plays in American History. 6 char
─────. Louisiana. In Walsh, H. Six Plays in American History. 12 char
─────. Mutiny on the Mayflower. In Walsh, H. Six Plays in American History. 19 char+
─────. The spy. In Walsh, H. Six Plays in American History. 17 char+
─────. Young Hickory. In Walsh, H. Six Plays in American History. 10 char+
WAR
    Miller, S. Dangerous game
    see also specific wars
Ward, Douglas Turner. Day of absence. In Childress, A. Black Scenes. 5 char+
Ward, Muriel. Family affair. In Burack, A. Skits, Comedies and Farces for Teen-agers. 9 char
─────. Mr. Lazy Man's family. In Kamerman, S. Fifty Plays for Junior Actors. 6 char
Ward, Theodore. The daubers. In Childress, A. Black Scenes. 4 char
Washington and the first flight in America. Ross, L.
Washington at Valley Forge. Howard, V.
WASHINGTON, D.C.
    Carlson, B. To build a federal city
WASHINGTON, GEORGE
    Barbee, L. Guide for George Washington
    Boiko, C. Tale of two drummers
    Clark, B. Fires at Valley Forge
    Davis, L. A turtle, a flute and the general's birthday

Dias, E. Martha Washington's spy
Fisher, A. Washington marches on
Hark, M. In honor of Washington
Howard, V. Washington at Valley Forge
MacLellan, E. Needle fights for freedom
Martens, A. George slept here, too
Miller, H. Dolly saves the day
─────. General returns
Nicholson, J. Handwriting on the wall
Roberts, H. Washington's sacrifice
Ross, L. Washington and the first flight in America
Very, A. Boy who could not tell a lie
Walsh, H. The spy
Washington marches on. Fisher, A.
WASHINGTON, MARTHA
Dias, E. Martha Washington's spy
Washington Square. James, H.
WASHINGTON'S BIRTHDAY
Barbee, L. Guide for George Washington
Davis, L. David and the second Lafayette
Fisher, A. Washington marches on
Hark, M. Enter George Washington
─────. In honor of Washington
Miller, H. Birthday pie
─────. Call Washington 1 7 7 6
─────. General returns
─────. Mount Vernon cricket
─────. Old Glory grows up
Ross, L. Washington and the first flight in America
see also WASHINGTON, GEORGE
Washington's sacrifice. Roberts, H.
Watch out for Aunt Hattie. Shore, M.
Watkins, Martha Swintz. Nobody believes in witches! In Kamerman, S. Fifty Plays for Holidays. 6 char+
Watts, Frances B. Bridge to Killybog Fair. In Kamerman, S. Dramatized Folk Tales of the World. 16 char
─────. Crimson feather. In Kamerman, S. Fifty Plays for Junior Actors. 10 char
─────. Leprechaun shoemakers. In Kamerman, S. Dramatized Folk Tales of the World. 9 char+
─────. Leprechaun's pot of gold. In Kamerman, S. Fifty Plays for Holidays. 10 char
─────. Miss Louisa and the outlaws. In Burack, A. Popular Plays for Classroom Reading. 11 char; in Kamerman, S. Fifty Plays for Junior Actors. 10 char+
─────. Santa and the efficiency expert. In Kamerman, S. Fifty Plays for Holidays. 10 char

_____. Tiniest heart. In Kamerman, S. Fifty Plays for Holidays. 15 char
Way-out Cinderella. Cable, H.
Way to Norwich. Fisher, A.
Way, way down south. Cable, H.
Wayward witch. Boiko, C.
We, the people. Toles, M.
WEATHER
    Boiko, C. Sun up!
    Miller, H. Weatherman on trial
WEATHER-SPOOF
    Fontaine, R. Fair today, followed by tomorrow
Weatherman on trial. Miller, H.
Weathers, Winston. Vision of the silver bell. In Burack, A. Christmas Plays for Young Actors. 10 char
Weaver's son. Fisher, A.
Weeping willow's happy day. Oser, J.
Weik, Mary Hays. The bridge. In Weik, M. Scarlet Thread. 19 char+
_____. King's garden. In Weik, M. Scarlet Thread. 5 char+
_____. Moonlight. In Weik, M. Scarlet Thread. 4 char+
_____. The rehearsal. In Weik, M. Scarlet Thread. 8 char
_____. River risin'! In Weik, M. Scarlet Thread. 19 char+
Welcome, parents. Cole, E.
Werner, Sally. Choosing of Easter Rabbit. In Kamerman, S. Fifty Plays for Holidays. 13 char
_____. Home, sweet home. In Burack, A. Four-Star Plays for Boys. 6 char+
_____. King's bean soup. In Kamerman, S. Children's Plays from Favorite Stories. 12 char
THE WEST
    Boiko, C. All points west
    Fontaine, R. How the West was won
    Huff, B. Ride the Gooberville stage!
    Steinbeck, J. Leader of the people
    Taylor, L. Gold detector
WHALES
    Love, S. Moby Dick
What ever happened to Mother Nature? Boiko, C.
What happened in Egypt. Fisher, A.
What happened to the cakes. Very, A.
What he deserves. Howard, H.
What is it? Carlson, B.

What will the toys say? Bennett, R.
What's a penny? Asbrand, K.
What's in my soup? Alexander, S.
What's zymurgy with you? Nolan, P.
When do we eat? Hark, M.
Where banking is a pleasure. Fontaine, R.
Where there are no snags. Carlson, B.
Which piece is mine? Walker, B.
White, Alice M. G. Bailiff's daughter of Islington. In White, A. Saucy Sailor and Other Dramatized Ballads. 10 char+
———. Crabfish. In White, A. Saucy Sailor and Other Dramatized Ballads. 5 char+
———. Deaf woman's courtship. In White, A. Saucy Sailor and Other Dramatized Ballads. 2 char
———. Eight bells. In White, A. Saucy Sailor and Other Dramatized Ballads. 5 char+
———. In Bibberley Town. In White, A. Saucy Sailor and Other Dramatized Ballads. 4 char+
———. Lazarus. In White, A. Saucy Sailor and Other Dramatized Ballads. 16 char+
———. May I woo the lassie? In White, A. Saucy Sailor and Other Dramatized Ballads. 6 char
———. My son John. In White, A. Saucy Sailor and Other Dramatized Ballads. 3 char
———. Nice girls don't chase the boys. In White, A. Saucy Sailor and Other Dramatized Ballads. 8 char+
———. Prodigal son. In White, A. Saucy Sailor and Other Dramatized Ballads. 17 char+
———. Sailor's return. In White, A. Saucy Sailor and Other Dramatized Ballads. 2 char+
———. Saucy sailor. In White, A. Saucy Sailor and Other Dramatized Ballads. 2 char
———. Willie's gane to Melville castle. In White, A. Saucy Sailor and Other Dramatized Ballads. 5 char
———. Wonderous apple tree. In White, A. Saucy Sailor and Other Dramatized Ballads. 4 char+
———. Wraggle taggle gypsies, O. In White, A. Saucy Sailor and Other Dramatized Ballads. 6 char+
Whites of their eyes. Willment, F.
Whitman, Constance. School for jesters. In Kamerman, S. Fifty Plays for Junior Actors. 10 char+
Whittaker, Helene. Gift from Johnny Appleseed. In Kamerman, S. Dramatized Folk Tales of the World. 10 char
Whitworth, Virginia Payne. King and the bee. In Kamerman, S. Dramatized Folk Tales of the World. 6 char
———. Magic cloak. In Kamerman, S. Dramatized

Folk Tales of the World. 14 char+
———. Mechanical maid. In Burack, A. Popular Plays for Classroom Reading. 8 char
Who helped the lion? Jarvis, S.
Who killed Doc Robin? Fontaine, R.
Who started the fire? Urban, C.
Who will be king? Carlson, B.
Who will bell the cat? Boiko, C.
Whole city's down there. Nolan, P.
Why catch a leprechaun? Carlson, B.
Why don't you? Carlson, B.
Why the leaves of the aspen tree quake in a breeze. Carlson, B.
Why the nightingale sings gloriously. Carlson, B.
Why the owl is sacred in Hawaii. Carlson, B.
Why the sea is salt. Mahlmann, L.
Why the turtle does not talk. Jarvis, S. M.
Wild dreams. Howard, V.
Wild flowers. Hoff, S.
Wild rabbit chase. Boiko, C.
Wild, wild west. Howard, V.
Wilde, Charles F. Comic strip antics. In Durrell, D. Teen-Age Plays for Classroom Reading. 5 char
———. Junior prom. In Burack, A. Skits, Comedies and Farces for Teen-agers. 8 char
———. Susan goes Hollywood. In Durrell, D. Teen-Age Plays for Classroom Reading. 10 char
Wilde, Oscar. Happy prince. In Durrell, D. Favorite Plays for Classroom Reading. 15 char
———. Importance of being earnest. In Olfson, L. Classics Adopted for Acting and Reading. 9 char
———. On being too frequently proposed to (Ideal husband) In Kline, P. Theatre Student: Scenes to Perform. 1 char
Wilder, Thornton. Childhood. In Swortzell, L. All the World's a Stage. 5 char
Williams, Gweneira M. Kettle of brains. In Burack, A. One Hundred Plays for Children. 4 char; in Durrell, D. Thirty Plays for Classroom Reading. 5 char
Willie's gane to Melville Castle. White, A.
Willment, Frank. Whites of their eyes. In Burack, A. Skits, Comedies and Farces for Teen-agers. 19 char; in Durrell, D. Teen-Age Plays for Classroom Reading. 20 char
Wilson, Marie Lyon. First flowers. In Kamerman, S. Little Plays for Little Players. 14 char

WIND
    Boiko, C. Lion to lamb
Wind wand. Dennis, A.
The winners. Howard, V.
WINTER
    Bennett, R. Littlest artist
    ———. Winter wizards
    Boiko, C. Snowflake
    Lehman, J. Biskie the snowman
    Nolan, P. Double nine of Chih Yuan
Winter wizards. Bennett, R.
Winther, Barbara. African trio. In Kamerman, S. Dramatized Folk Tales of the World. 10 char
    ———. Great Samurai sword. In Kamerman, S. Dramatized Folk Tales of the World. 12 char+
    ———. Sleeping mountains. In Kamerman, S. Dramatized Folk Tales of the World. 11 char
WISDOM
    Andersen, H. Emperor's nightingale
    Blumenfeld, L. Another way to weigh an elephant
    Boiko, C. Peter, Peter, Peter!
    Foley, M. Emperor's new robes
    Garver, J. Father hits the jackpot
    Hawthorne, N. Dr. Heidegger's experiment
    Holmes, R. Heir of Linne
    ———. King John and the Abbot of Canterbury
    Howard, H. Doctor Know All
    Hughes, T. Tiger's bones
    Jacob, E. Crowded house
    Jarvis, S. M. Lion and the birds
    Leuser, E. Big stone
    ———. Little bird in the tree
    Leuser, E. D. Wise people of Gotham
    Lynch, M. Scheherazade
    Molloy, L. Fortune of Merrylegs and Tawny-whisers
    Murphy, H. Wise and clever maiden
    Nicholson, M. Wise wife
    Nolan, P. Double nine of Chih Yuan
    ———. Skill of Pericles
    Peterson, M. Magic box
    ———. Simple Olaf
    Phillips, E. Aesop, man of fables
    Rhodes, J. Crow and the corn
    Shakespeare, W. Katherina's obedience
    Spamer, C. Shy prince
    Thane, A. Three wishes
    Vahl, R. Indian boy without a name

Very, A. Puss-in-boots
Walker, B. Lion's den
Watts, F. Tiniest heart
Whitworth, V. King and the bee
Williams, G. Kettle of brains
Wise and clever maiden. Murphy, H.
Wise men of Gotham. Holmes, R.
Wise people of Gotham. Leuser, E. D.
Wise wife. Nicholson, M.
WISHES
    Burlingame, C. Three wishes
    Clapp, P. Magic bookshelf
    Cooper, E. Witch's pumpkin
    Leuser, E. Magic well
    Leuser, E. D. Secret of the wishing well
    Nathan, B. If wishes were horses
    Nolan, P. Our sister, Sitya
    _____. Wishing well or ill
    St. Clair, R. Miss Muffet's wish
    Swintz, M. Three wishing bags
    Watts, F. Crimson feather
Wishing stream. Miller, H.
Wishing well or ill. Nolan, P.
WITCH HUNTS--NEW ENGLAND
    Carlson, B. Let her ride!
WITCHES
    Alderman, E. Wonderful witchware store
    Alexander, S. Zabba, zabba, zoom!
    Andersen, H. The tinderbox
    Barr, J. Rapunzel
    Bennett, A. Little witch
    Bennett, R. In the witch's house
    _____. Scarecrow and the witch
    Boiko, C. Wayward witch
    Carlson, B. Goodbye, Snikke-snak
    _____. Operation satellite
    Chisholm, J. Enchanted, I'm sure
    Cooper, E. Magic spell
    _____. Witch's pumpkin
    Hark, M. Meet Mr. Witch
    Hawthorne, N. Feathertop
    Leuser, E. Little witch who tried
    MacLellan, E. Test for a witch
    Miller, H. Broken broomstick
    _____. Curse of hag hollow
    _____. Miss Frankenstein
    Olfson, L. Equal rights

WITCHES

    Sanders, S. Hansel and Gretel
    Simonds, N. Hansel and Gretel
    Swintz, M. Three wishing bags
    Thane, A. Hansel and Gretel
    _____. Rapunzel
    _____. Saucy scarecrow
    Watkins, M. Nobody believes in witches!
Witches and the crows. McGee, C.
Witch's pumpkin. Cooper, E.
With all my heart. Richards, L.
WIVES
    Shakespeare, W. Katherina's obedience
Wizard of Oz. Baum, L.
WOLVES
    Chermak, S. Peter and the wolf
    Jarvis, S. M. Two silly wolves
    Nolan, P. Stanislaw and the wolf
    Nutter, C. Red Riding Hood and the wolf
WOMEN'S LIBERATION
    Branch, W. To follow the phoenix
    Cable, H. Way, way down south
    Olfson, L. Equal rights
    _____. Meet Miss Stone-Age!
Wonderful circus of words. Boiko, C.
Wonderful witchware store. Alderman, E.
Wonders of storybook land. D'Arcy, A.
Wondrous apple tree. White, A.
Worcester, Natalie S. Mad tea party. In Durrell, D.
  Thirty Plays for Classroom Reading. 5 char
WORDS
    Boiko, C. On camera, Noah Webster!
    _____. Wonderful circus of words
    Hall, M. Language shop
    Nolan, P. What's zymurgy with you?
    Tobey, L. The test
WORLD WAR II
    Fisher, A. Of gods and men
WORMS
    Cleary, B. Henry and the night crawlers
Woster, Alice. All houses are hundred. In Kamerman, S.
  Little Plays for Little Players. 18 char
    _____. Hubbub on the bookshelf. In Burack, A. One Hundred Plays for Children. 9 char
Would-be gentleman. Molière
Wraggle taggle gypsies. White, A.
WRESTLING
    Ross, L. Young Abe wrestles Armstrong

WRIGHT, ORVILLE AND WILBUR
    Howard, V. First flight of the Wright brothers
    Ickler, L. Kitty Hawk--1903
Wrist watch. Howard, V.
WRITERS
    Dias, E. Dear Lottie
Wurst student. Fontaine, R.
Wuthering Heights. Brontë, E.
Wyss, Johann. Swiss family Robinson. In Olfson, L. Classics Adopted for Acting and Reading. 12 char

- Y -

Yankee-doodle kitten. Newman, D.
Ye olden festival of Christmas. Bennett, R.
Yellow fever. Burlingame, C.
Yes, officer! Howard, V.
Yes, yes, a thousand times yes! Boiko, C.
You look lovely, dear. Howard, V.
Young Abe Lincoln. Fisher, A.
Young Abe wrestles Armstrong. Ross, L.
Young Abe's destiny. Boiko, C.
Young forever. Cable, H.
Young Hickory. Walsh, H.
Young man of considerable value. Nolan, P.
YOUNG MEN
    Hawthorne, N. David Swan
    see also TEEN-AGERS
Young, Rebecca T. From nine to five. In McGee, C. Drama for Fun. 4 char
YOUNG WOMEN
    Hagy, L. Fire in a paper
    James, H. Washington Square
    see also TEEN-AGERS
Younger generation. Nolan, P.
Youngster named Danny. In McGee, C. Drama for Fun. 2 char+
Your happy friend. Howard, V.
Your own thing. Driver, D.
YOUTH
    Cable, H. Young forever
    DuBois, G. St. Patrick saves the day
    Hark, M. Good neighbors

- Z -

Zabba, zabba, zoom! Alexander, S.
Zeligs, Dorothy. Queen Esther saves her people. In Ross, E. Holiday Puppets. 6 char+
Ziegler, Esther see Brydon, Margaret Wylie, and Esther Ziegler

CAST ANALYSIS

The following listing is divided into four parts: female cast, male cast, mixed cast, and puppet plays. Under each part, the arrangement is from few to many characters.

FEMALE CAST

1 character

Fletcher, J. Jailer's daughter falls in love with a prince
Howard, V. Box of chocolates
_____ . Explanations
_____ . Grandma crosses the street
_____ . Look, George
_____ . My boy friend
_____ . My first football game
_____ . Party night
_____ . Romantic facts for women
_____ . The shopper
_____ . Size, please
_____ . Waiting for Grandma
Ibsen, H. Aase searches for her son
Milton, J. Eve decides to eat the fruit of the tree of knowledge
Pope, A. Belinda bemoans the loss of a lock of her hair
Shakespeare, W. Cleopatra's death scene
_____ . Katherina's obedience
_____ . Lady Macbeth receives a letter from her husband
Wilde, O. On being too frequently proposed to

2 characters

Carlson, B. In the dumps
Howard, V. Bus stop
_____ . Girl talk

CAST ANALYSIS   182

　　　　　　. Schoolwork

3 characters

Carlson, B.   Rebecca of Sunnybrook Farm
Cooper, E.   Witch's pumpkin

3 characters and extras

Love, S.   Madame Defarge

4 characters

Bennett, R.   Visitors for Nancy Hawks
Fontaine, R. Camping pictures
　　　　　.   Matter of taste
Ward, T.   The daubers

5 characters

Fontaine, R. On you it looks good
French, D.   Mud pack madness
Olfson, L.   Cinderella revisited
　　　　　.   Hen party

5 characters and extras

Hammack, B.   Night before Christmas

6 characters

Barbee, L.   Princess who couldn't dance
Bennett, R.   Valentine for Mary
Olfson, L.   Happy haunting!
Phillips, M. Hat for mother

7 characters

Barbee, L.   Friday foursome packs a box
　　　　　.   Letter to Lincoln

8 characters

Brydon, M.   May witch
Gross, N.   Mystery ring
Hill, K.   Midnight burial

Leuser, E. Little witch who tried
St. Clair, R. Spirit of Christmas

10 characters

Paradis, M. Santa goes to town

13 characters

Martens, A. Thirteen

14 characters

Sagoff, S. Hand-me-down Hildy

MALE CAST

1 character

Browning, R. My last duchess
Everyman's prayer
Howard, V. Call to a bride
_____. Calling all spies
_____. The colonel
_____. Dear Judy
_____. Freddie proposes
_____. Housework for hubby
_____. Kiss me good night!
_____. The letter
_____. Pep talk
_____. Roller coaster
_____. Romantic facts for men
_____. Stagecoach
_____. Strong man
_____. Walking with Wilma
_____. Wild, wild west
_____. Your happy friend
Ibsen, H. Peer Gynt leaves Solveig
Marlowe, C. Death of Zenocrate
Molière. Harpagon searches for his stolen money
Rostand, E. Nose speech
Shakespeare, W. Richard alone
_____. To be or not to be
Vanbrugh, Sir J. Lord Foppington's day

CAST ANALYSIS 184

2 characters

Carlson, B.   Home cooking
Childress, A.   African garden
Howard, V.   Comedy team
_____ .   Funny business
_____ .   Help wanted
_____ .   Saturday chatter
Jarvis, S. M.   Fisherman and the elf
Taylor, L.   Comedy skit
_____ .   Poetry
_____ .   Say, Dad
_____ . $25,000

3 characters

Fontaine, R.   Oh, medico!
Jarvis, S. M.   I think I know
_____ .   Turkeys are tricky
Taylor, L.   Not for one sandwich

4 characters

Dunsany, L.   Jest of Hahalaba
Fontaine, R.   Androcles and his pal
_____ .   Emergency
_____ .   Eyes have it
Geiger, M.   In the fog
Jarvis, S. M.   !Trip-trap! trip-trap!
Love, S.   Apache silver
Nicholson, M.   Crying clown
Olfson, L.   Avon calling!
_____ .   Couple of right smart fellows
_____ .   Great Caesar's ghost!
_____ .   Spying high
_____ .   Ten-year-old detective
Shine, T.   Shoes

4 characters and extras

Bennett, R.   Runaway pirate
Carlson, B.   What is it?

5 characters

Colson, J.   Top of the bill
Fontaine, R.   How the West was won

Love, S.   Black idol
McGee, C.   Russian quartet
_____ .   Spasm in three speeds
Mitchell, L. Land beyond the river
Olfson, L.   Three swine of most small stature
Spamer, C.   Dwarfs' beards
Stuart, M.   Abigail stands fast

5 characters and extras

Hammack, B.   Night before Christmas

6 characters

Bradbury, R. The meadow
Carlson, B.   Pirates
Doyle, A.   Sherlock Holmes and the stockbroker's clerk
Fontaine, R. It's frightening!
_____ .   Ride your hobby
Love, S.   One-eyed giant
Shore, M.   Catastrophe Clarence
Taylor, L.   Gold detector
Twain, M.   Celebrated jumping frog of Calaveras County
Walsh, H.   Jamestown

6 characters and extras

Hall, M.   Hearts of oak
Howard, V.   Boston tea party
_____ .   Columbus' discovery of America
Werner, S.   Home, sweet home

7 characters

Boiko, C.   Book that saved the earth
Doyle, A.   Sherlock Holmes and the red-headed league
Holmes, R.   King John and the Abbot of Canterbury
Love, S.   Clive of India
_____ .   Man who shot the president

8 characters

Carlson, B.   Seven Simons
Miller, H.   Jiminy Cinders
Sayre, G.   Final edition

CAST ANALYSIS

8 characters and extras

Carlson, B.　To build a federal city

9 characters

Clark, B.　Fires at Valley Forge
Harper, J.　First cat on Mars

10 characters

Fisher, A.　Day of destiny
Howard, H.　Little circus donkey
Stevenson, R.　Treasure Island

10 characters and extras

Bakeless, K.　Most memorable voyage
Peterson, M.　Beyond mutiny

11 characters

Howard, V.　Daring sailormen
Love, S.　Beowulf
———.　King Arthur
Molloy, L.　Fortune of Merrylegs and Tawny-whiskers

11 characters and extras

Colson, J.　Message from Robin Hood
Howard, V.　Treasure of Monte Cristo

12 characters

Burlingame, C.　Yellow fever
Love, S.　Moby Dick

13 characters and extras

Colson, J.　Robin Hood in Sherwood Forest

23 characters

Miller, H.　Half-pint cowboy

CAST ANALYSIS

26 characters

Suerken, E. John Crown's legacy

MIXED CAST

1 character [either male or female]

Howard, V. All washed up
- Arkwood two-four-two-four
- Around the world
- The artist
- But, doctor
- Calling all cooks
- Complaint desk
- Courtesy at the wheel
- Dear Mr. Loveletter
- Dizzy dinners
- Drive in the country
- Famous words
- The fisherman
- Flight fifteen
- Foot in the door
- Fortunes?
- Girl who did very, very well
- Golf lesson
- The golfer
- Help wanted
- High-jumper
- Hook and bait
- How?
- How are you?
- How I conquered worry
- How to be successful
- How to hypnotize
- How to improve your memory
- It's a mystery
- The juggler
- Larry's lesson
- Left turn
- Lincoln's middle name
- Little known facts
- Look here, boss

CAST ANALYSIS

	.	Lunch at Pierre's
	.	Meet me in the moonlight
	.	My vocal career
	.	Not exactly
	.	Our famous proverbs
	.	Our national sports
	.	Pay and be gay
	.	Perfumes
	.	Phonograph record
	.	School daze
	.	Setting the table
	.	Space talk
	.	Staff of life
	.	Supper in silence
	.	Texas cowboy
	.	Texas roundup
	.	Time of my life
	.	Valentines
	.	Wrist watch
	.	Yes, officer!
	.	You look lovely, dear
McGee, C.		Fun with Hamlet
	.	Henry
	.	Peanut butter
	.	Pure white

1 character and extras

Howard, V.   Birthday surprises
McGee, C.   Lion hunt

2 characters

Alexander, S.   Frog princess
_____ .   Goom-bya, room-bya, zerko!
_____ .   Hello, little dog
_____ .   What's in my soup?
_____ .   Zabba, zabba, zoom!
Barbour, F.   Bird cage
Bennett, R.   Lion and the mouse
Branch, W.   To follow the phoenix
Bullins, E.   Son come home
Carlson, B.   All about animals
_____ .   Make your own bed
_____ .   On myself
_____ .   Or make pot holders
_____ .   Smithtown, U.S.A.

_____. To play the piano
_____. Why don't you?
Furman, R. To kill a devil
Howard, V. Directions
_____. Fred and Lois
_____. Mechanical man
_____. Mirror stunt
_____. Ranch romance
_____. Telephone chuckles
Jarvis, S. M. Fried onions and marshmallows
_____. Who helped the lion?
Lincoln, A. Streak o' lean
McGee, C. Interview with Punchy McPugg
_____. Lover's errand
Pylant, A. Starring you
Sperling, L. Baby bird
_____. Day Canary met Sparrow
White, A. Deaf woman's courtship
_____. Saucy sailor

2 characters and extras

Bennett, R. Fire-face and the Indians
Breaking the ice
Browne, T. Natural man
Carlson, B. Follow-the-leader
Definition of a boy
The eskimo
Evolution
Hark, M. Santa Claus parade
Howard, V. In the jungle
_____. Salesman!
_____. Slow motion pantomime
_____. Tennis match
_____. Waiter!
Local frog stages comeback
Newman, D. Mrs. Santa's Christmas gift
Tree toad loved a she-toad
Two frogs
White, A. Sailor's return
Youngster named Danny

3 characters

Bennett, R. French doll's surprise
_____. Hare and the tortoise
_____. In the witch's house

CAST ANALYSIS   190

Carlson, B.   It had to be
_____ .   Let's fool someone
_____ .   Marked trail
_____ .   Nothing!
_____ .   Ship like this
_____ .   The $10,000 dog
_____ .   Touch one
Fly and a flea
Fontaine, R.   Can't get there from here, mebbe
Jarvis, S.   Sun and the wind
Jarvis, S. M.   Mitten tree
_____ .   Why the turtle does not talk
McCoy, P.   No garden this year
McGee, C.   Can'tsee Poorsight
Nolan, P.   Boshibari and the two thieves
O'Casey, S.   End of the beginning
Rhodes, J.   Crow and the corn
Simonds, N.   Unhappy Santa
Taylor, L.   Baseball
_____ .   Doctor's office
_____ .   The telephone
Walker, B.   Rabbit and the wolf
_____ .   Which piece is mine?
White, A.   My son John

3 characters and extras

Bennett, R.   Beaded moccasins
_____ .   Child who was made of snow
Boiko, C.   Wayward witch
Carlson, B.   Golden tooth
_____ .   Justice for all
_____ .   My treasure
_____ .   Where there are no snags
Howard, V.   Happy hikers
_____ .   How music made everyone happy
_____ .   Newspaper dramatics
_____ .   Pantomime orchestra
Jarvis, S. M.   Free bacon

4 characters

Barr, J.   Three little kittens
Bealmear, J.   Covetous councilman
Bennett, R.   Miss Muffet and the spider
_____ .   Rainbow's end
_____ .   Snowman who played Santa

Boyd, J.   Featherweight champ or tickled to death
Campbell, J.   Pink roses for Christmas
Carlson, B.   Shut the door!
Deming, D.   First aid first
Fisher, A.   Christmas cake
Fontaine, R.   The loafer
_____ .   Love seeks a way
_____ .   Personality problem
Hoff, S.   Children on the moon
_____ .   The family
Holmes, R.   In the days of King Alfred
Howard, H.   Thanks to Sammy Scarecrow
Hughes, L.   Soul gone home
Jarvis, S.   Giant's cat
_____ .   Supper with the queen
Jarvis, S. M.   King's gold
_____ .   Lion and the birds
Knight, L.   Flibber turns the tables
Maupassant, G.   The necklace
Mayfield, J.   417
Miller, H.   Magic cookie jar
Nicholson, M.   Price of eggs
Olfson, L.   Incredible housing shortage
_____ .   Last time I saw Paris
_____ .   Once and future frog
Poe, E.   Cask of Amontillado
Taylor, L.   How to live long
Walker, B.   Lion's den
Wallace, R.   Case of the frustrated corpse
Williams, G.   Kettle of brains
Young, R.   From nine to five

4 characters and extras

Bennett, R.   Littlest artist
_____ .   Scarecrow and the witch
Bradley, P.   Professor Countdown takes off
Campbell, C.   Morning maker
Carlson, B.   Another way
_____ .   Goodbye, Snikke-snak
_____ .   Why catch a leprechaun?
_____ .   Why the nightingale sings gloriously
Grahame, K.   Reluctant dragon
Howard, V.   The experts
_____ .   Personality machine
_____ .   Pony express
_____ .   Ride of Paul Revere

CAST ANALYSIS 192

| . Television tricks
Jarvis, S. M.   Lion and the mosquitoes
Olfson, L.   La farza del Miss Muffet
Reay, N.   Mr. Bates goes to the polls
Weik, M.   Moonlight
White, A.   In Bibberley Town
_____ .   Wonderous apple tree

5 characters

Andersen, H.   Princess and the pea
Ashrand, K.   Adalmina's pearl
Barnett, G.   Treasure in the Smith house
Barr, J.   Rapunzel
Bennett, R.   City mouse and country mouse
_____ .   Out of the clock
_____ .   Piccola
_____ .   Runaway pirate
_____ .   Santa's send-off
_____ .   School for scamperers
_____ .   Shoemaker and the elves
_____ .   Three terrors
_____ .   Waking the daffodil
Bowers, E.   Nobility
Brontë, C.   Jane Eyre
Brontë, E.   Wuthering Heights
Carlson, B.   Why the leaves of the aspen tree quake in a
                  breeze
Cooper, E.   Little white cloud
Davis, O.   Purlie Victorious
Dennis, A.   Wind wand
Dias, E.   Ghost from Genoa
Feather, J.   One wish too many
Fisher, A.   Best bargain in the world
_____ .   Get-together dinner
_____ .   Mother's day off and on
_____ .   Weaver's son
Fontaine, R.   Fair today, followed by tomorrow
_____ .   Good morning, your honor
_____ .   Graduation address
_____ .   No starch in the collars
_____ .   Sweetie-weeties!
_____ .   United spies
_____ .   Wurst student
Hark, M.   Enter George Washington
_____ .   Stuff of heroes
Hawthorne, N.   Dr. Heidegger's experiment

CAST ANALYSIS

Heine, H. Flying Dutchman
Henry, O. Last leaf
————. Romance of a busy broker
Holmes, R. Little Red Riding Hood
Howard, H. Ben Franklin, peace-maker
Jarvis, S. Dog's house
Jarvis, S. M. Two silly wolves
Koon, H. Pierre Patelin
McGee, C. Gransel and Hettal
————. Sofapillio
————. Trip to Mexico
McQueen, M. Mother's choice
Musil, R. Invisible dragon of Winn Sinn Tu
Nightingale, E. Ariadne exposed
Nolan, P. Double nine of Chih Yuan
Olfson, L. Bride of Gorse-braken Hall
————. Meet Miss Stone-age!
————. My son, the prince
————. Try data-date!
Pylant, A. Mellerdrammer
St. Clair, R. Miss Muffet's wish
Sayers, N. Story of Gransel and Hettal
Schwartz, M. Twin cousins
Sherwood, R. Abe Lincoln in Illinois
Shore, M. Watch out for Aunt Hattie
Simon, S. Tiger and the brahman
Simonds, N. Hansel and Gretel
Spamer, C. Candy canes
Stockton, F. Transferred ghost
Taylor, L. Don't be afraid
White, A. Willie's gane to Melville castle
Wilde, C. Comic strip antics
Wilder, T. Childhood
Williams, G. Kettle of brains
Worcester, N. Mad tea party

5 characters and extras

Alderman, E. Wonderful witchware store
Barbee, L. Columbus sails the sea
Blanton, C. Dulce man
Carlson, B. Operation satellite
————. Rock the baby, Granny
————. Why the owl is sacred in Hawaii
Gardner, M. King Midas
Hark, M. In honor of Washington
Howard, V. California gold discovery

CAST ANALYSIS   194

_____.   Children who found new friends
_____.   Daniel in the lion's den
_____.   David's battle with Goliath
_____.   First flight of the Wright brothers
Molloy, L.   Stolen tarts
Richards, L.   With all my heart
Smith, J.   King Midas
Smith, M.   Best gift of all
Stevenson, R.   Sire de Maletroit's door
Ward, D.   Day of absence
Weik, M.   King's garden
White, A.   Crabfish
_____.   Eight bells

6 characters

Barbee, L.   Guide for George Washington
Bellah, M.   Blue toadstool
Bennett, R.   King's holiday
Cable, H.   Big Red Riding Hood
Carlson, B.   Salt in the soup
Chekhov, A.   The upheaval
Chisholm, J.   Enchanted, I'm sure
Clapp, P.   Girl whose fortune sought her
Colbo, E.   Heroine of Wren
Cooper, E.   Greta and the prince
_____.   Magic spell
Coyle, R.   Matter of conscience
Deming, D.   Grey ghosts
Dias, E.   Dear Lottie
_____.   Printer's devil
Elfenbein, J.   Puss-in-boots
Fisher, A.   New hearts for old
Fontaine, R.   Another Cinderella
_____.   Great Caesar
_____.   Let sleeping beauties lie
_____.   Supermarket blues
_____.   To the moon
Grahame, K.   Reluctant dragon
Grimm, Brothers.   Frog prince
Hagy, L.   Fire in a paper
Hall, H.   The valiant
Hall, M.   King Horn
Hansberry, L.   Raisin in the sun
Hark, M.   Bobby and the Lincoln speech
_____.   Cupies and hearts
_____.   Father's Easter hat

CAST ANALYSIS

.	Johnnie Jump Up
.	Nothing to be thankful for
.	Our own four walls
.	Visit of Johnny Appleseed
Heath, A.	Gypsy look
Heiderstadt, D.	Girl from the sea
Hoff, S.	Giants
.	Lion in the zoo
.	Wild flowers
Howard, H.	I'll share my fare
.	Thankful indeed
Howard, V.	Men of Mars
.	Wild dreams
Ionesco, E.	The leader
Jarvis, S.	Foolish Fred
.	Mr. Maybe
Lane, M.	Is there life on other planets?
McGee, C.	Fatal quest
MacLellan, E.	Clock's secret
McMeekin, I.	Runaway balloon
McNair, J.	Blown with the breeze
Mantle, M.	Doctor for Lucinda
Miller, H.	Curse of hag hollow
.	Dolly saves the day
.	Part-time hero
.	Shady shadows
Murray, J.	Dead of night
.	Miss Forsythe is missing
Nolan, J.	Happy Christmas to all
Nolan, P.	Courters
.	Magic of Salamanca
Olfson, L.	Sail on! sail on!
Peterson, M.	Old Four-legs
Roberts, H.	For the glory of Spain
.	Washington's sacrifice
Saki.	Open window
Simonds, N.	Hansel and Gretel
.	Peter Rabbit
Steinbeck, J.	Leader of the people
Tennyson, A.	Enoch Arden
Urban, C.	Queen with the broken heart
Very, A.	President Lincoln's children
Ward, M.	Mr. Lazy Man's family
White, A.	May I woo the lassie?
Whitworth, V.	King and the bee

CAST ANALYSIS   196

6 characters and extras

Bennett, R.   Magic weaver
 ———————— .   Rumpelstiltskin
Carlson, B.   Impossible! unacceptable! preposterous!
 ———————— .   Summer maker
Fisher, A.   Christmas tree for kitty
 ———————— .   Fresco for UNESCO
Howard, H.   Magic jack-o-lantern
Howard, V.   The dancers
 ———————— .   Stagecoach step
Jarvis, S. M.   Honey and dough
McFarlan, E.   Pear tree
McGee, C.   Romance of Minnie Martin or it shouldn't happen to a dog
 ———————— .   The stand-in
Menotti, G.   Amahl and the night visitors
Mintier, W.   Othello
Very, A.   Boy who could not tell a lie
Watkins, M.   Nobody believes in witches!
White, A.   Wraggle taggle gypsies, O

7 characters

Barbee, L.   Holly hangs high
Barr, J.   Lion and the mouse
 ———————— .   Present for mother
Beach, H.   On the fence
Bennett, R.   Pixie in a trap
 ———————— .   Thanksgiving pageant
 ———————— .   Winter wizards
Boiko, C.   Book that saved the earth
 ———————— .   Young Abe's destiny
Cheatham, V.   Snow White and friends
Chisholm, J.   Enchanted, I'm sure
Colbo, E.   Heroine of Wren
 ———————— .   Littlest fir
Deming, D.   Old man river
Dias, E.   Bow-wow blues
 ———————— .   Express to Valley Forge
 ———————— .   Hippie and the bard
 ———————— .   Little man who wasn't there
 ———————— .   Martha Washington's spy
 ———————— .   Visitor to Gettysburg
Downing, R.   Shop girl's revenge
Ferguson, D.   Most special dragon
Fisher, A.   Ghosts on guard

_____. Turning the tables
_____. What happened in Egypt
Fontaine, R. Efficiency expert
_____. Great Caesar!
Freudenberger, H. Jack and Jill
Glass, G. Golden touch
_____. Miss Pickerell goes to Mars
_____. Pippi Longstocking
Goldsmith, S. Louisa Alcott's wish
Gould, J. Thanksgiving is for everybody
Grabe, Mrs. K. I know an old woman
Graham, M. Unusual flower
Gregg, L. Miniature darzis
Hark, M. Christmas in the woods
_____. Christmas snowman
_____. Doctor Manners
_____. The dolls
_____. Five senses
_____. Hearts and flowers for mother
_____. Magic egg
_____. New-fangled Thanksgiving
_____. Not fit for man or beast
_____. See the parade
Heath, A. Much ado about ants
Howard, H. Mother's gift
Hughes, T. Beauty and the beast
Ickler, L. Kitty Hawk--1903
Jarvis, S. Six wise travelers
Leuser, E. Five brothers
Lindgren, A. Pippi Longstocking
Lipnik, E. Son of liberty
Love, S. Joan of Arc
McFarlan, E. Olive jar
MacGregor, E. Miss Pickerell goes to Mars
MacLellan, E. Birthday gift
Manning, S. Background for Nancy
Miller, H. Broadway turkey
_____. Puppy love
Molloy, L. Jenny-by-the-day
Musil, R. Peach tree kingdom
Newman, D. Green Leaf's lesson
Nicholson, J. Mysterious stranger
Nicholson, M. Wise wife
Nolan, P. Anton Chekhov sort of evening
_____. Wishing well or ill
Pendleton, E. Bobby and the Lincoln speech
_____. Jingle bells

CAST ANALYSIS 198

Phillips, M. Hat for Mother
Sanderlin, O. Follow the north star
Sanders, S. Hansel and Gretel
Schwartz, M. All in favor
Shore, M. Catastrophe Clarence
Slattery, M. Patchwork princess
————— . Royal magic
Slingluff, M. Naughty Susan
Smith, F. Rhyme's the crime or the verse is yet to come
Tausheck, R. Saga of Davey Rocket
Turnbull, L. Magic shoes

7 characters and extras

Bennett, R. The plot
————— . What will the toys say?
Boiko, C. Cinder-riley
————— . Insatiable dragon
Carlson, B. Ghosts
————— . Let her ride!
————— . Remember the Christmas tree
Clapp, P. Other side of the wall
Dias, E. Video Christmas
Fisher, A. Caves of the earth
————— . Invasion from the stratosphere
————— . Story of a well
Fontaine, R. Carefree high school orchestra
Howard, V. In the army
————— . The picnic
McFarlan, E. Tiger catcher
McGee, C. King with the terrible temper
On being a senior adult
Peterson, M. Simple Olaf
Swintz, M. Posies for the potentate
Thane, A. Hansel and Gretel

8 characters

Asbrand, K. Crystal flask
Barr, J. Cinderella
————— . Lion and the mouse
Bennett, R. Prince of hearts
Blumenfeld, L. Another way
Boiko, C. Care and feeding of mother
Brown, T. Talent tree
Cable, H. Best of sports
————— . Young forever

CAST ANALYSIS

Carroll, L.   Through the looking glass
Clear, B.   Ellen Tebbits
Dias, E.   Cast up by the sea
─────── .   Christmas spirit
─────── .   Gift of laughter
Dorand, J.   Surprise party
DuBois, G.   Last laugh
Felsheim, J.   Ali Baba and the forty thieves
Fisher, A.   Abe's winkin' eye
─────── .   Angel in the looking glass
─────── .   Of gods and men
─────── .   On strike
─────── .   Skills to share
─────── .   Special edition
─────── .   Spirit of Christmas
Fontaine, R.   Where banking is a pleasure
─────── .   Who killed Doc Robin?
Garver, J.   My fair Linda
─────── .   Turkey, anyone?
Glass, G.   Ellen's secret
Hark, M.   Good neighbors
─────── .   Off the shelf
─────── .   Prize for mother
─────── .   T for turkey
─────── .   Three wishes for mother
─────── .   Too many kittens
─────── .   When do we eat?
Head, F.   Spouse for Susie Mouse
Heinzen, B.   Miss Cast
Holmes, R.   Heir of Linne
─────── .   King and the miller
Hoppenstedt, E.   Poet's nightmare
Howard, H.   What he deserves
Hugo, V.   Bishop's candlesticks
James, H.   Washington Square
MacLellan, E.   Small shoes and small tulips
─────── .   Swiss mystery
Martens, A.   George slept here, too
─────── .   Roscoe the robot
Martin, P.   Little Ugo and the foolish ones
Miller, H.   Dial M for mother
─────── .   Ghost in the house
Murray, J.   I want to report a murder
─────── .   Scaredy cat
Muse, V.   Town mouse and his country cousin
Nathan, B.   If wishes were horses
Nicholson, M.   Wise wife

CAST ANALYSIS

Nolan, P.   French cabinetmaker
———————.   Going steady
———————.   Hi down there
———————.   Leak in the dike
———————.   Our sister, Sitya
———————.   Tree to the sky
———————.   What's zymurgy with you?
Pyle, M.   Not on the menu
Rawls, J.   Pilgrim painting
Reines, B.   Turncoat
Sheridan, R.   The rivals
Slattery, M.   King in the kitchen
Spamer, C.   Bunnyland brigade
———————.   Shy prince
Stockton, F.   Lady or the tiger?
Streacker, L.   No-mother land
Thane, A.   Three wishes
Tolstoy, L.   How much land does a man need?
Vahl, R.   Indian boy without a name
Verne, J.   Five weeks in a balloon
Weik, M.   The rehearsal
Whitworth, V.   Mechanical maid
Wilde, C.   Junior prom

8 characters and extras

Barr, J.   Old Mother Hubbard
Barrows, M.   Valentine tree
Bennett, R.   First Easter eggs
———————.   Snow-white and Rose-red
Boiko, C.   Runaway bookmobile
Browning, R.   Pied piper of Hamlin
Buechler, J.   Stone soup
Carlson, B.   O little town
Colbo, E.   First New England Christmas tree
Dickens, C.   Magic fishbone
Fisher, A.   Invasion from the stratosphere
———————.   Time for Mom
Folmsbee, B.   Goblin parade
Holmes, R.   Wise men of Gotham
Howard, V.   Backward people
———————.   Bible pantomimes
———————.   Cake bake
———————.   Man who didn't like rain
———————.   Sour notes
———————.   Super sale
Hughes, T.   Tiger's bones

Leuser, E.   Broth of Christkindli
———— .   Little bird in the tree
McCarty, E.   Little cake
McKee, H.   Witches and the crows
Malone, M.   Last snake in Ireland
Miller, H.   Three little kittens
———— .   Wishing stream
Nesbit, E.   Long and short division
Nicholson, M.   Laughing princess
Nolan, P.   Gates of Dinkelsbuehl
———— .   Highland fling
Phillips, E.   Aesop, man of fables
Sanders, S.   Tragedy in the graveyard
Sealock, T.   Lincoln coat
Twain, M.   Tom Sawyer
Very, A.   Tom Tit Tot
———— .   What happened to the cakes
White, A.   Nice girls don't chase the boys

9 characters

Anderson, R.   Trouble in outer space
Arnold, E.   Make him smile
Asbrand, K.   Friendly as can be
———— .   What's a penny?
Barbee, L.   Enter Juliet
Bennett, H.   Rumpelstiltskin
Bennett, R.   Good morning, Mr. Rabbit
Boiko, C.   Franklin reversal
———— .   Roman romance
———— .   Who will bell the cat?
Bulla, C.   Ghost town treasure
Burlingame, C.   Three wishes
Cable, H.   Deputy for Broken Bow
———— .   Last stop
———— .   Way-out Cinderella
Cleary, B.   Henry Huggins
Colson, J.   Baron Barnaby's box
Corbett, S.   Lemonade trick
Dias, E.   Cleanest town in the West
———— .   Madison Avenue merry-go-round
Dickens, C.   Martin Chuzzlewit
Dorand, J.   Surprise party
———— .   Teen and twenty
DuBois, G.   Governor Bradford's scissors
Elfenbein, J.   King who couldn't be fooled
———— .   Ten-penny tragedy

CAST ANALYSIS 202

Fisher, A.　One-ring circus
Glass, G.　Early life of George Washington Carver
_____.　Ghost town treasure
_____.　Henry and the night crawlers
_____.　Lemonade trick
Hark, M.　Pleasant dreams
_____.　Too many kittens
Hill, K.　Midnight burial
Hollingsworth, L.　Silent night
Howells, M.　Christmas every day
Kane, E.　How we got our numbers
Lehman, J.　Biskie the snowman
Lello, E.　Mystery at Tumble Inn
Leuser, E.　Courage piece
Leuser, E. D.　Magic grapes
_____.　Thanksgiving scarecrow
MacLellan, E.　Needle fights for freedom
_____.　Secret of the windmill
Melcher, M.　Princess who would not smile
Miller, H.　All-American thank you
_____.　Gathering sticks
_____.　Man like Lincoln
_____.　Mistletoe mystery
_____.　Pink parasol
_____.　Rabbit who refused to run
_____.　Return of Bobby Shafto
_____.　Valentine for Kate
_____.　Visit to Goldilocks
Miller, S.　Dangerous game
Molière.　Would-be gentleman
Molloy, L.　Broom market day
Munro, H.　Pom-pom
Murray, J.　Case of mistaken identity
_____.　Impossible room
_____.　Mad about art
_____.　Spies and dolls
Myrick, N.　Day is bright
Nicholson, M.　Princess Nimble-wit
Nolan, P.　Johnny Appleseed
_____.　Stanislaw and the wolf
_____.　Take it from the beginning
_____.　View of the sea
Pyle, H.　Apple of contentment
Rawls, J.　Pilgrim painting
Roberts, H.　Builder of the wall
Smith, G.　Tiger, the brahman, and the jackal
Spamer, C.　Pot of gold

Swintz, M.   King's creampuffs
Thane, A.   King Alfred and the cakes
Urban, C.   Who started the fire?
Van Druten, J.   I remember Mama
Ward, M.   Family affair
Wilde, O.   Importance of being earnest
Woster, A.   Hubbub on the bookshelf

9 characters and extras

Bennett, R.   Pudding-bag string
Boiko, C.   Number one Apple Tree Lane
Carlson, B.   Murky monster foiled again
Carter, S.   One last look
Chermak, S.   Peter and the wolf
Collodi, C.   Pinocchio goes to school
Duvall, L.   Valentine's Day
Fisher, A.   Hearts, tarts and valentines
Hark, M.   Father keeps house
Howard, V.   Building of the Panama Canal
Hughes, T.   Orpheus
Murphy, H.   Wise and clever maiden
Nolan, P.   Golden voice of Little Erik
Nutter, C.   Red Riding Hood and the wolf
Parsons, M.   Too much of a good thing
Peterson, M.   Pedro and the burro
Shakespeare, W.   Julius Caesar
Simon, S.   Baking contest
Swintz, M.   Three wishing bags
Thane, A.   Dick Whittington and his cat
_____.   Magic nutmeg-grater
Watts, F.   Leprechaun shoemakers

10 characters

Anderson, R.   Gold mine at Jeremiah Flats
Apolinar, D.   Your own thing
Atwater, R.   Mr. Popper's penguins
Barrington, P.   I had a hippopotamus
Bierce, A.   Shipwreck
Boiko, C.   Marvelous time machine
_____.   Meet the pilgrims!
_____.   One hundred words
_____.   Operation litterbug
_____.   Scaredy cat
_____.   Take me to your marshal
_____.   Yes, yes a thousand times yes!

CAST ANALYSIS 204

Bright, R.   Richard Brown and the dragon
Buck, D.   Floating stone
Burnett, F.   Little princess
Cable, H.   Reform of Sterling Silverheart
Carlson, B.   Fit for a king
Chisholm, J.   Shades of ransom
Clapp, P.   Magic bookshelf
Corson, H.   Fish in the forest
Dorand, J.   Teen and twenty
Driver, D.   Your own thing
DuBois, G.   Two strangers from Nazareth
Fay, M.   Saving the old homestead
Fisher, A.   One-ring circus
_____ .   Voice of liberty
Foulk, C.   Floating stone
Garver, J.   Father hits the jackpot
_____ .   Howling success
Glass, G.   How to put out a dreadful dragon
_____ .   Mr. Popper's penguins
Gould, J.   Seven little seeds
Greth, R.   Two masks
Hark, M.   Day for trees
_____ .   Junction Santa Claus
_____ .   New broom
_____ .   Rainbow colors
Hawthorne, N.   Feathertop
Henderson, N.   Look behind the mask
Hester, H.   Your own thing
Hoppenstedt, E.   Christmas house
Howard, V.   Happy holidays for little women
_____ .   Take-turners
Huff, B.   Case of the missing masterpiece
Kane, E.   Children of chocolate street
King, W.   Little Snow White
Lello, E.   Mystery of Tumble Inn
Leuser, E.   Little clown who forgot how to laugh
Lipnik, E.   Angel of mercy
MacLellan, E.   Cross princess
_____ .   Needle fights for freedom
Manning, S.   Background for Nancy
Mapp, F.   Ogre who built a bridge
Martin, P.   Invitation to supper
Miller, H.   General returns
_____ .   Horn of plenty
_____ .   Mount Vernon cricket
_____ .   Thankful's red beads
Molloy, L.   Cat and the queen

Murray, J.   Looking glass murder
_____ .   Spies and dolls
Nolan, P.   Happiest hat
_____ .   Moon's up there
_____ .   Trash and treasure
_____ .   Whole city's down below
_____ .   Young man of considerable value
Peterson, M.   Abe buys a barrel
Pyle, M.   Perambulating pie
Roberts, H.   Lonely fir tree
Roberts, W.   Musicians of Bremen Town
Robinson, C.   Boat club dance
Slattery, M.   Queen's mirror
Stevenson, R.   Kidnapping of David Balfour
Thane, A.   Rapunzel
Vandevere, J.   Mother Goose gives a dinner
Watts, F.   Crimson feather
_____ .   Leprechaun's pot of gold
_____ .   Santa and the efficiency expert
Weathers, W.   Vision of the silver bell
Whittaker, H.   Gift from Johnny Appleseed
Wilde, C.   Susan goes Hollywood
Winther, B.   African trio

10 characters and extras

Asbrand, K.   Pandora's box
Boiko, C.   Small crimson parasol
Cable, H.   Way, way down south
Hark, M.   That Christmas feeling
Howard, H.   Christmas train
Howard, V.   Pilgrim's first Thanksgiving
_____ .   Washington at Valley Forge
Kane, E.   Elves and the shoemaker
Kaufman, T.   Piffle! It's only a sniffle
McGee, C.   Dr. Quack's medicine show
Nolan, P.   Robin Hood and the match at Nottingham
_____ .   Skill of Pericles
Thane, A.   Baker's neighbor
_____ .   Jack and the magic beanstalk
Very, A.   Three sillies
Walsh, H.   Young Hickory
Watts, F.   Miss Louisa and the outlaws
Weik, M.   River risin'!
White, A.   Bailiff's daughter of Islington
Whitman, C.   School for jesters

CAST ANALYSIS   206

11 characters

Andersen, H.   The tinderbox
Bennett, R.   Christmas pie
Bierling, J.   No braver soldier
Boiko, C.   All hands on deck
_____.   The "T" party
_____.   Take me to your marshal
Brydon, M.   Reluctant ghost
Dias, E.   Treasure at Bentley Inn
Draper, C.   Emperor's daughters
DuBois, G.   St. Patrick saves the day
Dumas, A.   The duel
Fisher, A.   Nickel and a dime
_____.   Way to Norwich
Fletcher, L.   Sorry, wrong number
Hark, M.   Princess and the rose-colored glasses
Harper, J.   First cat on Mars
Homer.   The Iliad
Hoppenstedt, E.   Not only the strong
King, W.   Snow White
Kingman, L.   Mr. Thanks has his day
Leuser, E.   Legend of the Christmas rose
_____.   Mixing stick
_____.   Tommy's adventure
Lynch, M.   Finn McCool
_____.   Scheherazade
Miller, H.   Cupid in demand
_____.   Thanksgiving riddle
Moore, E.   Mr. Longfellow observes book week
Murray, J.   Case for two detectives
_____.   Looking glass murder
Nicholson, J. Valentine stardust
Nolan, P.   Happy ending
_____.   Son of William Tell
_____.   Younger generation
Oser, J.   Running the country
Perrault, C.   Puss in boots
Peterson, M.   Soup stone
Pirandello, L. The jar
Spyri, J.   Heidi
_____.   Heidi finds the way
Stockton, F.   Lady or the tiger?
Thane, A.   Aladdin and his wonderful lamp
_____.   Rumpelstiltskin
Very, A.   Jonathan's Thanksgiving
_____.   Puss-in-boots

Watts, F.   Miss Louisa and the outlaws
Winther, B.   Sleeping mountains

11 characters and extras

Bennett, R.   On New Year's Eve
Boiko, C.   Snowman who overstayed
_____.   Star bright
Carlson, B.   There's always a leader
Hark, M.   House is haunted
MacLellan, E.   Return of the Nina
_____.   Test for a witch
Newman, D.   Plum Blossom and the dragon
Ramsey, H.   In the name of Miles Standish
Thane, A.   Brownie who found Christmas
Tobey, L.   The test

12 characters

Baher, C.   Cinder-rabbit
Boiko, C.   All hands on deck
_____.   Peter, Peter, Peter!
_____.   Tale of two drummers
Burnett, F.   Little princess
Cole, E.   Welcome, parents
DuBois, H.   Perfect gift
Fisher, A.   Three and the dragon
_____.   Unexpected guests
Glass, G.   Dick Whittington and his cat
Hale, L.   Lady who put salt in her coffee
Hark, M.   Christmas party
_____.   House is haunted
Hervey, M.   Virtue is her own reward
Howard, V.   Strange tale of King Midas
Hughes, T.   Coming of the kings
Lehman, J.   Good health trolley
Leuser, E.   Big stone
MacLellan, E.   Return of the Nina
Melchior, H.   Little Ki and the Serpent
Miller, H.   Birthday pie
_____.   Peter Rabbit volunteers
_____.   Red carpet Christmas
_____.   Red flannel suit
_____.   Tomboy and the dragon
Murray, J.   Publisher's choice
Nolan, P.   In-group
Oser, J.   King's calendar

CAST ANALYSIS

Thane, A.   King who was bored
Tolstoy, L.   Little girls wiser than men
Twain, M.   Tom Sawyer, pirate
Walsh, H.   Louisiana
Werner, S.   King's bean soup
Wyss, J.   Swiss family Robinson

12 characters and extras

Blaine, B.   Rosy-cheeked ghost
Boiko, C.   Beware the genies!
_____.   Little red hen
_____.   Pepe and the cornfield bandit
_____.   Punctuation proclamation
Cable, H.   Reluctant Columbus
Chandler, A.   Chinese Rip Van Winkle
Fisher, A.   Merry Christmas elf
_____.   On Halloween
Foley, M.   Emperor's new robes
Howard, V.   David and Goliath
_____.   Johnny Appleseed in danger
_____.   Oliver Twist asks for more
_____.   The winners
Huff, B.   Feast of the thousand lanterns
Jacob, E.   Crowded house
Kennedy, L.   Pied piper of Hamelin
Pyle, M.   Mrs. Gibbs advertises
Shakespeare, W.   Romeo and Juliet
Stockton, F.   Old Pipes
Streacker, L.   Bob's armistice parade
Thane, A.   Big Paul Bunyan
Winther, B.   Great Samurai sword

13 characters

Bennett, A.   Little witch
Boiko, C.   Mother Goose's Christmas surprise
Chisholm, J.   Prince is where you find him
Collodi, C.   Pinocchio
Davis, L.   St. Patrick and the last snake in Ireland
Dias, E.   Ballad for the shy
_____.   Hold back the redskins
_____.   The mantle
Dumas, A.   Count of Monte Cristo
Enright, E.   The Saturdays
Fisher, A.   Accident of birth
Fox, D.   Littlest month

Glass, G. Little witch
———. The Saturdays
Hall, M. Trial of Billy Scott
Hark, M. Books a la mode
Hartley, C. Children of the calendar
Howard, H. Doctor Know All
Huff, B. Ride the Gooberville stage!
Leuser, E. Honored one
Miller, H. Paper bag mystery
———. Wait and see
Murray, J. Mechanical man
Nicholson, J. Ghost walks tonight
Thane, A. Magic nutmeg-grater
Twain, M. Tom Sawyer, pirate

13 characters and extras

Baum, L. Wizard of Oz
Boiko, C. Jack Jouette's ride
Davis, L. David and the second Lafayette
Fisher, A. Thanks a million
Miller, H. Teddy bear hero
———. Weatherman on trial
Murray, J. Triumph for Trimbly
Nicholson, J. Haunted bookshop
Poe, E. Masque of the red death
Rowland, E. Hans, who made the princess laugh
Sanders, S. Wizard of Oz
Swintz, M. Panic in the palace
Twain, M. Tom Sawyer and Injun Joe

14 characters

Andersen, H. Emperor's nightingale
———. The swineherd
Baum, L. Wizard of Oz
Boiko, C. How to choose a boy
———. What ever happened to Mother Nature?
Cervantes, M. Don Quixote
Faux, D. Littlest month
Fisher, A. Getting in line
Hark, M. Nursery rhyme diet
Howard, V. Don Quixote saves the day
Hughes, T. Sean, the fool, the devil, and the cats
Huntsberry, W. Minor developments
Love, S. Fifth of November
Miller, H. Call Washington 1 7 7 6

CAST ANALYSIS 210

_____. Christmas peppermints
_____. Haunts for hire
Murray, J. Health, wealthy, and wild
Newman, Looking for Lincoln
Nolan, P. America is a song
Peterson, M. Magic box
Schaaf, A. Jump for Joy
Simon, S. Doctor farmer
Spamer, C. Pop-up books
Very, A. Golden bell for mother
Wilson, M. First flowers

14 characters and extras

Barbee, L. Flag of the United States
Boiko, C. Big shoo
_____. Lady Moon and the thief
_____. Search for the sky-blue princess
Corson, H. Dame Fortune and Don Money
Hark, M. Meet Mr. Witch
Howard, V. The bus
_____. Lincoln's Gettysburg Address
Irving, W. Legend of Sleepy Hollow
Miller, H. Broken broomstick
Murray, J. Sixth juror
Nolan, P. America is a song
_____. Licha's birthday serenade
Pyle, M. Three royal r's
Schwartz, E. Little Red Riding Hood
Shakespeare, W. Hamlet
_____. The tempest
Thane, A. Saucy scarecrow
Whitworth, V. Magic cloak

15 characters

Asbrand, K. Silver coffeepot
Boiko, C. Terrible Terry's surprise
_____. Trouble in tree-land
Fisher, A. King's toothache
Jacob, E. Snow White
Malory, T. Crowning of King Arthur
Miller, A. Grandpa and the statue
Miller, H. Circus daze
_____. Damsels in distress
_____. Matter of health
_____. Shirley Holmes and the FBI

CAST ANALYSIS

Murray, J. National everything
Newman, D. Cinderella
Schaaf, A. Jump for Joy
Thane, A. Gift for Hans Brinker
Watts, F. Tiniest heart
Wilde, O. Happy prince

15 characters and extras

Boiko, C. Melinda's incredible birthday
_____. Tall-tale tournament
Brydon, M. Dreadful dragon
Cable, H. Peace, pilgrim
Fisher, A. All the world around
Hale, E. Man without a country
Hoppenstedt, E. Naomi-of-the-inn
Howard, V. Sir Galahad and the maidens
Miller, H. Mother beats the band
_____. Mother Goose bakeshop
Murray, J. Airport adventure
_____. Come to the fair!
Newman, D. Yankee-doodle kitten
Pyle, M. Clever Peter
Rowland, E. Three aunts
Thane, A. Cinderella

16 characters

Alderman, E. Hamelot
Baum, L. Wizard of Oz
Boiko, C. Spaceship Santa Maria
Chaloner, G. The bookworm
D'Arcy, A. Cinderella
Dias, E. Landslide for Shakespeare
Dickens, C. Christmas carol
Fisher, A. Alice in Puzzleland
_____. Mother of Thanksgiving
_____. Once upon a time
Hark, M. A B C for safety
Henderson, N. Automa
Kingman, L. Magic pumpkin
Leuser, E. D. Wise people of Gotham
Miller, H. S. O. S. from Santa
_____. Shirley Holmes and the FBI
Newman, D. Rebellious robots
Thane, A. Elves and the shoemaker
Watts, F. Bridge to Killybog fair

CAST ANALYSIS

16 characters and extras

Boiko, C.	All about mothers
———.	All points west
———.	Christmas revel
Campbell, C.	Bell of Dolores
Davis, L.	Turtle, a flute, and the general's birthday
Hark, M.	Cupid's post office
McArthur J.	Fiesta the first
Miller, H.	Wake up, Santa Claus!
Olfson, L.	Equal rights
Patterson, E.	No room at the inn
Roberts, H.	Pocahontas, the tomboy princess
———.	Test for William Tell
Rybak, R.	Day the moonmen landed
Shakespeare, W.	Comedy of errors
White, A.	Lazarus

17 characters

Bennett, H.	Sleeping Beauty
Boiko, C.	Pandora's perilous predicament
———.	Penny wise
Carroll, L.	Alice's adventures in Wonderland
Colbert, M.	Salt in the sea
Fitz-Adcock, I.	Royal cloth of China
Hall, M.	Language shop
Hark, M.	Lincoln reminders
———.	Mind your p's and q's
McQueen, N.	Magic egg
Miller, H.	Captain Castaway's captives
———.	Gentle giant
Smith, G.	Star Light and the sandman
Thane, A.	Twelve dancing princesses

17 characters and extras

Bennett, R.	Ye olden festival of Christmas
Boiko, C.	Cupivac
———.	How mothers came to be
———.	Snowflake
Capell, L.	Tongue-cut sparrow
Cooper, J.	The spy
Fisher, A.	Young Abe Lincoln
Hawthorne, N.	David Swan
Irving, W.	Rip Van Winkle
Murray, J.	One in a million

CAST ANALYSIS

Walsh, H.   The spy
White, A.   Prodigal son

18 characters

Boiko, C.   Ah See and the six-colored heaven
_____ .   Honorable cat's decision
Cable, H.   Bailey, go home
Corson, H.   Triumph for two
Dickens, C.   Oliver Twist
Miller, H.   Garden holdup
_____ .   Real princess
_____ .   Simple Simon's reward
Newman, D.   Magic goose
_____ .   One night in Bethlehem
Orczy, B.   Scarlet Pimpernel
Oser, J.   Weeping willow's happy day
Perrault, C.   Sleeping beauty
Very, A.   Gift of the fairies
Woster, A.   All houses are haunted

18 characters and extras

Cable, H.   Another man's family
Hark, M.   Dish for the king
Henderson, N.   Harvest for Lola
Irving, W.   Rip Van Winkle
McArthur, J.   Fiesta
Sanders, S.   Julius Caesar
_____ .   Rip Van Winkle
Shakespeare, W.   Julius Caesar
_____ .   Taming of the shrew

19 characters

Asbrand, K.   China comes to you
Baher, C.   Robin Hood outwits the sheriff
Boiko, C.   Crocus who couldn't bloom
Burtle, G.   Mystery of the gumdrop dragon
Corey, C.   Dancing princesses
D'Arcy, A.   Wonders of storybook land
Dickens, C.   Christmas carol
Hark, M.   Many thanks
Irving, W.   Rip Van Winkle
McCarty, S.   Tree friends
Melchior, H.   Visit to the planets
Miller, H.   Rabbits who changed their minds

CAST ANALYSIS   214

_____ .   Safety clinic
Verne, Jules.   Around the world in eighty days
Willment, F.   Whites of their eyes

19 characters and extras

Boiko, C.   On camera, Noah Webster!
Jacob, E.   Robin Hood tricks the sheriff
Leuser, E.   Magic well
Leuser, E. D.   Secret of the wishing well
Miller, H.   Miss Frankenstein
Rowland, E.   Precedent in pastries
Rybak, R.   Election day in Spooksville
Sanders, S.   Three sillies
Thane, A.   Brave little tailor
Walsh, H.   Benjamin Franklin
_____ .   Mutiny on the Mayflower
Weik, M.   The bridge

20 characters

Boiko, C.   Exterior decorator
_____ .   Song goes forth
Cable, H.   Little Jackie and the beanstalk
Hark, M.   Spring is here
Jacob, E.   Robin Hood tricks the sheriff
Willment, F.   Whites of their eyes

20 characters and extras

Boiko, C.   Wild rabbit chase
Howard, V.   Return of Rip Van Winkle
Miller, H.   May Day for mother
_____ .   Shower of hearts
Moessenger, B.   Man in the red suit

21 characters

Asbrand, K.   Little hero of Holland
Boiko, C.   Hotel Oak
_____ .   Sun up!
Fisher, A.   All in the UN
_____ .   Play without a name
Holmes, R.   Golden goose
Miller, H.   Lost Christmas
_____ .   Ten pennies for Lincoln

CAST ANALYSIS

21 characters and extras

Conrad, E. Show boat
Henderson, N. The pledge
Shakespeare, W. Midsummer night's dream

22 characters

Boiko, C. Lion to lamb
Chaloner, G. Court of King Arithmetic
Miller, H. Friendship wheel
———— . Spunky Punky
Twain, M. Prince and the pauper

22 characters and extras

Lawrence, J. Inside a kid's head
Shakespeare, W. Macbeth
Toles, M. We, the people

23 characters

Miller, H. Forgetful Easter rabbit
Rittenhouse, C. Children of the sun

23 characters and extras

Boiko, C. Long table

24 characters

Boiko, C. Clean sweep
———— . May basket fantasia
Cable, H. Fairest pitcher of them all
Carroll, G. Merry, merry, merry
D'Aulnoy, M. Princess Rosette
Fisher, A. Treasure hunt

24 characters and extras

Dickens, C. Christmas carol
Miller, H. Toy scout jamboree
Thane, A. Merry Tyll and the three rogues
Very, A. Everywhere Christmas

CAST ANALYSIS   216

25 characters
==============

Miller, H.   One to grow on
  ———   . Trouble in Tick-tock Town
Nolan, P.   And Christmas is its name
Saroyan, W. Man with the heart in the highlands

25 characters and extras
========================

Miller, H.   Library circus

26 characters
=============

Fisher, A.   Empty bowls
  ———   . Let there be bread
Miller, H.   Case of the giggling goblin

26 characters and extras
========================

Mills, G.   Christmas comes to Hamelin

27 characters
=============

Miller, H.   Country store cat

27 characters and extras
========================

Boiko, C.   Next stop--spring!
Hark, M.   Christmas eve news

28 characters
=============

Biggs, L.   Key to understanding
Boiko, C.   Wonderful circus of words
Fisher, A.   Time out for Christmas

28 characters and extras
========================

Thane, A.   Dummling and the golden goose

29 characters
=============

Miller, H.   Old Glory grows up

29 characters and extras
========================

Boiko, C.   Anywhere and everywhere

CAST ANALYSIS

Morley, O. King Arthur and his knights

30 characters and extras

Richards, L. Chop-chin and the golden dragon

31 characters

Miller, H. Trial of Mother Goose

31 characters and extras

Feather, J. Quick-witted Jack
Henderson, N. Get on board, little children

32 characters and extras

Benson, I. Long live Christmas

33 characters

Hark, M. Book revue

33 characters and extras

Boiko, C. Destination: Christmas!
Fisher, A. Washington marches on

37 characters

Miller, H. Busy barbers

38 characters

Miller, H. Santa calls a conference

38 characters and extras

Preston, C. Born in a stable
_____. In a manger laid

39 characters and extras

Fisher, A. Cavalcade of human rights

40 characters and extras

Preston, C. Old Christmas

CAST ANALYSIS   218

PUPPET PLAYS

2 characters

McKay, H.   Suprise for Mr. Winkle

3 characters

Boylan, E.   Jack the giant killer
Mahlmann, L.   Magic mushrooms

3 characters and extras

Cochrane, L.   Moon dragon
Ross, L.   Washington and the first flight in America

4 characters

Boylan, E.   Prince and the dragon
_____.   Three billy goats gruff
Carlson, B.   Trailing arbutus

4 characters and extras

Carlson, B.   Robin Hood meets Little John
_____.   Who will be king?
Ross, L.   Admiral and the feathered pilots
_____.   Young Abe wrestles Armstrong

5 characters

Bennett, R.   Three terrors
Boylan, E.   Runaway pancake
Canadian fairy tale
Mahlmann, L.   Princess and the pea
Thomson, J.   Pepi and Sobrero

5 characters and extras

Carlson, B.   Golden spike
_____.   Turn south at Voorhees' farm
Philpott, V.   The egg
Ross, L.   Three kings

CAST ANALYSIS

6 characters

Mahlmann, L. Frog prince
_____ . Reluctant dragon
Pantopuck. Owl's birthday

6 characters and extras

Cochrane, L. Karagiosis and the dragon
_____ . Story of Rama and Sita
Lonely giant
Taylor, J. Lazy leprechaun
Zeligs, D. Queen Esther saves her people

7 characters

Bennett, R. First Easter eggs
Boylan, E. Musicians of Bremen

8 characters

Gertler, L. Punch and the heartless giant

9 characters

Gingerbread boy
Mahlmann, L. Magic shoes
_____ . Why the sea is salt
Silver key

9 characters and extras

Carlson, B. Happy nesting

10 characters

Mahlmann, L. Jack and the beanstalk

10 characters and extras

Irving, W. Rip Van Winkle

11 characters

Mahlmann, L. The tinderbox
Tichenor, T. Jack and the beanstalk

CAST ANALYSIS   220

<u>12 characters</u>

Fisher, A.   Unexpected guests

<u>13 characters</u>

Mahlmann, L.   Pinocchio

<u>13 characters and extras</u>

Mahlmann, L.   Wizard of Oz

<u>14 characters</u>

Mahlmann, L.   Snow White and the seven dwarfs

<u>17 characters</u>

Mahlmann, L.   Alice's adventures in Wonderland

<u>17 characters and extras</u>

Lorea, F.   Billy-club puppets

DIRECTORY OF PUBLISHERS

Abingdon Press
201 Eighth Ave., S.
Nashville, TN 37202

Allyn & Bacon
470 Atlantic Ave.
Boston, MA 02210

Atheneum Publishers
122 E. 42 St.
New York, NY 10017

Books for Libraries, Inc.
One Dupont St.
Plainview, NY 11803

R. R. Bowker Co.
1180 Avenue of the Americas
New York, NY 10036

Broadman Press
127 Ninth Ave., N.
Nashville, TN 37203

Burgess Publishing Co.
426-428 S. Sixth St.
Minneapolis, MN 55415

Citation Press
(Scholastic Book Services)
50 W. 44 St.
New York, NY 16036

Delacorte Press
(dist. by Dial Press)
1 Dag Hammarskjold Plaza
245 E. 47 St.
New York, NY 10017

Doubleday & Co.
245 Park Ave.
New York, NY 10017

E. P. Dutton & Co.
201 Park Ave., S.
New York, NY 10003

Stephen Greene Press
P.O. Box 1000
Fessenden Rd., Indian Flat
Brattleboro, VT 12833

Harcourt Brace Jovanovich
757 Third Ave.
New York, NY 10017

Lothrop, Lee & Shepard Co.
(div. of William Morrow & Co.)
105 Madison Ave.
New York, NY 10016

Macmillan Publishing Co.
866 Third Avenue
New York, NY 10022

Julian Messner
(dist. by Simon & Schuster)
One W. 39 St.
New York, NY 10018

Parents' Magazine Press
52 Vanderbilt Ave.
New York, NY 10017

Plays, Inc.
Eight Arlington St.
Boston, MA 02116

G. P. Putnam's Sons
200 Madison Ave.
New York, NY 10016

Richards Rosen Press
29 E. 21 St.
New York, NY 10010

Scholastic Book Services
(div. of Scholastic Magazine)
50 W. 44 St.
New York, NY 10036

Seabury Press
815 Second Ave.
New York, NY 10017

Van Nostrand Reinhold Co.
(div. of Litton Educational Publishing)
450 W. 33 St.
New York, NY 10001

Viking Press
625 Madison Ave.
New York, NY 10022

Henry Z. Walck
19 Union Square West
New York, NY 10003

Walker and Co.
720 Fifth Ave.
New York, NY 10019

H. W. Wilson Co.
950 University Ave.
Bronx, NY 10452

BIBLIOGRAPHY OF COLLECTIONS

Alexander, Sue. Small Plays for You and a Friend. New York: Seabury Press, 1973. 48 pp. (gr. k-3).

Bennett, Rowena. Creative Plays and Programs for Holidays. Boston: Plays, Inc., 1967. 368pp. (gr. 3-6).

Boiko, Claire. Children's Plays for Creative Actors. Boston: Plays, Inc., 1967, 1971. 368p. (gr. 3-6).

⸺. Plays and Programs for Boys and Girls. Boston: Plays, Inc., 1972. 306pp. (gr. 3-6).

Boylan, Eleanor. How to Be a Puppeteer. New York: E. P. Dutton, 1970. 132 pp. (gr. 4-6).

Burack, Abraham Saul, ed. Christmas Plays for Young Actors. Boston: Plays, Inc., 1969. 308 pp. (gr. 3 up)

⸺. Four-Star Plays for Boys. Boston: Plays, Inc., 1969. 237 pp. (gr. 1-12).

⸺. One Hundred Plays for Children. Boston: Plays, Inc., 1970. 886 pp. (gr. 1-6).

⸺. Skits, Comedies and Farces for Teen-agers. Boston: Plays, Inc., 1970. 433 pp. (gr. 7-12).

Burack, Abraham Saul, and B. Alice Crossley, eds. Popular Plays for Classroom Reading. Boston: Plays, Inc., 1974. 353 pp. (gr. 5-9).

Cable, Harold. Plays for Modern Teen-Age Actors. Boston: Plays, Inc., 1971. 320 pp. (gr. 7-12).

Carlson, Bernice Wells. Funny-Bone Dramatics. Nashville:

Abingdon Press, 1974. 96 pp. (gr. k-3).

_____. Play a Part. New York: Abingdon Press, 1970. 240 pp. (gr. 3-6).

Childress, Alice, ed. Black Scenes. Garden City, N.Y.: Doubleday, 1971. 154 pp. (gr. 7 up).

Cochrane, Louise. Shadow Puppets in Color. Boston: Plays, Inc., 1972. 48 pp. (gr. 4 up).

Conrad, Edna, and Mary Van Dyke. History on the Stage: Children Make Plays from Historical Novels. New York: Van Nostrand Reinhold, 1971. 128 pp. (gr. 7-9).

Cullum, Albert. Shake Hands with Shakespeare. New York: Citation Press, 1968. 320 pp. (gr. 3-6).

Dias, Earl J. One-Act Plays for Teen-Agers. Boston: Plays, Inc., 1971. 339 pp. (gr. 7 up).

Durrell, Donald D., and B. Alice Crossley, eds. Favorite Plays for Classroom Reading. Boston: Plays, Inc., 1965, 1971. 288 pp. (gr. 5-8).

_____. Teen-Age Plays for Classroom Reading. Boston: Plays, Inc., 1971. 338 pp. (gr. 7-12).

_____. Thirty Plays for Classroom Reading. Boston: Plays, Inc., 1968. 206 pp. (gr. 3-6).

Fisher, Aileen. Holiday Programs for Boys and Girls. Boston: Plays, Inc., 1970. 374 pp. (gr. 2-7).

_____, and Olive Rabe. United Nations Plays and Programs. Boston: Plays, Inc., 1965. 285 pp. (gr. 3-10).

Fontaine, Robert. Humorous Skits for Young People. Boston: Plays, Inc., 1965. 184 pp. (gr. 4-10).

Gilfond, Henry, ed. Plays for Reading: Classic Short Stories in Dramatic Form. New York: Walker and Co., 1967. 152 pp. (gr. 5 up).

Glass, Gerald G., and Muriel Walzer Klein. From Plays into Reading: Plays to Read in the Classroom. Boston: Allyn and Bacon, 1969. 189 pp. (gr. 4-6).

Hark, Mildred, and Noel McQueen. Junior Plays for All Occasions. Boston: Plays, Inc., 1969. 576 pp. (gr. 2-6).

Henderson, Nancy. Walk Together: Five Plays on Human Rights. New York: Julian Messner, 1972. 128 pp. (gr. 4 up).

Hoff, Syd. Giants and Other Plays for Kids. New York: G. P. Putnam's Sons, 1973. 40 pp. (gr. 2-5).

Howard, Vernon. Complete Book of Children's Theater. Garden City, N.Y.: Doubleday, 1969. 544 pp. (gr. 3-8).

Hughes, Ted. The Tiger's Bones and Other Plays for Children. New York: Viking Press, 1974. 141 pp. (gr. 5-9).

Jarvis, Sally Melcher. Fried Onions and Marshmallows and Other Little Plays for Little People. New York: Parents' Magazine Press, 1968. 60 pp. (gr. k-3).

Kamerman, Sylvia E., ed. Children's Plays from Favorite Stories. Boston: Plays, Inc., 1970. 583 pp. (gr. 3-6).

_____. Dramatized Folk Tales of the World. Boston: Plays, Inc. 1971. 575 pp. (gr. 5-6).

_____. Fifty Plays for Holidays. Boston: Plays, Inc., 1969. 652pp. (gr. 4-7).

_____. Fifty Plays for Junior Actors. Boston: Plays, Inc., 1966. 676 pp. (gr. 4-6).

_____. Little Plays for Little Players. Boston: Plays, Inc., 1969. 335 pp. (gr. 1-6).

Kline, Peter. The Theatre Student: Scenes to Perform. New York: Richards Rosen Press, 1969. 190 pp. (gr. 7 up)

Love, Stewart, and William D. Cumming. Plays for Reading and Recording. Boston: Plays, Inc., 1966. 118 pp. (gr. 6-10).

McGee, Cecil, ed. Drama for Fun. Nashville: Broadman Press, 1969. 175 pp. (gr. 4-12).

Mahlmann, Lewis, and David Cadwalader Jones. Puppet Plays for Young Players. Boston: Plays, Inc., 1974. 194 pp. (gr. 3 up).

Maloney, Henry B., ed. Plays to Remember. New York: Macmillan, 1967. 186 pp. (gr. 6-10).

Martin, Judith, ed. Little Plays for Little People. New York: Parents' Magazine Press, 1965. 60 pp. (gr. k-4).

Martin, Patricia Miles. Two Plays about Foolish People. New York: G. P. Putnam's Sons, 1972. 48 pp. (gr. 1-5).

Miller, Helen Louise. First Plays for Children. Boston: Plays, Inc., 1971. 295 pp. (gr. 1-6).

_____. Modern Plays for Special Days. Boston: Plays, Inc., 1965. 352 pp. (gr. 7 up).

_____. Short Plays for Children. Boston: Plays, Inc., 1969. 338 pp. (gr. 3-8).

Murray, John. Comedies and Mysteries for Young Actors. Boston: Plays, Inc., 1972. 339 pp. (gr. 4-12).

Nolan, Paul T. Drama Workshop Plays for Young People. Boston: Plays, Inc., 1969. 309 pp. (gr. 7 up).

_____. Round-the-World Plays for Young People. Boston: Plays, Inc., 1970. 285 pp. (gr. 4-8).

Olfson, Lewy, ed. Classics Adopted for Acting and Reading. Boston: Plays, Inc., 1970. 294 pp. (gr. 6-12).

_____. Dramatized Classics for Radio-Style Reading, Vol. II. Boston: Plays, Inc., 1965. 236 pp. (gr. 5 up).

_____. Skits and Short Farces for Young Actors. Boston: Plays, Inc., 1973. 171 pp. (gr. 5-12).

Philpott, A. R., ed. Eight Plays for Hand Puppets. Boston: Plays, Inc., 1968. 74 pp. (gr. 4-10).

Picozzi, Raymond, ed. Plays to Enjoy. New York: Macmillan, 1967. 169 pp. (gr. 6-12).

Preston, Carol. A Trilogy of Christmas Plays for Children. New York: Harcourt, Brace & World, 1967. 135 pp. (gr. 4 up).

Ross, Laura, ed. Holiday Puppets. New York: Lothrop, Lee & Shepard, 1974. 223 pp. (gr. 6 up).

Sanders, Sandra. Creating Plays with Children. New York: Scholastic Book Services, 1970. 95 pp. (gr. 3-6).

Smith, Moyne Rice, ed. 7 Plays and How to Produce Them. New York: Henry Z. Walck, 1968. 148 pp. (gr. 4-6).

Swortzell, Lowell, ed. All the World's a Stage: Modern Plays for Young People. New York: Delacorte Press, 1972. 610 pp. (gr. 7 up).

Taylor, Loren E. Stunts and Skits. Minneapolis: Burgess Pub. Co., 1965. 112 pp. (gr. 3-8).

Thane, Adele, ed. Plays from Famous Stories and Fairy Tales. Boston: Plays, Inc., 1967. 463 pp. (gr. 4-8).

Tichenor, Tom. Tom Tichenor's Puppets. Nashville: Abingdon Press, 1971. 223 pp. (gr. 5 up).

Walsh, Henry H. Six Plays in American History. Brattleboro, Vt.: Stephen Greene Press, 1969. 216 pp. (gr. 7-12).

Weik, Mary Hays. The Scarlet Thread. New York: Atheneum, 1968. 109 pp. (gr. 5 up).

White, Alice M. G., and Janet E. Tobitt. The Saucy Sailor and Other Dramatized Ballads. New York: Books for Libraries, 1969. 185 pp. (gr. 5-12).